Spiritual Growth and Care
in the Fourth Age of Life

Box 2.1 and Table 2.5 are reproduced from 'Understanding the ageing process: A developmental perspective of the psychosocial and spiritual dimensions' by Elizabeth MacKinlay in *Journal of Religious Gerontology 12*, B/4, 111–122 (2001). Reproduced with permission from The Haworth Press.

First published in 2006
by Jessica Kingsley Publishers
116 Pentonville Road
London N1 9JB, UK
and
400 Market Street, Suite 400
Philadelphia, PA 19106, USA

www.jkp.com

Library of Congress Cataloging in Publication Data
MacKinlay, Elizabeth, 1940-
    Spiritual growth and care in the fourth age of life / Elizabeth
MacKinlay. -- 1st American pbk. ed.
        p. cm.
    Includes bibliographical references and index.
    ISBN-13: 978-1-84310-231-1 (pbk. : alk. paper)
    ISBN-10: 1-84310-231-5 (pbk. : alk. paper)
    1. Older people--Religious life. 2. Older people--Pastoral coun-
seling of. 3. Older people--Care.   I. Title.
BL625.4.M33 2006
259'.3--dc22
                                                2005036451

British Library Cataloguing in Publication Data
A CIP catalogue record for this book is available from the British Library

ISBN 978 1 84310 231 1

Contents

Figures

Tables

Preface

I remember when I was about ten years of age, my grandmother had the first of a series of strokes. At the time of her first stroke, I was staying with my grandparents on their farm. Later, my grandfather couldn't continue to care for her and work the farm too, so she came to stay at our place. When my mother couldn't care for her any more at home, Gran was admitted to a nursing home. Visiting her was my first experience of aged care. It was a large old home, converted to a number of rooms for the residents. Some of the rooms were large with a number of elderly people in each room. The room my gran was in was a single room. I would sometimes visit her and help feed her. This experience was an important one for me, as by age 13, I had decided that I would become a nurse.

Through my more than 40 years of nursing, I have worked in a variety of nursing specialities, but I have always been drawn back to my roots of caring about, and for, elderly people. For a number of these years, I have taught nurses.

Ageing is not all one. The term 'old' as understood currently by many in western society covers a range of perhaps some 50 years. This would have been almost a lifetime for many people not long ago. In the short time since *The Spiritual Dimension of Ageing* (MacKinlay 2001a) was published there has been a proliferation in writing in this field. So, why add yet another book?

Life is a spiritual journey. This journey does not end when an elderly person can no longer live independently. The study that this book is based on follows from the first major study that culminated in *The Spiritual Dimension of Ageing*. When I completed the earlier study it seemed that I was just beginning. I had searched the literature, I had collected the data, I had examined the data using grounded theory, I had extracted the themes and constructed a model of spiritual tasks of ageing. But did that model work or was it only valid for the group of independent older adults I had interviewed in that first study? The spiritual dimension seemed important to this group of older people, but was the same true for the frailer group of elderly people resident in nursing homes or receiving care at home? What is it like living in an aged care facility? Are there differences in the spiritual dimension for these people, and would the model I had constructed be supported in further study with this frail and vulnerable group?

There still seemed to be so many questions to be asked. When I had completed the first study, it seemed necessary to move to the next stage. This study is the second wave, if you like, of a process of filling out a picture of the spiritual dimension in later life. It was with excitement and some apprehension that I began yet another study of spirituality. Excitement, because I find it a joy and a privilege to listen to the stories of older people. At the same time, I felt some apprehension because I was not sure how the model I had constructed from the group of well older people could be applied to the situation of these nursing home residents.

Chapter 1 of this book outlines the latest research in the growing field of study in ageing, spirituality and religion. While there is still much to be achieved in mapping out the spiritual dimension in later life, much has been accomplished in the last decade.

The study

Chapter 2 outlines the research that lies behind this book. The main study reported here was based on the same methodology developed and used in the earlier study. I considered it important to continue to explore the spiritual dimension, again not foreclosing on any issues that these frail older people may find important to them. Thus in-depth interviews were again conducted, using a broad framework of open-ended questions, allowing the participants to address issues that were important for them.

Assessment of the spiritual needs of older people

Chapter 3 examines spiritual assessment. This is an important area for practice, and instruments are needed that will provide guidance for practice of spiritual and pastoral care. It is now possible, based on the data from the two studies, to construct an assessment tool to enable more effective assessment of the spiritual needs of older people.

Chapters 4 and 5 describe two of the spiritual tasks of ageing, the search for ultimate meaning and how we respond to life's meaning. Chapter 6 is on spiritual reminiscence, that is, reflecting on the life journey and finding my story, and its links with my community and finally with God's story. We need to recover the skills both to listen to people's stories and to tell our stories. Kenyon

(2003) says that we are co-authors of our stories and, importantly, that we 'are story'. Story goes to the heart of who we are.

The next two chapters examine the important areas of mental health and dementia in later life. I invited Corinne Trevitt to write Chapter 8 on dementia, as she and I have worked closely together on a recent project: 'Finding meaning in the experience of dementia: The place of spiritual reminiscence work' (MacKinlay, Trevitt and Coady 2002–2005).

Chapter 9 considers worship and use of ritual among older people. The chapter includes a context of multifaith and multicultural western ageing societies. Chapters 10 and 11 tackle the important topics of vulnerability and transcendence, considering the many physical and chronic health problems that many older people face and the implications of living in a disintegrating body and the syndrome of failure to thrive.

The need for intimacy becomes complex in the fourth age of life, and Chapter 12 addresses relationship and intimacy needs among nursing home residents. The needs for relationship continue to be important for all human beings, no matter what their age. Chapter 13 is about grief, death, dying and spirituality in an aged care facility. Many older people spend their last days either in an aged care facility or in a hospital. Support in the dying process, so that people do not need to die alone, is discussed in this chapter.

Chapter 14 brings together the main ethical issues of later life, many of which have been addressed implicitly through the book. No book on the care of frail elderly people would be complete without such a chapter. Ethical issues include the worth and dignity of human beings, end of life issues and use of health resources with elderly people. The final chapter brings the components of the model of spiritual tasks together, to consider them in a wholistic frame.

Acknowledgements

A number of people have provided valuable assistance in this book, but I wish particularly to acknowledge the work of Corinne Trevitt. Corinne and I have worked closely together for a number of years, in teaching nurses, in ageing research and especially in research on spirituality and dementia. Corinne has written the chapter on dementia in this book and provided valuable advice on other parts of the book. Ruwan Palapathwala has provided guidance in some of the multicultural and multifaith aspects of the book in Chapters 1 and 9. Appreciation is also extended to Graham Lindsay for the figures, to Karen Woodward for assistance with design of assessment instruments, and to Merrie Hepworth and Karen MacKinlay for reading and critiquing the manuscript.

CHAPTER 1

The Spiritual Dimension of Ageing and People in Need of Care

This is a book about growing older in the fourth age of the human life cycle. If the third age is defined as being older and still remaining independent (without specifying a chronological age range), then the fourth age is the age of frailty, dependency and being in need of care. It is for these people and their carers that this book is written. Even though this is a book about the fourth age, it has a focus of well-being and spiritual care and development, in other words the approach taken is wholistic.

What is it that allows one person to continue to hope against the most difficult of circumstances, while another in very similar circumstances may give up all hope? These are difficult questions that have engaged human intellect from early times; such questions were posed in the story of Job in the Old Testament.

Towards an understanding of the spiritual dimension

A continuing search for what makes a difference in recovery from illness and healing has unearthed a missing and unexplained phenomenon, the spiritual dimension. This search has traversed the disciplines of medicine, nursing, social work, chaplaincy and pastoral care. All have a share in this aspect of being human (MacKinlay 2001a). The first developments in spiritual care came from within palliative care and mental health.

End of life care for people living with cancer raised questions of the spiritual dimension. Why did some people continue to live when their prognosis pointed to an imminent death, while others died much before their time? These events could not be charted clearly by scientific means alone. The questions that people face in the process of dying, such as the search for life-meaning, for hope, issues of guilt, the need for forgiveness and reconciliation, pain – existential as well as physical – have meant that spiritual issues are continually being raised in palliative care practice. In mental health practice issues around religion are common, and there has been much debate over many years regarding the relationship between religion and mental health; some studies have claimed a positive relationship between religion and mental health, some claim that poor mental health may be associated with religion, while other studies are non-conclusive. Koenig has researched and written extensively on this area and supports an association of well-being and religion (1994; 1998; Koenig and Lawson 2004).

The debate continues to develop in defining the spiritual dimension. In my earlier book (MacKinlay 2001a) I argued that the spiritual dimension is part of being human; just as we have a body, so we have a mind and a spirit.[1] Perhaps it could be more correctly said that this domain is the soul. The word 'soul' was little spoken of during the latter decades of the twentieth century, and it was during these same decades that the word 'spiritual' began to be more widely used in society, and not confined to religious use. David Tacey (2003) teaches and writes of the emergence of what he calls 'contemporary' spirituality. His experience of spirituality within secular Australian society is based on work with university students and their search for the spiritual. Tacey wants to take the debate outside the churches, as he sees that traditional religion is not what these young people are searching for, yet they seek for something more that seems to be of a spiritual nature. In both the study of the spiritual dimension of independent living older people (MacKinlay 1998) and in a similar study of frail older people resident in nursing homes (MacKinlay 2001b) the search for the spiritual was evident. In comparison with groups of younger people, such as Tacey was working with, more of these older people worked through their spirituality in traditional forms of worship, but some also lived out their spirituality outside of the churches.

If religion is understood as used in Greeley's work (1969; 1973; 1982), as answering the most basic questions that humans ask: 'It is concerned with the Ultimate on which reality rests' (1973, p.60), then religion has a major part to play in the ordinary lives of people. Palapathwala (in press) suggests that Christianity as a religion for western societies 'has almost ceased to be a source of meaningful spirituality in later life'. Indeed, a sticking point arises when attempting to use the term 'religion' in everyday life, certainly within Australian society (Tacey 2003), where the term 'religion' has become associated with hypocritical behaviour, as one of the elderly participants in my first study (MacKinlay 2001a) said, 'being religious' was being a 'do-gooder'.

The relationship between spirituality and religion

I have heard it said by a number of people, 'I'm spiritual, but not religious.' Can one really separate out the two dimensions? Koenig, McCullough and Larson (2001, p.18) distinguish between religion and spirituality:

> Religion is an organized system of beliefs, practices, rituals, and symbols designed
>
> (a) to facilitate closeness to the sacred or transcendent (God, higher power, or ultimate truth/reality) and
>
> (b) to foster an understanding of one's relationship and responsibility to others in living together in a community.

They define spirituality as:

> the personal quest for understanding answers to ultimate questions about life, about meaning, and about relationship to the sacred or transcendent, which may (or may not) lead to or arise from the development of religious rituals and the formation of community.

These two definitions are important in clarifying the dimensions under discussion. What is essential to an understanding of these dimensions is that religion cannot be completely divorced from spirituality; spirituality is the dimension from which religion arises. Put another way, religion is part of spirituality. The practice of religion is a way that humans relate to the sacred, to otherness. Not all humans practise religion, but all do have a spiritual dimension, thus a person may work out their spirituality in a variety of ways, as shown in Figure 1.1. It could be said that spirituality is mediated through a variety of ways.

The field of spirituality is still being explored to determine the exact nature of the spiritual. Tanyi (2002) studied the literature applying a conceptual analysis process. She proposed a definition of spirituality that includes recognizing a personal search for meaning and purpose in life; religious or non-religious and connection to self-chosen or religious beliefs, values and practices that give meaning to life. She states that 'this connection brings faith, hope, peace and empowerment', with outcomes of 'joy, forgiveness, awareness and acceptance of hardship and mortality, a heightened sense of physical and emotional well-being and the ability to transcend beyond the infirmities of existence' (p.508). This definition closely matches the model of spiritual tasks of ageing developed in my studies (MacKinlay 2001a).

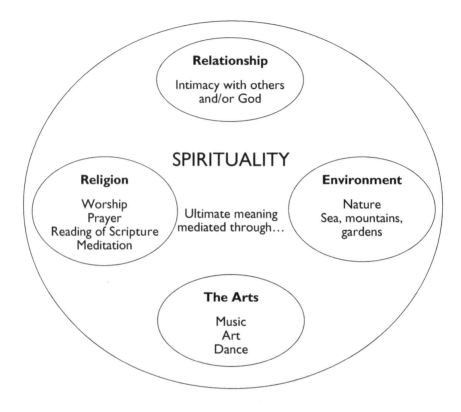

Figure 1.1 Ways of mediating the spiritual dimension

In my earlier work based on listening to the life stories of independent living older adults, both Christians and those who did not have any faith affiliation (MacKinlay 1998; 2001a), I defined spirituality as:

> That which lies at the core of each person's being, an essential dimension which brings meaning to life. It is acknowledged that spirituality is not constituted only by religious practices, but must be understood more broadly, as relation-ship with God, however God or ultimate meaning is perceived by the person, and in relationship with other people. (MacKinlay 1998, p.36)

This definition attempts to show both the breadth and depth of the spiritual dimension taking into account the range of possibilities that human spirituality may encompass. It is the definition used in the study reported in this book.

In my book (MacKinlay 2001a) I wrote of each person having a generic spirituality, which would be open to continued development by the individual as they grew older. As an athlete would develop particular skills in the physical dimension, and not every one is an athlete, so too with the development of the spiritual dimension. Thus, some people pay little attention to the development of their spiritual dimension, while for others it is central within their lives, and one could say they may become spiritual athletes. So, it may be asked, is it appropriate to speak of a generic spirituality for every human being? Taking this perspective, I think it is. Each person has the potential and the choice to develop and become more aware of, and more in touch with, their spiritual dimension.

In recent debate, another term has been introduced (Jewell 2004), that of a 'universal' spirituality. It appears this term is applied in a similar way to 'generic' spirituality. Which term will be of more use in describing the spiritual dimension that is a part of each person? Does universal spirituality mean a spirituality that is found everywhere, or does it mean a kind of spirituality that each person has? I would argue that it is useful to propose that each person has a spiritual dimension and that this dimension is an essential part of being human. However, that dimension cannot be universal in the sense of being the same for everyone. I prefer the term generic, taken to mean that each person has an undifferentiated spiritual dimension that may develop across the lifespan. I have differentiated the undeveloped (generic spirituality) from the developed spirituality, that is, specific spirituality. This is specific in that the individual has developed and focused their spiritual dimension in certain ways. These ways may be from the taking on and the practice of a religion and faith, for instance, Christianity, Judaism, Islam, Buddhism, Hinduism, humanism, or from finding meaning and thus feeding the spirit through depth of relationship, through the Arts and the environment.

Study of religion and spirituality

In the early stages of research into religion and spirituality, measures of religiosity or extrinsic religion were often studied, for example, frequency of church attendance. It is unlikely that these measures will produce useful findings as frequency of attendance only measures behaviour, and that cannot explain *why* the person attended church, or what meaning attendance had for the person. It needs to also be asked, did the person attend church because they met other people there and perhaps this met their need for socialization? Perhaps the person attended church because they wanted to worship God; the study of frequency of church attendance does not provide answers to these important differences.

How might we understand these phenomena more adequately? It is suggested that new ways of studying the spiritual dimension are needed to adequately explore this dimension. In many ways, the spiritual dimension does not seem amenable to study through traditional scientific methods. This does not mean that it should not be studied but, just as ways amenable to the study of the human body and the human mind were developed, so now appropriate ways to study the human spirit also need to be developed. We already have a basis for study from methods in social science research. These methods may be adapted for use in spirituality study. More is needed than the anecdotal material that already abounds.

Hill and Pargament (2003) state that most measurements of religion and spirituality have used paper-and-pencil measures, and that such measures may not be effective ways of studying this field. They write that 'alternative religion and spirituality measures are needed' (p.70). They note that social psychology measures for the centrality or importance of religion and spirituality may be useful. Working with children who had cystic fibrosis they assessed their religious and spiritual coping strategies by asking them to draw pictures of God and themselves. They also suggested using unobtrusive observational techniques of religious, spiritual and health practices and rituals. A current study of people with dementia comprising small group work using spiritual reminiscence uses the participants' words, observational techniques drawn from grounded theory and phenomenology, as well as quantitative data (MacKinlay *et al.* 2002–2005).[2] This and other similar studies may be valuable through building the picture we have of spirituality in ageing.

A number of studies have considered aspects of religious coping (Koenig, McCullough and Larson 2001; Pargament 1997). Other studies have examined aspects of social support and religion, most considering the broad range of social support, but not specifically the place of religion in this. Fiala, Bjorck and Gorsuch (2002), basing their work on the model of general perceived social support of Cutrona and Russell (1987) and recognizing the importance of specifically defining support, developed a measure of religious support measures. This new scale has three hypothesized categories: God support, congregational support and church leader support. Factor analysis was used to test reliability and validity of the scales, and all three of their scales of religious support were related to lower depression and greater life satisfaction. They found, as others have found, that religious attendance alone does not imply religious support, and that 'religious support can provide unique resources for religious persons, above and beyond those furnished by social support' (Fiala *et al.* 2002, p.761). This being so, it is important to develop more intentional ways of providing such support, for both community dwellers and for people in residential care. Care of the spirit is not an optional extra of care.

It is important to consider what aspect of religion and/or spirituality is being studied and why. Is the purpose of study to find out how to improve health, as many of the medical-based studies are? Or is it to discover aspects of religion and spirituality that may lead to renewed or continued spiritual growth and development? Perhaps the purpose of study in these fields is to engage with these dimensions in current twenty-first-century western societies. There is a sense in which we have lost some of the skills and strategies for spiritual well-being, and need to rediscover or find new ways of meeting our needs for the spiritual.

Chronic illness and spirituality

Other important components of particular spiritual need are living with chronic illness and pain. Older people, particularly those in aged care facilities, commonly live with multiple chronic conditions. In many ways the experience of chronic illness and pain is often simply regarded as part of the ageing process, examples of the downside of living longer. However, simply to regard chronic illnesses as medical conditions to be treated is not to deal with the conditions wholistically. Medical diagnosis does not necessarily correlate with functional capacity, let alone a sense of well-being for the individual.

Well-being in later life has to include the spiritual dimension too, and it is through this that people may work towards attaining greater quality of life and still live life to the full, even with chronic illness. Thorn and Paterson (1998), in a 15-year study of the literature, found changing conceptualizations held by individuals with chronic illness, from a focus on loss and burden toward images of health within illness, transformation and normality. Over the same period they noted a parallel change in conceptualizations of health care relationships to chronic illness, from client-as-patient to client-as-partner. Including the person living with the chronic illness is an important change of emphasis in care that may lead to a greater sense of control for these people and thus greater quality of life.

Ethics and spiritual care

As understanding of the concept of spirituality develops there are other aspects of this field that need attention. One aspect is ethical behaviour with patients and clients. Faith is both individual and community. At an individual level the person's beliefs must be respected both in acting and failing to act. For example, if the person does not want spiritual advice or guidance, and has no religious affiliation, then it is offensive and unethical to recommend spiritual or religious activities to the person. It is equally unethical to fail to address the religious and spiritual needs of an individual.

How does one know who to provide spiritual care for, or what a person's spiritual needs are? This is simple: ask the person, in language that he or she can understand, what their spiritual and/or religious needs are. Spiritual assessment should form an important and integral aspect of multidisciplinary practice in aged care. The topic of spiritual assessment is dealt with in a separate chapter. It is essential that even subjects that staff may not feel comfortable with are dealt with appropriately, always according respectful attitudes and care towards each individual, regardless of their gender, ethnicity and religion or spiritual beliefs.

Prayer is one area where nurses and other health professionals may ask questions, for example, is it ethical to pray with patients? Winslow and Winslow (2003) have suggested guidelines for praying with patients: first, gain an understanding of the person's spiritual needs; second, pray only with permission; third, spiritual practices must be voluntary; fourth, be aware of and appreciate your own spirituality; and finally, spiritual care requires preserving the integrity of both the patient or resident and the health or aged care provider.

Spiritual care: whose role?

Traditionally spiritual care has been the role of chaplains, however in recent years there have been moves to include spiritual care within the role of other health professionals. It is important that the roles developed are consistent with and complementary to the core functions of each of these health professions. It will achieve little for the recipients of care if professional care-givers try to make a universal 'spiritual' role for all.

Understanding of spirituality by nurses

Like other health professionals, nurses are studying the concept of spiritual care, what it entails, how it might be delivered and the likely outcomes. However, there is as yet no substantial body of research to back practice. Most of the early research and writing has been in palliative care, mental health and gerontology, possibly because matters of religion and spirituality are more likely to come to consciousness among people experiencing cancer, mental health problems, ageing and dying. Indeed, in one of these speciality fields, a review of research on religious and spiritual variables published in two gerontological nursing journals from 1991 to 1997 (Weaver, Flannelly and Flannelly 2001) found only 40 articles (5.1%) referred to religion or spirituality, and of these 52.5 per cent were on religious behaviours, not spirituality. Recent writings in nursing and spirituality include work by McSherry (2000), Strang, Strang, and Ternestedt (2002), Swinton (2001) and Touhy (2001), with much of the work attempting to define spirituality and study nurses' perceptions and practice of spiritual care. A study of raising staff awareness of spirituality was conducted by MacKinlay (2001e) and is reported in Chapter 2.

Spiritual care in medicine

Much research has been undertaken within the field of religion and health in recent years. Koenig, McCullough and Larson (2001) provide an excellent review of current literature in the *Handbook of Religion and Health*. Sloan *et al.* (2000) and Sloan and Bagiella (2002) provide a critique of research in this field with a caution; they found 266 articles published in 2000 through a Medline search claiming health benefits associated with religious involvement. However, they noted that few were relevant and many were misrepresented or had flaws of methodology. They acknowledged that few of the articles could truly be described as indicating beneficial effects of religious involvement. It is noted too that the higher proportion of the population in the US who regularly attend church compared with the UK and Australia means that studies based on religion and health may have different findings depending on the country in which they are based.

Sloan *et al.* (2000) also question whether spiritual care can be the province of physicians, noting that although there is a high level of religion in the US, and surveys have found that patients would like their physicians to ask them about their spiritual needs, that does not mean that it is in the best interests of patients for physicians to prescribe religious activities. This is a reasonable assumption as indeed physicians do prescribe treatments, while strategies and interventions for spiritual care do not seem to fit into this type of construct. Indeed spiritual care does not appear amenable to dispensing! Does this mean that physicians cannot have a role in spiritual and/or religious care? Perhaps the greatest role that physicians have in spiritual care is to recognize the spiritual needs of their patients, and if they do not have preparation in this field, to refer their patients to specialists who do. Sloan *et al.* (2000, p.1917) suggest that 'to make religious activities adjunctive medical treatments' comes dangerously close to validating religion by its effect on health, which is in fact demeaning. As they note, 'religion does not need science to justify its existence or appeal.

Religion and science, and religion and medicine, exist in different domains and are qualitatively different' (p.1917). It is vital to acknowledge this fact as researchers who try to make religion and spirituality fit a scientific mode of inquiry may be doing both religion and spirituality a major disservice.

The spiritual dimension of older people residing in aged care facilities

As people in western societies continue to age, it is important to consider what effects this will have on the requirements for aged care accommodation and how these people may best be cared for into the future. Rowland, Liu and Braun (2002) studied the probability of being in a nursing home over the period of one's lifetime in Australia. They studied three constructs: the probability of someone in the community ever entering an aged care home, the probability of someone in the community entering an aged care home *between two ages*, and the probability of *being in or entering* an aged care home. They found that a female at birth faces a more than two in five (0.42) chance of entering an aged care home, while the chance for a male at birth is about one in four (0.24). They note importantly that the probability for women over 65 years entering an aged care home is 0.42 and for men, 0.24, this is despite the fact that only 7 per cent of women and 3 per cent of men aged 65 and over were residents on any one day in the period 1999–2000 (p.121). The likelihood of spending some time in an aged care home for permanent care after age 85 increases to 0.62 for women, but only 0.46 for men. These figures indicate that in later life and with increasing frailty, many will require full-time and permanent residential care.

As Rowland *et al.* (2002) suggest, these figures are of considerable significance, not only for Australia but also internationally, in the planning and financing of aged care. I suggest these figures have further implications for the type of care that is needed for these mostly frail and older people. This care will need to take account of the particular issues that these people are likely to face. This will include effects of isolation prior to coming into care and establishing new relationships at an advanced age within a new community (the aged care home). The care will also entail being able to deal with the particular and significant losses these older people face and the task of finding meaning in the face of continuing disability and loss of control. This care must also focus on the final career that each of us inevitably faces: the preparation for dying and death itself.

It is imperative too that those of us who work in aged care are aware of our own ageing, and of our own denial of the ageing process and associated fears of growing old and dying. It is hard for health professionals and chaplains to step outside the society that has formed us (Meador and Hensen 2003) even for those who are Christian. We live in a society that wishes not to struggle with issues of suffering and dying, but to abolish them, and the myth is that science can achieve that end. Research into longevity seeks to maintain perpetual youth, restore youth/rejuvenate, postpone biological ageing, prolong life and achieve physical immortality (Kirkwood 1999; 2000).

It is possible that into the future, as the baby boomers grow older, different modes of aged care will develop. The current trend toward larger and more complex aged care facilities may fail to meet the needs of the coming cohorts of older people. The current trend will continue as long as ageing is cast into a medical model and is seen largely as a disease to be cured.

Wholistic care in aged care facilities

The need for wholistic care for nursing home residents is only now being recognized, yet much still is to be done before such care can be provided. First, what is wholistic care? It is care that includes appropriate physical, mental, social and spiritual care. Let me begin with the barriers; it seems necessary to address these first. A number of barriers for wholistic care have been identified (MacKinlay 1998). These include the perception by policy makers, aged care providers and staff that the main care required by frail older nursing home residents is physical care. Results of these perceptions are first that funding is not set to include spiritual care as it is seen as an optional extra. Second, many staff feel uncomfortable about the boundaries of spiritual care and there is a perception that religion and spiritual care are very private and thus not matters that come into the realm of care. Third, training in spiritual care is as yet often lacking in basic educational programmes of most professional groups. Even when aged care accreditation guidelines include it, spiritual care may still be seen as simply providing church services. Finally, spiritual care is still not recognized as an integral component of aged care.

While it is not suggested in any way that physical care is unimportant, it is strongly argued that physical care alone is not enough. In recent years aged care accreditation guidelines in Australia have more obviously identified psycho-social needs as being important and these are more often being planned into care now. However, the spiritual dimension of care remains the forgotten component of care (Swinton 2001). Perhaps this is because both the need and the fulfilment of the need are often not visible. Yet, there is another aspect of the problem: the content and outcome of spiritual care is not recognized by numbers of those who develop policy, plan and/or provide aged care. An important basis for introducing appropriate spiritual care into aged care is the development of models of spiritual care.

The model of spiritual tasks and process of ageing

Based on the interviews of independent older people, a model of spiritual tasks of ageing was developed. This is outlined in detail in *The Spiritual Dimension of Ageing* (MacKinlay 2001a) and is based on the premise that all humans have a spiritual dimension, and that there are certain common tasks that all face related to spirituality. It is acknowledged that there are variations in how individuals will work out their spiritual dimension, even among members of the same religious faith, and even among members of the same religious denomination. However, a generic model can be suggested that forms a basic model for spirituality in later life. It is also acknowledged that the importance of the spiritual dimension will vary between individuals, however, it is maintained that the spiritual dimension is part of being human, even if at a relatively unconscious level. The spiritual journey is one of 'becoming' that is part of being human, and consciousness of the process is likely to be heightened at certain points of the life cycle. An effective model for spiritual development should show how the process of becoming is facilitated across the life journey, influenced by the meeting of both developmental and situational crises. The spiritual journey often becomes more intentional in the latter part of life.

An interactive model for ageing spiritually

It is important to regard the model (shown in Figure 1.2) as a dynamic interactive model, where the core and ultimate meaning will influence the response to meaning and hope, and so forth. Likewise, loss and grief may influence the individual's sense of ultimate life-meaning. The model is also to be understood as a process, the 'tasks' are not simply tasks that the person completes and then moves on. It is rather, as Erikson (Erikson *et al.* 1986) has written of his stages of psychosocial development, that one stage may weave back on another. Thus, according to this model the individual is always in the process of becoming.

Further reflection on the model (MacKinlay 2001a) has led me to suggest that, even though it was constructed from the data from older people, it may be relevant for younger people too. For example, people facing a life-threatening illness and people living with mental disabilities such as Down Syndrome.[3]

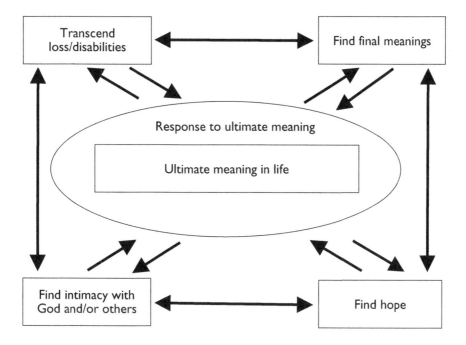

Figure 1.2 A generic model of spiritual tasks and process of ageing. Adapted from MacKinlay 2001a, p.224

The model of spiritual tasks and process of ageing (MacKinlay 2001a) may be used as a generic model for understanding the process of spiritual development in later life and for health professionals who work with older people. It could also be used for providing palliative care and working with people who have mental disabilities. This model does not assume a background of theological knowledge and training. However, to work effectively and in a more intentional manner with spiritual development and care, specialist training is a prerequisite. Models based on the major faiths would be of benefit for practitioners of pastoral care.

A CHRISTIAN MODEL OF SPIRITUAL TASKS AND PROCESS OF AGEING

The generic model forms the basis for spiritual tasks for Christians. A new model spells out the Christian tasks of ageing within the spiritual context of life. In this model (Figure 1.3), ultimate meaning in later life becomes life centred in God through Jesus Christ; response to meaning is mediated through worship, prayer, study, meditation and other spiritual strategies. Transcendence of loss and disabilities becomes, for the Christian, a dying to self, or self-forgetting. The move towards final meanings in later life becomes a search through spiritual reminiscence to articulate my life story and to see this in the context of God's story. This is both an individual and community search for meaning. Finding intimacy with God and others becomes a growing into Christ, just as it is a finding of intimacy with others. The generic hope becomes, for the Christian, hope both now and in the life to come. There is interaction between the parts of the model, indicated by the arrows.

A JEWISH MODEL OF SPIRITUAL TASKS OF AGEING

An understanding of the Jewish perspective must take account of three major themes: God, Torah and Israel (Zedek 1998, p.255). Israel connects the Jewish people culturally and with their faith story as spiritual heirs of Abraham, Isaac, and Jacob. The Jewish faith has strong connections through a unique history, community and culture. A great deal has been written about the distinctive nature of Jewish families, from the intensity of care-giving to low incidence of alcoholism. However, with increasing secularism in many places, this seems to not be as clearly marked as it perhaps was in previous decades (Zedek 1998). Jewish people generally adopt an attitude of responsibility for their health and well-being, and are open to change. This attitude allows for continued spiritual development borne out in the search for meaning in later life. Thus the generic spiritual tasks and process of ageing (MacKinlay 2001a) could be used with Jewish residents, while making provision for specific Jewish rituals and cultural requirements.

Pastoral care in a Jewish context arises from the Jewish notion of *mitzvah* or *chesed*, meaning acts of loving kindness (Friedman 2001). There are a number of forms of *chesed* relevant to aged care: inviting guests into one's home, visiting the sick and comforting the mourner, and the latter two correspond with Christian understandings of pastoral care. In fact, for Jews, the act of visiting the sick implies establishing a healing relationship between the sick person and the visitor.

AN ISLAMIC MODEL OF SPIRITUAL TASKS OF AGEING

There are increasing numbers of Muslims and ageing Muslims in many western countries. Diversity exists among Muslims, however: 'Islam is a discrete cosmology with a number of widely held tenets' (Hodge 2002, p.6). It is seen as a complete way of life, having a world view 'that unifies the metaphysical and material and gives structure and coherence to personal existence' (Hodge 2002, p.6). In contrast to the world view of western secularism, Muslims do not view

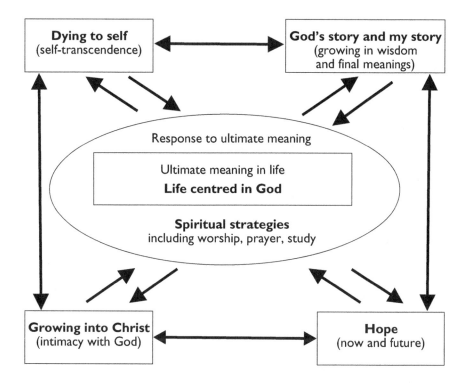

Figure 1.3 A Christian model of spiritual tasks of ageing. Adapted from MacKinlay 2001a, p.224

life as having separate arenas of a secular public sphere and a private religious sphere. 'Islam means "Peace" and "to submit to the will or law of God"' (Husain 1998, p.279).

As for Jews and Christians, a model of spiritual tasks and process of ageing would have Allah or God at its centre. Response to Allah forms an essential component of the Islamic faith, especially in relation to prayer. Aspects of relationship would also be important as the family and community have a place of importance in the lives of Muslims. Transcendence of loss and disability and self-transcendence also feature as submitting to the will of Allah.

A HINDU MODEL OF SPIRITUAL TASKS OF AGEING

The underlying philosophy of Hinduism includes an understanding of the law of Karma: that all deeds of humans have effects, either good or bad (Juthani 1998). This is tied to the cycle of reincarnation, where the person has to continue to be recreated in new body until the person has achieved *moksha*, which is understood as receiving liberation from the world of illusion (*maya*), and *avidya*, the ignorance that keeps people in bondage to the world. Hindus may strive to achieve *moksha* by three paths: the paths of illumination, action and devotion. Older Hindus may be pursuing one or more of these paths. *Dharma* is the way of living through rightness, justice, goodness and purpose through selflessness. This brings integrity and harmony to the universe.

Thus a model of spiritual tasks of ageing for Hindus would look rather different from a model based on the Abrahamic faiths (Jewish, Islamic and Christian). Brahma (God) is at the centre of the lives of Hindus and they hold to an underlying philosophy by which to live. The Hindu view of God is monotheistic in an ultimate sense, but is also polytheistic, pantheistic and panentheistic[4]. Hindus are likely to have a number of pictures or idols of gods in their homes. While an afterlife is acknowledged in one way or another in the Abrahamic faiths, there is no concept of that from within Hinduism. Hindus acknowledge the cycle of life and death where reincarnation of the person into different life forms continues until the person achieves *moksha*. Transcendence would certainly form a part of the spiritual tasks of ageing for Hindus, and to an extent, relationship would involve good works towards others. However, as Thursby notes, the spiritual journey for Hindus constitutes a path of spiritual development towards 'The cessation of a desire-driven identity, toward release, toward *nirvana*.' Thus release from suffering is not so much the transcendence of it, as it is a dissolution of the 'self'. It follows then that 'impermanence is the actual condition of life in the world and the sense of a separate selfhood is inevitably a failing, a false refuge from it' (Thursby 2000, p.171).

The traditional Hindu view of life acknowledges four stages of life across the lifespan; these are:

1. *Brahmacharya Ashrama:* childhood, building character and learning duty to others.

2. *Grhasha Ashrama:* begins at marriage.

3. *Vanaprasha Ashrama:* when one's children have reached adulthood.

4. *Sannyasa Ashrama:* the final life stage, when the person mentally renounces all worldly ties. The elderly person entering this stage spends all their time in meditation and contemplation, pondering the mysteries of life.[5]

A BUDDHIST MODEL OF SPIRITUAL TASKS OF AGEING

The numbers of adherents of Buddhism are increasing in western countries and these people are growing older. In Buddhism there are 'four seals' of belief derived from observations of consciousness. The first seal is *dukkha*, meaning 'ill'. It recognizes that suffering is a universal component of being human. The second is *anatta*, or 'no-self', and it states that there is no separately existing self:

> Buddha's analysis of consciousness concluded that a separate self could not be found in any of the parts of awareness nor in the sum of the parts of awareness. All that could be found to exist was a set of connected events, objects, emotions, and thoughts. (Scotton 1998, p.264)

It was therefore clear that 'reality' and 'self' were only a constantly changing scene of different events, and realizing that is an essential step towards release from suffering.

The third seal is *annicca* (impermanence), the idea that nothing lasts, whether material or emotional, not even the planets. Only the rate at which things change differs. The fourth seal is that *nibbana* (release from suffering) exists; this is achieved through giving up attachment to the 'false sense of a separate self and all that it produces' (Scotton 1998, p.264). Buddhism too differs markedly from the western secular world view. Buddhist thought supports a spiritualistic world where physical reality is merely delusion, constructed by our consciousness. In Buddhism physical reality is construction of the *pnacha-khanda* – the five instruments of clinging (Palapathwala, in press).

Thus, like Hinduism, Buddhism has no central concept of self, nor does it have one God at the centre. Therefore, a model of spiritual tasks of ageing for Hinduism and Buddhism must take account of the world view of both these major faiths for the way these people face ageing.

The aged care environment

In recent years there has been a move by some to renew the environment of residential aged care. The current trend to increase the size of aged care facilities does little to create a home-like environment. The Eden Alternative begun by Thomas in the US (www.edenalt.com) is one method for humanizing aged care. The movement is based on presenting both residents and staff with friendly environments that include the use of animals, plants and children in a therapeutic manner. The project also seeks to include residents in decisions of their daily care. Their vision (stated on their website, accessed 24 March 2005) is to eliminate loneliness, helplessness and boredom. Findings from research have so far failed to provide convincing results. Coleman *et al.* (2002) found no statistical differences between two groups of nursing home residents after one year of using the Eden Alternative. In another study using a treatment (Eden Alternative) group in a nursing home and a control group in another nursing home and studying the differences on loneliness, helplessness and boredom, Bergman-Evans (2004) found that while the treatment group decreased on scores of helplessness and boredom, there was no difference between the two groups in regard to loneliness, noting:

> There is little doubt that the risk of loneliness for individuals who enter and reside in a nursing home is significant. However, if the individual was isolated in the community because of decreased functioning, the loneliness may have preceded the move. It is probably naive to imagine that any intervention is powerful enough to balance the tremendous loss that follows changes in health status as well as the relinquishment of the family home, friends, pets, and self-image. (p.31)

Decreased levels of helplessness and boredom are important findings, and reports of the benefits of plants, animals and children around nursing homes suggest that this concept of deinstitutionalization has some very positive effects for residents and staff. It is noted, however, that while environment is important in aged care facilities, changing the environment alone will not alleviate the deep need for human connection. There is a great need that care for frail elderly people should be truly wholistic, including meeting needs for physical, psychosocial and spiritual needs, in an environment that empowers the older people and at the same time, is pleasant for staff and family to be in.

Conclusion

This is a book about the fourth age of life, the potential for continued spiritual growth, and also the need for spiritual care. This first chapter has examined the recent literature on ageing, spirituality and religion. It has outlined current understanding of religion as a component of the broader dimension of spirituality and examined recent research on the relationship between religion, spirituality and health in ageing. A model for spiritual tasks of ageing has been introduced, and spirituality in the major faith groups outlined. Issues of wholistic care and the importance of the aged care environment for quality of life have been discussed. This chapter has set the scene for a journey into ageing and well-being in later life.

Summary

- *The topic is the fourth age of life; the focus is on spiritual growth, well-being and spiritual care.*

- *Questions in the process of dying are the search for life-meaning, for hope, issues of guilt, the need for forgiveness and reconciliation, pain – existential as well as physical – all linked to the spiritual dimension.*

- *Definitions of spirituality are still being developed; however, a greater consensus is forming of the content of spiritual care.*

- *In essence spirituality must consist of finding core meaning in life, response to meaning, and relationship with God and / or others.*

- *A model of spiritual tasks of ageing is offered.*

- *In countries that are increasingly multicultural and multifaith some knowledge is needed of the faiths and cultures of other lands.*

- *Possible roles for multidisciplinary staff are suggested.*

Notes

1   For an account of the coming to a definition of spirituality used in my work see *The Spiritual Dimension of Ageing* (MacKinlay 2001a).

2   E.B. MacKinlay, C. Trevitt and M. Coady 'Finding meaning in the experience of dementia: The place of spiritual reminiscence work', was funded by Australian Research Council Linkage Grant 2002–2005. The Linkage Grant is a grant that seeks to fund research that is administered through one or more universities with industry partners; in the case of this grant, the industry partners are from the aged care industry.

3   Personal conversations with a number of family members of people with Down Syndrome.

4   'Panentheism is the term – first coined by Karl Christian Friedrich Krause (1781–1832) – to describe the understanding that all is in God and God is in all. Panentheism makes a subtle but important distinction from pantheism; it does not maintain that God and the world are identical' (personal communication from Ruwan Palapathwala).

5   Personal communication from Ruwan Palapathwala.

CHAPTER 2

The Studies of Frail Older People and Staff in Aged Care

The purpose of this chapter is to outline the main study, of frail elderly nursing home residents, and to discuss relevant findings of three other studies. These studies provide evidence on which to base care for frail older people, at home or in residential aged care. These studies cover both an elderly person's perspective and a staff perspective. Both are important in considering care needs.

Studies of spirituality of older people

In a study of nursing home residents that I conducted, which I completed in 2001, Violet was one participant who lived with multiple physical health problems, including large and painful leg ulcers, breathing difficulties and incontinence, yet she was often a source of joy to those who cared for her. She had a deep sense of the nearness of God to her as she struggled with her physical disabilities. Violet was one example of the frail older people in nursing homes who were not afraid of what lay ahead of them; in spite of, and perhaps because of her disabilities, she had a strong sense of hope.

Healing and wholeness occur in some cases that cannot be adequately explained by scientific methods. Healing and wholeness are not the same as cure, and it could be said that Violet was moving towards wholeness, continuing to grow spiritually as she learnt to transcend her disabilities. What was happening? Are the answers to be found in the spiritual domain?

The studies

A framework for care was developed from the work of mapping the spiritual dimension of independent living older people (MacKinlay 2001a) and from the subsequent study of frail elderly residents of nursing homes (MacKinlay

2001b). The data from these studies were collected using in-depth interviews, which were then transcribed and analysed (Minichiello *et al.* 1995). Grounded theory was used in these qualitative studies to find the important spiritual themes for elderly people. The initial project was conducted for my doctoral studies, and the themes identified in that first study were used to construct a model of spiritual tasks and process of ageing (MacKinlay 1998). This model was supported by the subsequent study of frail older people residing in aged care facilities (MacKinlay 2001b). Further study has since been conducted with aged care residents who live with dementia (MacKinlay *et al.* 2002–2005).

Another study is reported here to complete the picture: a study of raising the spiritual awareness of staff in aged care facilities (MacKinlay 2001b). This study examined what staff knew about ageing and spirituality and used workshops to raise awareness and knowledge of spiritual needs in later life.

DEMOGRAPHIC DATA

The sample of frail elderly residents (Table 2.1), having a mean age of 78.7 years with a minimum of 69 years and maximum of 94, were older than those in the independent living group, with a mean age of 75.3 and a range of 65–90 years. In both groups only 50 per cent of participants had completed primary or part secondary education (Table 2.2). In the frail elderly group 10 per cent had completed secondary education, 25 per cent had trade qualifications, and one had attended university. In contrast 30 per cent of the independent living sample had tertiary education and most of these had studied at university in middle age or later, showing an engagement in life-long study. There were 30 per cent males and 70 per cent females in the sample of frail elderly people. In the earlier study of independent living people only 46.7 per cent were widowed, compared with 80 per cent of the frail group.

In the study of frail elderly people, all informants were cognitively intact and were able to answer both the demographic questionnaire and the in-depth interview questions. Most of these interviews were from half an hour to one and a half hours in length, not as long as those conducted with the independent living group. The latter group ranged from one to two hours. This was probably for one or two reasons: first, this group may have been closer to finding final meanings in life and hence not exploring as many aspects of their lives; second, the interviews may have been shorter as 75 per cent of these informants reported having less energy than they used to have.

There were a number of differences between the participants in the two groups. Obviously, the group in aged care were more frail, and as a criterion for this group was cognitive competence the number of potential participants in

Table 2.1 Comparison of ages of participants in the two groups

Age	Independent living (n=75)	Resident in aged care (n=20)
Age range (years)	65–90	69–94
Mean age (years)	75.3	78.7

Table 2.2 Comparison of education of participants in the two groups

Education	Independent living* (%) (n=24)	Resident in aged care (%) (n=20)
Completed primary or part secondary education	50	50
Completed secondary education	0.12	10
Completed trade qualifications	0.08	25
Completed tertiary education	30	0.05

* Education data available only from in-depth interview (24 of 75 participants)

residential aged care was restricted as increasing numbers of these residents have dementia. In total, 20 aged care residents participated in the study with the in-depth interviews being conducted during 1998–1999. All residents lived with multiple chronic illnesses.

It is noted that nursing home populations are rapidly ageing, and a repeat of this study now, only six years later, would find an even older group and fewer who do not have dementia of some form.

THE PROCESS OF STUDY

The studies were based on grounded theory (Glaser and Strauss 1967; 1999; Morse 1992; Morse and Field 1995; Strauss and Corbin 1990) and the study of frail elderly people followed from doctoral studies using the same methodology with independent living older adults. The study of elderly people in residential care was conducted using residents from two different nursing homes in the Australian Capital Territory (ACT). This second set of interviews aimed to compare the responses from the two groups of informants and to test the model of spiritual tasks of ageing designed from the data of the first study of independent living older people.

The participants were recruited following information sessions for residents, relatives and staff letters. Institutional ethics approval was obtained and participants gave written consent. Potential participants were approached by registered nurses in the nursing homes with a letter explaining the project and inviting them to participate in the study and consent was obtained by the nursing home staff. Each resident was seen by the researcher at least twice; first to meet, to collect demographic data and conduct a questionnaire; second to conduct the in-depth interview, lasting from half an hour to one-and-a-half hours, and this session was audio tape recorded. It was necessary on several occasions to return a second time to complete the interview as the participant could become very tired during the interview process. Great care was taken not to continue when a participant was too tired. All interviews were audio taped and transcribed. The data were analysed using the QSR N4 (NUD*IST) qualitative data program. Analysis was completed using grounded theory (Glaser and Strauss 1967; 1999; Strauss and Corbin 1990).

Grounded theory was used to find the themes of spirituality that were important to these frail older people. Grounded theory is a valuable means of exploring data, particularly in areas where little is known as is the case with spirituality among frail older residents of aged care facilities. It would have been of little use to construct a questionnaire without first knowing what themes (categories) were important to the target group. This method of research empowers the participants as it brings the full focus of the research process onto them, and allows them to provide the data for the study, rather than imposing a structure on the participants. The researchers then analyse the data, including the stories of these older people.

The number of people in this study was based on the idea of theoretical saturation (Glaser and Strauss 1999, p.61) meaning that no additional data was being found from further interviews whereby any of the existing categories could be further developed, nor were any further new categories discovered. In the case of these frail nursing home residents, in the course of 20 interviews similar circumstances and experiences were seen over and over again, without the addition of any new data to any category or its properties.

The residents' self-perception of health

Despite the fact that these residents all lived with multiple chronic health conditions and had been classified for high level residential care, their perceptions of health were overall positive (Table 2.3). It would be expected that a higher proportion of these frail people would say they were in poor health than the 20 per cent who said they were. It is also interesting that the same percentage of both the independent and the residential groups (20%) said they were in very good to excellent health. It is noted that this range of 'very good to excellent' is used here, as in the original study (MacKinlay 1998) the highest level of health that participants were given as a choice was 'very good health'. It was a decision of the researcher not to provide the 'excellent health' option to the independent living participants. This illustrates clearly how parameters set by researchers can limit the findings of a project. As the data were collected it soon became evident that numbers of these elderly people were in better than 'very good health'. The options on the questionnaires were adjusted for the residential aged care participants, allowing them to choose from five categories, with a resulting 20 per cent reporting they were in 'very good to excellent health'.

It is important to consider the meaning of these self-perceptions of health, which are perhaps more correctly recognized as self-perceptions of well-being. The self-perceptions will influence the degree to which these older people can enjoy life, and fully participate in living, to flourish and find peace, joy and integrity in the latter years of their lives. These participants gave self-perceptions of their health that were much more positive than a medical diagnosis would provide.

Comparing the residents' perceptions of their health with a medical history perspective may produce a very different picture. It is contended that a medical diagnosis does not provide the whole story, especially in regard to well-being of older people. However, many nursing homes still work on a framework of medical care.

A new framework is needed that will affirm residents as people who need assistance with various aspects of daily life, who can still find quality of life and move away from the idea that ageing is a disease. Box 2.1 outlines the content of spiritual care, based on the model of spiritual tasks of ageing (MacKinlay 2001a). It is noted that these same spiritual tasks were identified from analysis of the data from the frail older people as from the earlier independent group of older people, thus supporting the findings of the original study and the model designed then. Box 2.1 uses these spiritual tasks as a means of grouping the spiritual behaviours of the raising spiritual awareness workshop. It can be seen

Table 2.3 Self-reported perception of health

Self-reported perception of health	Independent group (%)	Nursing home group (%)
Very good to excellent health*	20	20
Good health	38.7	15
Moderately to fairly good health	40	45
Poor health	1.3	20

* Independent participants were offered a choice of four categories – poor to very good health, while nursing home participants were offered a choice of five categories – poor to excellent health. These categories have been collapsed here to include very good and excellent health together.

that these behaviours fit well into the framework from the model. These behaviours may act as guides to spiritual practice.

A new framework of wholistic care will openly acknowledge the spiritual needs of older people. This will be an important development in care and will help address current practice issues that are often not accounted for in management and budgeting processes. A recent illustration of the need for wholistic care was from a manager of an aged care facility who said 75 per cent of her work involved assisting residents with issues of fear, guilt and grief. These are definitely issues of a spiritual nature. Thus, while retaining provision of good physical care, spiritual care should be developed as a critical component of care in aged care facilities. Yet, in studies of staff in aged care and in talking with aged care workers, many do not feel confident in having skills to either identify spiritual needs or provide spiritual care. There is still more to do in research and also in effectively communicating the findings into courses and training for workers in aged care.

A study of nurses working in aged care facilities and their understanding of 'spirituality'

During 1994–1995 a project was conducted to raise nurse awareness of their own spirituality and assist them to recognize the spiritual needs of their residents in six nursing homes (MacKinlay 2001e). A total of 96 participants

Box 2.1 Spiritual care and the spiritual tasks of ageing

To find ultimate meaning (for themselves)

- Facilitating relationship with an elderly person.

- Facilitating reconciliation among family members.

- Assisting a person to deal with feelings of guilt.

- Facilitating reconciliation with God.

- Supporting a person in their feeling of being loved by others/God.

Transcendence: Assisting a person in the move from self-centredness to self-transcendence

- To achieve a sense of self-acceptance.

- To accept and deal with the process of ageing.

- To live with chronic conditions and disabilities.

- To find meaning in increasing frailty.

- To deal with anger.

- To deal with grief.

Spiritual strategies: Response to ultimate meaning

- Praying with the resident.

- Reading the Bible or other sacred and religious material.

- Assisting an elderly person to worship according to their faith.

- Assisting the resident to develop spiritual strategies according to the individual's needs, including use of music, art and meditation.

- Referral of a person who needs forgiveness to chaplaincy or pastoral care.

Being 'with' the resident: Intimacy in relationship with God and/or others

- Listening and being present to a patient.

- Connecting with the resident.

- Developing a trusting relationship with the resident.

- Caring with integrity for an elderly person.

- Honouring a person's integrity.

Meaning making: From provisional life meanings to final meanings

- Facilitating reminiscence and life review.

- Assisting an elderly person to find final meanings in life.

- Assisting a person to find meaning in growing older.

- Assisting a person to find meaning in suffering and death.

Hope

- Assisting an elderly person who is fearful of their future.

- Caring for a person who feels hopeless.

- Affirming a person in their search for hope.

- Supporting a person in the process of dying (spirituality in palliative care).

- Supporting a person in their hope of life after death.

took part in the project: 31.3 per cent registered nurses, 17.7 per cent enrolled nurses, 33.3 per cent assistants in nursing and 17.7 per cent other workers in aged care. Only six of the participants had any specific preparation in gerontology, 30 per cent said they had some preparation in how to meet patients' spiritual needs and 64.3 per cent said they felt comfortable in meeting residents' spiritual needs, yet 94.3 per cent stated more preparation in spiritual care would help in their practice. The study consisted of a pre-test that examined participant understanding of the term 'spirituality' and asked them to identify a number of behaviours as physical, psychosocial or spiritual domains, or a combination of psychosocial and spiritual (see Box 2.2). The participants then took part in a workshop on raising awareness of spirituality, then, approximately one week later, they were asked to complete the post-workshop test, identical to the pre-test. The analysis, using SPSS, was set up to take account of moves from psychosocial to spiritual or the reverse.

First, participants were asked to describe the term 'spirituality', which 69 of 96 (72%) did (27 did not attempt the question). Seven participants said that not everyone has a spiritual dimension, and nine did not answer, making a total of 16 non-responses to that question. If the non-response is counted as a negative response, 15.5 per cent of participants did not believe that everyone has a spiritual dimension and 84.5 per cent agreed that everyone has a spiritual dimension. Of the 63 who completed the post-workshop survey, 93.7 per cent stated that everyone has a spiritual dimension. A variety of definitions of spirituality were received from the workshop participants; these were written down and ranged from spirituality being the essence of life, the soul, through life-meaning, to religion, morals and values, a belief in self.

There was little in these descriptions and definitions that included the human need for relationship and deep connection with others. Yet this formed an important aspect of spirituality for all older people interviewed; in fact relationship formed one of six major themes for all older people in the studies. It is noted that the aged care workers were (except for some older volunteers) of a younger and different cohort than the elderly residents. It is possible that spirituality is not seen to include this theme of relationship among younger aged care workers, or it may be simply a perception of the content of spirituality. It is noted, however, that the post-workshop participant definitions did change to include relationship. There was still a range of descriptions and definitions, including one participant who in the post-workshop questionnaire stated: 'I don't believe in the word [sic] Human Spirituality.' While I acknowledge that some older people may agree with this, at the same time, I hope that this participant would be open to the spiritual needs of those they were caring for. If this carer is working solely from their own perspective, they may fail to acknowledge important care needs of residents and this would be detrimental to the provision of wholistic care. More useful data were obtained from the analysis of pre- and post-tests of identifying behaviours.

The pre- and post-session test: identifying behaviours as spiritual or psychosocial

All participants were asked to identify items on a list of behaviours as physical, psychosocial or spiritual (Box 2.2). Comparison of pre- and post-session test items (MacKinlay 2001e) was performed to identify changes in respondents' perceptions of the spiritual aspect of each activity on the inventory. Significant

Box 2.2 List of spiritual behaviours/actions developed for the study

1. Praying with a patient.

2. Assisting a person to find meaning in suffering and death.

3. Listening to a patient.

4. Supporting a person in their hope of life after death.

5. Developing a trusting relationship with a patient.

6. Reading the Bible or other religious material.

7. Calling the chaplain or minister.

8. Facilitating reminiscence.

9. Assisting an elderly person to find meaning in life.

10. Caring with integrity for an elderly person.

11. Assisting a person in the process of dying.

12. Facilitating relationship with an elderly person.

13. Assisting an elderly person to worship according to their faith.

14. Assisting an elderly person who is fearful of their future.

15. Supporting a person in their feeling of being loved by others/God.

16. Assisting a person to deal with feelings of guilt.

17. Caring for a person who feels hopeless.

18. Referral of a person who needs forgiveness.

19. Facilitating reconciliation among family members.

20. Facilitating reconciliation with God.

21. Assisting a person to achieve a sense of self-acceptance.

22. Honouring a person's integrity.

23. Assisting a person to deal with anger.

24. Assisting a person to deal with grief.

Reproduced from MacKinlay 2001e, p.118

changes in participant identification of the spiritual dimension were shown between the pre- and post-surveys for 10 items (Table 2.4). In the pre-session inventory, the only items which were rated high as spiritual behaviours were those associated with worship, or that contained the word 'God' or 'Bible'; this is consistent with a common perception that religion and spirituality are synonymous, yet human spirituality encompasses a far broader perspective. Using McNemar's test, at the 95 per cent level of significance, 10 items were significant (Chi sq (1 df) critical value at 95% was 3.84).

Table 2.4 Change in participant assignment of behaviours as psychosocial or spiritual from pre- to post-test*

Item	Behaviour	Score
3	Listening to a patient	6.23
8	Facilitating reminiscence	4.76
11	Assisting a person in the process of dying	6.00
14	Assisting an elderly person who is fearful of their future	9.00
15	Supporting a person in their feeling of being loved by others/God	4.50
16	Assisting a person to deal with feelings of guilt	11.27
17	Caring for a person who feels hopeless	4.45
19	Facilitating reconciliation among family members	8.89
22	Honouring a person's integrity	7.36
23	Assisting a person to deal with anger	8.07

* Only significant changes are listed

Reproduced from MacKinlay 2001e, p.119

The nurses who participated in this study subsequently identified the spiritual dimension more frequently in their work with nursing home residents; however, a number of them said that, although they were now able to identify spiritual needs more readily, they did not feel comfortable in providing spiritual care. It is apparent that if spiritual care is to become part of the nursing role, then adequate preparation for the role must be provided in nursing education. Certainly evidence-based practice must support teaching and thus practice.

Implications for spiritual care arising from the studies

Spirituality, seen as life-meaning, ways of responding to meaning including religion, music, art and the environment, transcendence of losses and difficulties of ageing, the need for intimacy and hope, is important to frail older people in residential care. Care in aged care facilities needs to reflect this important area for intervention, yet in the study of aged care staff, while awareness of spiritual needs might be raised through the workshops provided, although 64.3 per cent said they felt comfortable in meeting residents' spiritual needs, 94.3 per cent stated that more preparation in spiritual care would help in their practice. The role of nurses in spiritual care needs to be clearly described. There is mounting evidence to do this now (Carson and Green 1992; Koenig and Lawson 2004; MacKinlay 2001a; 2001e; McSherry 2000; Swinton 2001). There is also a need to examine the way care is provided in aged care facilities to see how spiritual care may be effectively introduced into the roles of care providers, for example, of diversional therapists, or activity officers, social workers, psychologists and medical practitioners. It has always been assumed that spiritual care was the province of clergy, chaplains and pastoral carers, but even these care providers need knowledge of the potential developments of the spiritual dimension in ageing.

Conclusion

This chapter has outlined the studies that are applied in this book. The first of these was a study of independent living older people, mapping their spiritual dimension. Analysis of the data, using grounded theory, led to the construction of a model of spiritual tasks and process of ageing. This was followed by a similar study, this time extending the project to map the spiritual dimension among older residents of aged care facilities. The model developed in the first study was supported by the findings of the second study. A further study that included pre- and post-tests of aged care staff and of their identification of spiritual behaviours used a workshop to raise staff spiritual awareness.

Summary

This chapter has outlined two main studies, mapping the spiritual dimension of frail older but cognitively intact residents of aged care.

- *Comparisons made of the residential elderly study participants and an earlier study of independent living older people, showed the frail group were more likely to be older, to be widowed and have lower education. However, the residential aged care group had similar levels of self-perceived health to the independent group.*

- *The model of spiritual tasks of ageing constructed from data of the independent living group was supported from the findings of the residential aged care group.*

A further study of raising aged care staff awareness of spirituality in older people outlined staff awareness of spirituality of older people and their needs for care.

- *There were significant changes from pre- to post-workshop identification of spiritual behaviours by aged care staff, showing a greater awareness of spiritual care.*

- *Changes in the way aged care is delivered are needed to provide for wholistic care that includes the spiritual dimension as an integral component of care.*

CHAPTER 3

Assessment of Spirituality and Spiritual Needs

A Developmental Approach

Against a background of increased interest in the spiritual dimension, and in particular, the spiritual dimension in later life, it is important that any ministry to, or care of, the spiritual dimension is based on effective assessment of spiritual needs. This chapter considers a developmental approach to spirituality in ageing, and hence to the assessment of spiritual needs. A developmental approach assumes that there is at least a potential for spiritual growth in later life. In fact it has been noted by a number of authors that spiritual development does continue into later life (Fowler 1981; MacKinlay 2001e; Moberg 1990). Further, Kane and Kane (2000) devote a chapter (Olson and Kane) to spiritual assessment in their latest edition of *Assessing Older Persons*. They note that gerontologists increasingly acknowledge the importance of the spiritual lives of older people, urge practitioners to include spiritual well-being as an aspect of health and include spiritual care as a 'sought-after outcome, however elusive to measure'(p.300).

The term 'spiritual' in this context means that which brings greatest or deepest life-meaning for the person, typically this may be through relationship with God or some sense of other, and/or through relationship with other people (MacKinlay 2001a).

Wholistic assessment

Best practice supports the use of wholistic assessment, as physical and psycho-social health problems may impinge on spiritual well-being. It is also possible that spiritual distress may adversely influence physical and/or mental well-being. The spiritual dimension is of a different nature than the physical dimension, and it differs also from the psychological dimension. Acknowledging the human needs for meaning, connection and hope as components of the spiritual, it is obvious that appropriate assessment means are required.

We would not dream of providing physical care without first assessing the care recipient's needs. For example, with any new resident, it is important to assess their basic needs for nourishment, for mobility, safety, elimination, skin integrity, needs for and response to medications and their risk of infection. Nor should assessment for depression be neglected as 40–60 per cent of residents admitted to residential aged care may be depressed (Fleming 2001) and depression lowers quality of life for those who experience it. Most commonly the Geriatric Depression Scale (GDS) is used to identify levels of depression. Likewise, in recent years a high level of awareness of dementia has developed in aged care, and assessments such as the Mini Mental State Examination (MMSE) (Folstein, Folstein and McHugh 1975) are routinely used for screening for dementia.

The case for spiritual assessment

No less important are the basic needs for spiritual care and nourishment. I would contend that touching into the spiritual and connecting deeply with others is essential for spiritual well-being, both for care providers and for recipients of care. Unless we can accurately identify spiritual needs, these will not be addressed and these needs may perhaps be mistakenly treated as psychological needs. For example, we may identify a frail elderly person as failing to thrive and treat the person physically and psychologically to overcome the symptoms of weight loss, depression and loss of interest in life, with little effect. However, the real underlying issue may be lack of nourishment of the soul, the need for love and care of the spirit. Thus it is essential to accurately identify such conditions as a requirement for determining appropriate strategies for care.

It is argued that it is important to assess spiritual needs to give best care to the spiritual concerns. Facilitating spiritual growth and well-being amongst older adults is a multidisciplinary concern. Health professionals from different disciplines are now beginning to realize this. Yet many are still unsure of what the spiritual dimension looks like, and despite the fact that more interest has been shown in spirituality over the last couple of decades, there remains little agreement as to what constitutes spirituality (Draper and McSherry 2002; McSherry 2002; Swinton and Narayanasamy 2002; Wright 2000). In addition, McSherry (2002) notes that little research has been published that can provide nurses with a framework for assessment, let alone delivery of spiritual care. Nevertheless, work is continuing in this area, with one example being a pilot scheme to routinely assess spiritual needs of patients at Bradford Teaching Hospitals (Nursing Standard 2004).

Assessment is important to determine where the individual is on their spiritual journey; this is a necessary first step to be able to meet the individual at their point of need. Care is only wholistic when the spiritual dimension is assessed and considered together with the physical and psychological dimensions in care planning. Aged care health professionals need guidelines to effectively make spiritual assessments as a starting point for effective spiritual care.

Spiritual assessment is more often used in residential aged care facilities and people who live independently are assumed to be able to provide for their own spiritual needs. However, it is noted that many people in society at the beginning of the twenty-first century do not even know what spiritual needs they have, nor do they have a repertoire of spiritual strategies that they may draw on to assist them to develop spiritually. Perhaps as gymnasiums for physical development and well-being became increasingly popular in the latter decades of the twentieth century, so we may be in need of establishing ways of developing spiritual strategies, perhaps spiritual gymnasiums? These may form part of the facilities that will be provided in residential aged care in the future.

What does a spiritual assessment consist of?

First, it is acknowledged that both religiosity and spirituality are multi-dimensional constructs and so far, little work has examined the independence or correlation among the domains (Olson and Kane 2000). It is important first to consider why spiritual assessment is being done. Much of the assessment attempted so far has examined spirituality and its relation to health and well-being, thus the assessment instruments have often focused on research rather than on clinical assessment of spiritual needs (Fiala *et al.* 2002; Hays *et al.* 2001; Hill and Pargament 2003; Koenig 1998). Even to assess for spiritual well-being is probably of more interest academically than clinically. Some would argue, quite rightly, that we must be careful not to reduce spirituality and spiritual care to a spiritual questionnaire that can simply be 'ticked off' and the person slotted into a particular routine.

It seems there is still often confusion as to what to assess – is the assessment really an assessment of religion, or spirituality? What is gained by assessing church attendance? Are there more important aspects of spirituality that should be assessed? Wright questions the use of objective measures to assess spiritual needs, noting importantly, that 'spiritual needs do not lend themselves to objective questionnaires' (Wright 2004, p.26). In fact, as McSherry (2002) has noted, it may be quite misleading to attempt to put a score on spiritual needs or spiritual well-being. However, to be at all helpful, it is necessary to have both an indication of the person's religious affiliation and preferences, if any, and some information regarding their spiritual needs. What is needed in clinical settings is an instrument that will enable optimal identification of spiritual needs so that best care may be delivered. Thus the content of a spiritual assessment should include questions about meaning in life, source of hope, coping strategies in crises, and any spiritual or religious practices.

Assessing religious needs versus assessing spiritual needs

Assessment of religious needs has long been the province of clergy and chaplains. It is only recently that other health care professionals have become interested in assessment and provision of spiritual care. One of the factors involved in this move may be an increasing realization that spirituality is closely related to overall well-being and health (Carson 1989; Hays *et al.* 2001; Hill and Pargament 2003), while a second factor is a growing acknowledgment by secular society that religion and spirituality are different concepts. It currently seems acceptable to acknowledge having spiritual needs, while rejecting religious needs (Tacey 2003). Not all practitioners or researchers would agree on the latter point. Many would say that religion is part of spirituality (Koenig, McCullough and Larson 2001; MacKinlay 2001a), see Chapter 1. Where the individual practises a religion, the term 'religiosity' may be used and this may be regarded as a part of spirituality.

It is in this context that the separation of religious from spiritual needs seems an artificial one. This raises important issues around assessment. For example, if health care providers are to assess spiritual needs, and religious needs are seen as part of these, then the question of knowledge of religious needs arises. It cannot be realistic to expect health care providers to also study religion, thus assessment of religious needs would seem to be impossible. However, if assessment of spiritual needs can be seen as not requiring study in religion, then health care providers may be able to both assess spiritual needs and provide spiritual care. Even if religion is seen as being part of the spiritual dimension, this approach may be possible. Thus spiritual assessment becomes a possibility for health care providers, with the proviso that these practitioners are both aware of their own spiritual dimension and have some basic preparation in assessing and providing spiritual care. Otherwise it is possible that health professionals who are not spiritually self-aware may unknowingly project their own spiritual needs onto the person they are working with.

On this basis, it is argued that the assessment of religious needs is the role of clergy, chaplains and pastoral workers, while still acknowledging that other health care providers may at least ask the questions of whether a person wishes to receive religious services and care.

Comfort levels of staff related to assessing spiritual needs of patients

An early study by Soeken and Carson (1987) pointed out the discomfort that some nurses experienced when confronted with the spiritual needs of patients. Several studies in recent years have examined staff beliefs regarding spiritual assessment. Wahby, Born and Montagnini (2004) described the attitudes and practices of palliative care physicians regarding spiritual assessment. In this small study, they noted that physicians were more likely to utilize spiritual interventions when they felt comfortable with their own spirituality. This was also found in a study of nurses (MacKinlay 2001e). In a paper on integrating spirituality in counselling with older adults, Driscoll-Lamberg (2001) notes both the need for counsellors to use spiritual assessment and their lack of preparation for doing so.

Typically, staff who do not feel comfortable with their own spirituality do not feel comfortable in providing spiritual care. Staff do not need to have a personal faith to be able to respect the faith of a person that they provide care for.

Who should assess spiritual needs?

There has been some debate on this issue, asking whose domain is the spiritual, is it the province of chaplains? Is it a broader responsibility for health professionals, for example, nurses, social workers, pastoral carers? It would seem that as the spiritual dimension is being recognized as a multidisciplinary responsibility, so the responsibility for its assessment is also multidisciplinary. It would be fair to say that aged care chaplains are the specialists in the field; however, for maximum benefit to all residents, it should be acknowledged that spiritual assessment is multidisciplinary.

Workshops or continuing education to raise spiritual awareness are important for staff working with older people (MacKinlay 2001e). Without an understanding of the spiritual dimension, health professionals may not recognize spiritual needs, so these will remain unmet. Thus, spiritual assessment is everyone's concern, while recognizing the special role of aged care chaplains and pastoral carers.

Where a person has needs related to their faith or religious practices, with the person's permission, an appropriate person of that faith (Jewish, Christian, Islamic, Buddhist, Hindu, or other) should be contacted to provide specific religious care and/or rituals or liturgies.

Spiritual needs of older people

Koenig defines spiritual needs as 'conscious or unconscious strivings that arise from the influence of the human spirit on the biopsychosocial natures' (1994, p.283). He lists 14 spiritual needs of older persons, for convenience, these have been summarized in Box 3.1.

It is argued that all 14 spiritual needs listed by Koenig are important areas for assessment. It is also affirming that in recent literature many authors are pointing to very similar content for an understanding of the spiritual. Thus it appears that a consensus is developing for understanding the spiritual dimension. It is therefore logical to consider spiritual assessment tools that will include the most commonly cited aspects of spirituality. A basis of research should be used to provide evidence for the construction of assessment tools.

The basis for development of a spiritual assessment instrument to assess spiritual needs of older adults

My thesis is that spiritual development continues across the lifespan and healthy ageing is dependent on spiritual health and well-being as well as physical and psychosocial wellness. It is my contention (MacKinlay 2001a) that spiritual health in ageing can be enhanced by:

1. sensitizing older people to their own spiritual journeys

2. assessing the spiritual needs of frail older people

3. assisting older people to effectively meet their spiritual needs.

I consider the spiritual dimension to be a generic dimension, just as the psychosocial and physical dimensions are. The spiritual dimension is part of being human, however, the way that people choose to develop their spiritual dimension may differ. For some, this will include the practice of a religion; for others a particular life-focus may be followed, for example, with engagement in music, art or the environment.

Box 3.1 Fourteen spiritual needs of physically ill elders

1. The need for meaning, purpose and hope.

2. The need to transcend circumstances.

3. The need for support in dealing with loss.

4. The need for continuity.

5. The need for validation and support of religious behaviours.

6. The need to engage in religious behaviours.

7. The need for personal dignity and sense of worthiness.

8. The need for unconditional love.

9. The need to express anger and doubt.

10. The need to feel that God is on their side.

11. The need to love and serve others.

12. The need to be thankful.

13. The need to forgive and be forgiven.

14. The need to prepare for death and dying.

Based on Koenig 1994, pp.283–293

Constructing a spiritual assessment instrument

Perhaps the earliest spiritual assessment designed by a nurse was a spiritual history guide (Stoll 1979, p.1574). This guide was divided into four areas of concern: the person's concept of God or deity; the person's source of strength and hope; the significance of religious practices and rituals to the person and the person's perceived relationship between their spiritual beliefs and health status. Stoll's guide was for general use, not specifically for older people. It was a valuable guide designed at the time when nursing diagnoses were being classified. More recent work has focused on developing psychometrically sound instruments to measure aspects of spirituality, an example is the Functional Assessment of Chronic Illness Therapy – Spiritual Well-Being Scale (FACIT-sp) (Peterman *et al.* 2002).

The type of assessment may vary, according to the background of the assessor and the sorts of assumptions they make about spirituality. In fact, how do they define spirituality? This will make a difference to the way questions are asked. Spirituality is hard to be objective about, yet we do not hesitate to discuss and measure personality (Moberg 2001). A number of assessment tools are already in use: Olson and Kane (2000, pp.310–316) review measures of private and organizational religious practices (Idler 1999; Levin 1999), measures of commitment (Hodge 1972; Williams 1999), measures of religious/spiritual history (George 1999), measures of religious support (Krause 1999), selected measures from the Fetzer working party (Idler 1999; Pargament 1999), and measures of spiritual well-being (Ellison 1983).

The assessment tools described in this chapter are based on research conducted by MacKinlay (1998; 2001a; 2001b; 2001d). I originally set out to test a spiritual assessment instrument that had been designed for assessing spiritual health amongst people who had cancer: Spiritual Health Inventory (SHI) (Highfield 1989). The SHI was modified for a sample of elderly people and was renamed Spiritual Health Inventory, Elderly (SHIE, MacKinlay 1998), making the assumption that there would be a number of similarities between those who have cancer and older people, resident in aged care facilities. This assumption was based on vulnerability and heightened spiritual awareness associated with a diagnosis of cancer and possible situational crises on the one hand and, on the other hand, admission to an aged care facility and the associated losses experienced in the case of the older person. However, this instrument designed by a group of experts (but not including the target audience of older people) failed to give sufficient loading on factor analysis (Hair *et al.* 1995), accounting for only 30.1 per cent of the total variance (MacKinlay 1998), and so was rejected. Analysis of the factors contained in the SHIE and the themes obtained from the data of the exploration of in-depth interview material showed SHIE did not connect with the following major themes from the data: ultimate meaning; response to ultimate meaning; transcendence; relationship and final meanings.

These findings illustrate the importance of including members of the group being assessed in the construction of any assessment instrument. There were no consumers of health care included in the construction of the SHI, and the team who constructed that questionnaire failed to identify questions that tapped into the fullness of the spiritual dimension for this group of people. The findings also point to the need to use qualitative methods to explore new fields of learning, as the results of survey and questionnaire instruments will only be as good as the questions that are asked. It may be that the 'wrong' questions are asked, and questions that are central to meaning for the population being studied are left unasked. Reliance on a quantitative instrument that fails to tap into the relevant questions is at best misleading. However, once the area is mapped out using qualitative means, this data can then be used to construct questionnaires that can be used in surveys and assessment.

A model for spiritual development in later life

A model for spiritual development in later life was constructed based on the main themes from the data of in-depth interviews (MacKinlay 2001a). These themes were:

1. *Ultimate meaning* (for each person): relationship with God, sense of other, absence of religious belief, or other centres of ultimate meaning.

2. *Response to the ultimate* includes: worship, prayer, reading scripture, symbols of meaning, meditation, experience of 'otherness' and response to music, the Arts and environment.

The following four themes seem to develop in interaction with and dependence on the first two listed above.

1. *Vulnerability/self-sufficiency:* this includes disabilities and effects of physical ageing; that is, perceived and/or actual vulnerability. An outcome of this theme is the development of transcendence to move through and beyond vulnerabilities.

2. *Wisdom/final meanings:* wisdom includes discernment, the move from provisional towards final meanings, an increased ability to tolerate ambiguity, and increased sense of interiority. An outcome of this theme is to come to an increased self-awareness and some understanding of the questions that life asks of each of us (Frankl 1984). For example, the question: 'What is (and has been) my purpose in life?' This question also pushes forward into the future, searching and affirming that there is still purpose and meaning in life. There may be times when this meaning is hard to find, but it is

still to be found. Spiritual reminiscence and the possibilities of reframing of past experiences may well be important strategies here.

3. *Relationship/isolation:* relationship with others, whether this is satisfied or not satisfied and the possibility of social and/or spiritual isolation. This theme is related to loss of relationships in later life. An outcome of this theme is to search for and find new intimacies.

4. *Hope/fear/despair:* includes spiritual integrity, contentment, peace, joy, searching, despair, hopelessness and meaninglessness. Outcomes of this theme are finding peace, joy, contentment and hope in the face of increasing losses and frailty.

The six themes drawn from the data outlined above form the basis for the model of spiritual tasks or processes of ageing (see Figure 1.2). The term 'task' as used in this chapter is understood as a dynamic and continuing process, and not simply something to be completed. In fact the spiritual tasks or processes of ageing may not be completed during this life. However, the process of moving towards the fulfilment of these tasks is what is of concern. At times there is tension and struggle in this process.

The spiritual assessment instrument presented in this chapter (see Appendices 1 and 2) is based on the model of spiritual development and tasks in later life developed by MacKinlay (1998). It is acknowledged that this tool is based on several studies but needs further refinement; it is, however, offered here as an assessment instrument that may be used in clinical settings, pending further work. It is constructed at two levels. The first level is an initial screening assessment, to be completed as soon after admission to an aged care facility as possible, or at first meeting with a community-dwelling older person. This first level assessment aims to identify immediate spiritual needs. The second level assessment instrument provides a structure for spiritual assessment that may be easily administered through an interview with an older adult. It is suggested that this instrument is used in an interview process to provide an opportunity for the person to share important aspects of their spiritual journey that may be critical to their spiritual well-being, both in settling into a new residence and in developing longer term planning for spiritual care and well-being.

Assessment of spiritual needs at admission to an aged care facility

Elderly people admitted to aged care facilities may be experiencing a crisis of meaning and multiple losses as they enter residential aged care. All too often the decision to enter long term care has been a difficult one, involving grief and loss, and not infrequently guilt, experienced by the older person entering care, but also by the family who may have been involved to varying degrees in the process.

Combined with the aged care assessment and process that has resulted in their admission to an aged care facility, they may now face a complexity of health problems of a physical, mental and spiritual nature including settling into a new and strange environment. Add to that the multiple losses experienced prior to admission such as loss of independence, loss of community, loss of residence, loss of many of their belongings. For some, this move will mean loss of intimacy and lessened contact with family and friends. All of these factors, including the need of the person to accept that long-term care may be the best decision in the circumstances, as well as the need to feel accepted and comfortable in the new environment, may produce a sense of spiritual crisis at the time of admission. On this basis, spiritual assessment at admission is important. Based on the assumption that spirituality is generic and universal, spiritual assessment should be for all residents, not just those who have a religious affiliation.

In recent years the increasing requirements of accreditation within aged care facilities have begun to recognize and document spiritual and cultural needs. In this environment the need for intentional spiritual assessment assumes even greater importance.

Two levels of spiritual assessment

The spiritual assessment instrument suggested here is set out in two levels, the first (Appendix 1) is to be administered when the person is initially admitted to residential aged care. The second (Appendix 2) is to be administered by a member of the pastoral care team, or a health professional specially trained in spiritual assessment and care. The aim of the two level assessment is to screen for spiritual needs at admission and to make referrals as required. It is assumed that there will not be time to make a full assessment at the time of admission, thus the first level assessment asks essential information that will enable special and immediate spiritual needs to be identified and followed up. The Level 1 assessment is designed so that, if possible, the new resident and/or their family may complete the form, or if that is not possible, then the admitting staff member may complete the initial assessment. This Level 1 assessment form will ideally be kept with the resident's notes.

The Level 1 assessment asks two types of questions, the first are related to broad questions of meaning and coping: 'What makes your life worth living?' 'Are there things that are hard for you now?' These initial questions are followed by a focusing question: 'What is hardest for you now?' And finally, 'How do you cope with difficult things in your life?' The second set of questions on this first assessment instrument includes one optional question on religious denomination. The remaining questions relate to religious and spiritual practices, whether the person is a member of a faith community and whether the person wishes to have someone of that community notified. Where the new resident is a member of a congregation or faith community that is within a reasonable distance of the aged care facility, it is often valuable to maintain the connections with that community, if the person desires. It is too easy in a busy residential aged care facility for communications with the outside community to be broken or weakened. Connections are vitally important to these new residents, who have already lost so much.

The Level 2 assessment is then conducted by a member of the pastoral care team, the chaplain, or a health care professional with special preparation in spiritual care. This assessment tool includes questions on the person's life story, and spiritual reminiscence. See Appendix 2.

When should assessment be done?

Admission is a critical time for the elderly person coming into a new environment. Therefore, admission assessment of spiritual needs is essential. It may be possible to complete spiritual assessment at a later time, but as spiritual needs at time of admission may be heightened, it is important to assess these needs then. It is stressed that these needs are just as important as assessing risk for pressure ulcers or any other physical or psychosocial measures, yet too often spiritual needs are relegated to optional status and given lower priority.

Spiritual needs should continue to be assessed over the longer term, during the person's stay in residential care, as changes in physical status, issues of grief and loss or any other major events for the individual may serve to highlight emerging spiritual issues. Again, a team approach is valuable. Nursing staff seeing the resident regularly may be the first to identify an emerging spiritual need. Unfortunately, diagnosis of depression is too often missed amongst older people in residential care (Fleming 2001). Spiritual assessment and care forms part of the team approach to early identification and care of depression (MacKinlay 2003). Physical problems too, for example incontinence, may impinge on spiritual well-being. It is not uncommon for people who have incontinence to experience a sense of shame, that is, a spiritual concern arising from a physical problem.

Conclusion

Spiritual assessment should form an integral component of admission assessment for all older people in residential care. Spiritual assessment may also be used when working with fourth age people living in the community. Spiritual assessment, based on the literature, should be understood as more than religious assessment. Further spiritual assessment may be required at intervals throughout the person's stay in residential care. Effective spiritual assessment provides guidance for meeting individuals' spiritual needs, thus enabling provision of truly wholistic care. The assessment instrument presented in this chapter is based on research that examined the spiritual dimension of older people, and is suggested as a way to developing effective spiritual assessment tools for use among older people in residential care.

Summary

- *Spiritual assessment should be for all residents, not just those who have a religious affiliation.*

- *Assessment at first meeting with the older person is important.*

- *Assessment is important to determine where the individual is on their spiritual journey; this is a necessary first step to meet the individual at their point of need.*

- *Health professionals who are not spiritually self-aware may unknowingly project their own spiritual needs onto the person they are working with.*

- *Spiritual health and well-being in ageing can be enhanced by:*

  1. sensitizing older people to their own spiritual journeys

  2. assessing the spiritual needs of frail older people

  3. assisting older people to effectively meet their spiritual needs.

CHAPTER 4

Meaning in Life and Frailty in the Later Years

For many people, as they grow older, the search for life-meaning becomes more focused and intentional. What is held as providing central or ultimate life-meaning is critical to each person's sense of well-being. It is out of this core sense of well-being that hope can flow or, on the other hand, if there is no sense of well-being, hope and the will to live may be lost. The stories used in this section are based on analysis of in-depth interviews of elderly nursing home residents during 1998–1999.

The image of God held by a person may provide an important way into understanding that person's spiritual well-being. It is from what lies at the core of our being that we respond to the whole of life. For those who hold some belief or understanding of God or god, that will provide the lens through which they look at life. Pastoral questions may focus on asking, 'Does that lens provide a framework for hope?' or 'Does it provide a framework for despair?' For a Christian, that image of God may be of a loving father, or it might be of a stern judge who stands far off. In other religions, for example, for ageing Buddhists, the search is to face and accept physical decline and death, while in humanism, the person sees their 'self' as being the seat of life meaning, without the need for anything outside or 'other than' themselves. Whatever the focus of life-meaning, this will influence the way in which the person responds to life and it is an important place to begin exploring a person's spirituality.

Where do nursing home residents find meaning?

To begin one step back, what is it that produces quality of life for residents of nursing homes? Is it prevention of pressure ulcers, good hydration and nutrition, good continence management, falls prevention, effective medication management and pain management? There is no argument against any of these; they are essential components of good aged care. Does quality of life for nursing home residents depend on activities such as diversional therapy, outings and a pleasant environment? These too are valuable aspects of aged care. But beyond all of these, and deeper, is finding meaning in life. Finding meaning involves the psychosocial and especially the spiritual dimensions of life.

The model of spiritual tasks of ageing forms the basis for assessment (see Figures 1.2 and 1.3). One of the tasks of ageing, based on this model, is to search for final life-meaning. Working from the assumption that people construct provisional meanings throughout life, only coming to grapple with finding final meanings as they perceive they are nearing the end of their lives, it could be assumed that these older and more frail nursing home residents might be more focused on the search for final meanings (Frankl 1984; Kimble *et al.* 1995; MacKinlay 1998).

A constant or changing image of God (variety of experiences)

More of the frail elderly people in residential care held an image of God, and found that God was important in bringing meaning into their lives, than a previous study of independent living people (MacKinlay 2001a; 2002). More viewed God as being at the centre of their lives. As would be expected, among the aged care residents interviewed, there was a variety of images held of God.

For some, the image they have of God has changed over the years; for others, it has remained constant. Alice, for example, did not think her image of God had changed with the passing years; God was to her now much as she had imagined him when she was a child going to Sunday school. She said: 'Well, I think He's up there somewhere and has rules over us and any of these accidents or plane crashes or anything like that I think that He does that for a purpose.' And she went on to explain, 'I think if it's meant to be that nobody can stop it, 'cause there's some terrible things happen in the world now.' Alice said: 'Everything that God does for us, it's for a purpose, we mightn't think so at the time but it's all for a purpose.' She could see this as she looked back over her life.

She still prays every night when she goes to bed, just as she did as a child, she remembers her mother getting them all to kneel beside their beds to say their prayers. She still remembers some of the set prayers from then: 'Now I lay me down to sleep I pray thee Lord my soul to keep, if I should die before I wake, I ask you God…' Alice did feel that she gained comfort from these set prayers. When I asked her whether she felt close to God, or felt she had any kind of relationship with God, she did not seem to have any concept of what this could be like. It is important to support Alice in finding comfort through her prayer life, and the continuity of her sense of God affirmed.

Andrew, like Alice, said his belief in God started when he was a child. In his case, he remembered being a choirboy. He also recalled having religious instruction at school and says, 'So I've always got my own feelings about those sort of things and just don't say "well, I've given up going to church that [has] done nothing for me" and now at my time of life I find they [the church] are doing things for me.' He said he feels closer to God since his wife's funeral.

Agnes spoke of her reliance on God, and said: 'Well I don't think I could do without Him'. On the other hand, Angus, a Catholic, said: 'Well the way I am at the present time he's [God] not a real good friend of mine' [laughs]. He didn't want me to pursue the topic. Angus was typical of some of the men who did not want to talk about religion, or to reflect deeply on life. It is also important to accept Angus' perspective of his relationship with God, while leaving possibilities of conversation open.

A faith of my own

Bonnie had studied spiritualism for many years. She had developed a religion of her own, with a deep sense of the spiritual, and she had come to accept that in her view reincarnation was a reality, very much the style described by Bellah *et al.* (1985) as 'Sheilaism', after one of his subjects who named her religion after herself (Sheila). It has some components of Christianity, but interprets biblical passages in ways not understood by Christians, for example, she said: 'Because Christ said in my Father's house there are many mansions and there is a room for everybody even dreadful people who have been dreadful on earth.' Later in her search for truth Bonnie said:

> So then I began to think about the Bible, because somewhere along the line I'd lost Jesus and this worried me. And I thought now, reading the Old Testament and the New Testament, I don't think the God of Jesus, is the God of the Old Testament. They're two totally different people.

This perceived 'loss of Jesus' seemed to continue to concern her to some extent. Bonnie had rejected the concept of 'free will' from her studies in astrology, mixed with spiritualism and an understanding of reincarnation, saying:

> So with my sort of new spiritual beliefs I was forced to accept reincarnation, not in the sense that we've told reincarnation, but the fact that in spirit we may or may not decide to be reborn and live a certain life to teach us whatever…I'm still not sure what I've learnt in this life yet. I think it could be patience, I think it

could be or it may be just wisdom, it may be just understanding of people, I don't know.

Bonnie clearly distinguished between spiritual beliefs and religious beliefs, saying she could not believe in religious beliefs and she maintained that her spiritual beliefs had no place in a religious context. She also acknowledged experiencing her spiritual journey as what she thought was a universal spiritual search. She said that there must be some reason for living. Her interview had been a fascinating mixture of misinterpretations of Christian scripture; accounts of answered prayer; thoughts on astrology and spiritualism; reincarnation and then this summary of the journey. It was indeed an example of Sheilaism (Bellah 1985), but one wonders if on the journey the Holy Spirit was not guiding her. The question of her journey remains. She has not reached a sense of her final meaning of life yet.

Taking another perspective, Dora has a firm faith and belief in an afterlife. Her life has been characterized by a gradual growth of faith. When I asked her how she sees God now she replied: 'Just as a, a being in the distance, he's there [pause], it might be more that I see Jesus before I see God…and it's more the, the, the image of Jesus that I see.' She went on to describe how he would be dressed and then she said: 'just that he's always there'. This is an intimate image of Jesus and God that Dora carried in her everyday life.

Grace described God and her faith saying: 'He's a person that we can't see, He knows, He knows how you feel you know. He knows what we look like, I'm alright and I'll be with him.'

Charlie described God as 'an ever loving Father'. Charlie expressed a fear of death that had been with him since childhood – he had spent seven years in the navy and inferred that experiences during this time had left a deep impression on him. He seemed reflective, but not wanting to share too much about his fears. He said he drew comfort from prayer.

Joyce has muscular dystrophy and sometimes finds it hard to understand the many losses she has experienced. She describes God as: 'Well just a presence that's there and there's got to be somebody there, I don't know, I don't really know!' Later I asked Joyce what things in life touch her spiritually, and she replied:

Oh I don't know really, I mean, the flowers and gardens always make me feel that there's got to be someone there to create the most beautiful colours and things, you know and I just…no I'm not really a strong believer, I mean, I'm not an atheist either.

Rebecca, a Christian Scientist, described God as 'the all-knowing, all-wise, creating all good'. Of Jesus she said: 'The Christ…a spiritual identity, he's not a person at all.'

Max said that God is a part of his life: 'I would say so yes, I'm not as stupid now as I was when I was younger.' He thinks more about God these days, and noted that he had changed and deepened his spiritual journey over the years.

Margaret said she first became aware of God, 'Well before I made my First Communion and we were taken to the church and I suppose it was then, and He's still close to me.' Of a changing relationship with God as she has grown older: 'Well I suppose it's I've got that much closer [to God] that's all I can say.' Now Margaret was confident as she faced her future: 'I hope I get to Heaven and I know Heaven's the very best place to be, I mean that!'

Bob had obviously pondered questions of his faith long and deeply, which was clearly evident when he spoke:

> I've taken life seriously and I've been prepared to believe [rather] than scoff. There [are] sort of esoterical things, that I believe in God and I believe fiercely, if you like in a God. Mainly it's keeping my hope, you know, and I might have trouble confiding it to somebody in the terms of clarity but it's always there and I know what it is. And if I set out to examine it I reckon I could tell you what it is.

Of his image of God, Bob reflected:

> I think the truth is there for all those who like to tap it. Might be just in the spiritual sense, incomplete, or it's more likely to be I'd say the sort of combination of mind and body and experience… I think it's there for you all the time. I personally think that what my mind and self can be is going to give fairly good sensation to this thought… I think the answer comes, it's all there for anybody and it's all there to make up a belief that can be followed by anybody.

Bob says of his faith journey: 'I'm familiar with all the Scriptures. See I'm not the kind of a boy who was unimpressed by Sunday school and church and that, just took up to thinking about God you know.'

Sonya talked about her childhood days and attending Sunday school and games they used to play. She was never aware of having a relationship with God; she said now: 'If I stop to think about it I always felt very sorry for God.' She went on:

> I'm Catholic and I always as a child going around the Sorrowful Mysteries in our church, you know, I could cry when I did them, seeing Him pulling the cross and that and the big crucify, I used to be so broken hearted for Him, you know, and think what cruel men they were, those Romans, you know, poor

man, I thought poor man, the way he suffered and that's what I always think of even now. Come Easter time and…

She says she has a good relationship with God now: 'I think, I think that He's a marvellous person and one day he will answer my prayers and perhaps get me back in a unit somewhere, with His help. And then I'll have a bedroom to myself.'

Veronica says she has no image of God; she does, however, attend some church services in the nursing home and finds comfort from these. She has had little input into religion over her adult life until being admitted to the nursing home. She does acknowledge a spiritual dimension to life, and that this seems to be growing more important as she is growing older. At 75 years of age her hope is to 'go on for a good while'.

Centres of meaning in multicultural western societies

Although most of the frail older people were of Anglo-Celtic background there is still a wide range of spirituality and diverse ideas of religion and God.[1] There is a wide range of experiences of God among these older people; more of this group of frail people have reflected on and felt near to God than those in the independent living group. It is suggested that this may be associated with a growing sense of frailty and lessened energy among this group and the move from doing to becoming and being that occurs in later life. Most of them could only walk with assistance, if at all, thus they were dependent on staff to take them to activities. Each of them spent many hours of the day alone and had time to contemplate and reflect on their life journey. A number of these people spent time in reflection of their relationship with God. Meaning for them was more often centred on God, however God was perceived by the individual.

It is also noted that a number of these older people have difficulty in understanding the content of their faith; some hold mythical views of religion and unhelpful concepts of scripture and faith. For some residents in aged care, learning more about their faith could be valuable, this may assist them to grow in their faith, and provide them with a sense of hope.

The starting point for spiritual care must be meeting the person at their place of meaning. Thus it is important to be able to dialogue openly about the source of the older person's life-meaning.

Meaning in relationship

In this study, core meaning was found both through relationship with God and with others. In the 1998 study most people found meaning through human relationship, of that group of independent living older people, 46.7 per cent were widowed, contrasted against 80 per cent widowed in the later study. Even though fewer of the residents have partners, for most in this study meaning is still through relationship, but often relationship with children or grandchildren was more important now. For some, however, there was little or no contact with families, due either to geographical isolation or to having few or no living relatives. It is suggested that the unavailability of close human relationships may be a stimulus to some older people to find life-meaning through a spiritual source or through God.

Alice, aged 80, gave a response typical of these informants. She said she finds meaning through: 'four children and nine grandchildren and they keep me going, especially the little five-year-old girl'.

Andrew's wife had died less than two months before the interview. He seemed to be clutching at meaning, reaching back into his memories for a sense of who he was. There seemed to be a thread of grief running through the whole interview. Although he did not specifically answer questions about meaning, it could be inferred by his talk of things he had shared with his wife, for instance gardening, and their plans for the future together. He found going to church now was important.

Agnes finds most meaning through her daughter. She is very concerned for her as she has Crohn's disease. She has no other family except a sister and brothers, who visit when they can. These frail elderly nursing home residents were often concerned for the well-being of one or more children or grandchildren.

Grace says she is living to see her great-grandchild born and this eagerly anticipated event is providing a sense of hope and meaning for her, and a reason to be alive. Violet also finds meaning through her family, daughter and son-in-law and grandsons and a granddaughter. Meaning for Veronica is also from family, from her grandchildren. When I asked her what were the good things in her life now she said: 'Oh [laughs] that I'm still alive I guess you'd say.'

Margaret finds deepest meaning in her life through God. She said: 'Well I ask God, and God listens to me and God answers me.' Margaret talked a lot about her husband, when she first met him and their relationship, she shared some special memories, including the night she first met her husband. She said they still love each other. Margaret spoke of the joy in her life saying: 'Oh yes, I've got lots of things to be happy about.' More of these frail older people in residential care found deepest meaning through their relationship with God than those in the independent living group. The independent living older people had more family and friends and were involved in more activities. On the other hand, the frail older people had lost more relationships and were less likely to be able to engage with activities in the aged care facility. It was in these situations that some seem to have turned more into themselves, and had become more contemplative and conscious of the presence of God in their lives.

Finding meaning in the face of increasing frailty

Humans are by nature meaning-makers. Frankl (1997) stated that there must be meaning to life under any circumstances, 'even the worst conceivable ones.' Thus meaning is not meant only as a surface, happy condition, but rather as something that exists and is real. Frankl defines it as 'suddenly becoming aware of a possibility against the background of reality' (p.141). It is well understood that no person can hand meaning to another; no person can construct the meaning of another person's life, meaning can only be realized by the individual whose life it is. As Frankl asserts, we cannot tell a person what their life means, but we may be able to convey the idea to the person that 'life never ceases to offer us a meaning up to its last moment, up to our last breath' (p.141).

Frankl contends there are three avenues that lead to meaning fulfilment; first, doing a good deed or creating a work; second, experiencing something or encountering someone; and third, facing a fate that we cannot change and making a stand. He says even through this final of the three ways we may find meaning, in fact, this is done through realizing that we have risen above ourselves, as it were, transcended ourselves. We then find that we have grown and changed in the encounter and process. This must include the process of facing pain and suffering as well as any other aspect of life. This is not, of course, to say that we should experience suffering and pain in order to change, grow and find meaning, but it does say that the way we face unavoidable suffering will make a difference to our well-being and our ability to find meaning.

For Dora, coming to terms with being in a nursing home means that she can't do anything to help her family now. She said that what keeps her going is her faith and the help she gets from the staff. But she also wonders 'why God doesn't take me when I pray every night that he will... Because I feel as though I'm no use to anyone.' This is in spite of her feeling loved and supported by her family. It is important to note that Dora is not asking to have her life terminated. She accepts God's will in her life, simply expressing a readiness to die when

God is ready to take her and she wishes it would be sooner rather than later. She said of being in a nursing home: 'I accept it. This is what God's willed for me [pause] and I'm quite happy here.' Her spiritual supports are very important to her.

The special meaning of birth was remembered as one of the most important events in Dora's life:

> I think the birth of your first child, when you hold that baby in your arms I, I think that's a highlight, when the second one comes along it's just the same. But you've had the first one, then you have your second one and you think, God's good to me, two healthy children.

Elaine says she finds life hard 'when you can't get around, but I'm quite contented if I don't get any worse.' Like Dora, she says the support of staff in the nursing home keeps her going. Staff may play an important part in the lives of these frail and elderly residents in supporting and affirming them as people of worth.

Joyce too finds meaning in her family. Faced with much tragedy in her life, including muscular dystrophy, that now restricts many activities and makes her quite dependent on staff for her care needs, yet she seems to have such a positive attitude to life. I asked her if she could:

> Perhaps put your finger on what it is that gives you this energy that you obviously have, that you're able to express about the good things in your life and about your relationship with your children and grandchildren, in spite of all the bad things that you've experienced?

Joyce responded:

> Well it's love for them and I think it's will power, you know, I mean the will to go on and be happy and that I think. I think you have to do it yourself, I really do, I think you have to do it yourself you know, I mean I don't think there's anybody's there helping me I think that it's just my nature.

I was reminded of Frankl's work here, and the 'will to meaning'. Joyce maintained a purpose for living throughout; this was a critical aspect of her sense of joy in life. She said: 'I'm thankful for every day I'm alive.' Joyce had a kind of spiritual resilience (Ramsey and Bleisner 2000); she seemed to have an ability to recover and be ready to face life after every knock-back.

Katie longed for intimacy with another human being. This lack of human relationship made it hard for her to examine her life journey and make sense of it. Katie related this to me when I asked what brought meaning to her life now:

> I keep wishing I'm getting better, the wishes I think might be coming true but very slowly. I'm on a lonely scale as a matter of fact, because my daughter had to have an operation for her heart and I can't see her and I don't ever see her daughter, she's only got the one, and I've got nobody in Canberra that I know. They just gave me 24 hours notice to come here and they have done a lot for me since I've been here, I'm much better.

Katie said that she often wishes there was someone she could talk to about her life: 'Before I've always had someone to go to you know, if I wanted anything or if I wanted to know about something.' I asked her: 'And you haven't got anyone now?'

> Not here, I haven't. No, it makes it very hard, you know… There are often times you feel like a talk even if you go back over the years, just something different, because I can't see well enough to read now and I've just got to live this…no one to talk to or no one that I know, I've just got to lay there and think things out and try and work out something but it's almost impossible when you can't…you don't know anybody,

Katie was trying to work out her life-meaning, and she found this hard to do by herself. Using reminiscence work, either as a one-on-one or in small groups, may be very helpful in assisting these people to find life meaning and purpose (see Chapter 6).

Bob said of meaning in his life:

> What gives most meaning to my life in the daily sense is the fact that…I'm not concocting this reason, is that the belief that I do have in the Maker, the God or whatever have you, you know, mainly from childhood memories of the gospel, but it gives meaning to my life because [it] makes sense… If I take that out nothing makes sense.

He went on:

> It's very hard to explain what it is, in everyday terms, but it's hard to be casual about it and it's hard to sort of not get too emotional about it. I can easily let that happen to me. But the meaning, that there is some meaning, and I believe that there is, and I think that all my life I have injected my life with that kind of meaning which came to my heart.

Speaking of meaning in his life Bob continued:

> Well sometimes it gets rather disturbed because of the everyday daily demands that one gets on one's time even though it might be a reasonable demand like yours is [my interviewing him] but they might just be demands that spring

from…you don't know where they come from but someone demands them and you've got to do them. Well fulfilling those demands in a way that'll satisfy myself and I'm the only one that's got to be satisfied in the final analysis, you know, I've got to make sense to myself. That keeps me going and sometimes when that is interfered with too much I find that perhaps I ought to be a bit perturbed about it. In other words I don't find life a complete mystery especially the good parts, but I'm interested in poetry and stuff like that might seem esoterical from Shelley and Yeats and most the standard sort of poets. And I found that the meaning for my life has come out of the voice that I gather from what I hear and see from the artistic fraternity of this world. I'm sure you can understand that.

Unlike some of the men in the study of independent living older people, Bob reflected deeply on his life and its meaning. Even though he talked about the demands on his time that he did not always appreciate, he seemed willing to share openly about where he found meaning, and this involved talking of his faith. In the oldest of older people, mostly, both men and women seemed willing to share. It could be said that gender differences that existed in earlier life seemed to be less marked as both men and women were exploring their lives and life-meaning.

Sonya was one person who said she had no meaning in her life now; but she would find meaning if she could 'just be well again'. She just wants to be able to go home to her family. When I asked her what she enjoys in life she responded: 'Listening to tapes from the Blind Society.' Sonya focused more on her lack of well-being, and did not seem able to transcend her health problems. She also seemed reluctant and unable to reflect on her life at the time of interview. Sonya was not finding meaning in the face of increasing vulnerability. This is discussed further in Chapter 10.

THE FARMERS

There were two farmers in this group of participants. For them, farming had provided a special source of meaning in life. Both had obviously regarded their farms as a way of life, not just a job. Both seemed even to have a deep sense of joy in speaking of their farms. It was with a degree of sadness that they spoke of no longer being able to work on their farms.

Angus found meaning through his farm and he still longs to go there. I attempted to draw Angus out in what the farm meant to him. I first asked him to tell me a bit more about the farm and how important it was to him. His initial response was: 'Well, it was income for a start.' It seemed to me that this was not all, so I asked: 'Do you enjoy the farm?' He responded: 'That's right, oh yes, yes.

I don't know anything else.' Angus seemed to find it hard to articulate his deep feelings for his farm. It seemed to be for him a sense of joy and meaning.

Bert, the other farmer, finds meaning through his wife and five sons; he had a sixth son who was accidentally shot about three years before. Bert had made a hard decision to come into a nursing home; he felt his wife could no longer care for him at home as he has Parkinson's disease.

MEANING THROUGH MUSIC

Rebecca is blind and is a member of Christian Science. She says meaning for her is from listening to the passages from the Bible and from *Science and Health* each morning. She also enjoys listening to classical music. Fewer of these very frail elderly people actively pursued meaning through music or art, and often their energy levels were too low for sustained activities.

THE STRUGGLE TO FIND MEANING FOLLOWING SUDDEN DISABLEMENT

Sometimes it is hard to find meaning in life; sudden disablement such as a stroke is one example where people are confronted by an event requiring a complete change of life and adjustment to major loss of physical health and independence. Max, who had a stroke, says he doesn't find meaning in his life now, although he does say he thanks God he is alive. He says: 'Well I wished I could work in some way, I can't now, I don't see, I'm very slow to what I used to be.' Prior to that, he was working in his own business with a lot of community interests and commitments. Max was suddenly disabled and found it hard to come to terms with. He was obviously still seeking to find meaning in life through doing; he had been a very active man, and his work as a builder was now denied to him. He had been a man characterized through his ability to work and to do practical things. His identity was based on his work role. Now life seemed to lack a sense of meaning and value. Max's situation is discussed further in Chapter 11.

Conclusion

Elderly people who have reached the fourth age of the life journey, that stage when they are no longer able to live independently and provide for their own needs, frequently find a renewed search for life-meaning. In fact they may begin to change from seeing life as sets of provisional meanings, to searching for final life-meaning. The search is likely to become more urgent. For some that search will include a shift in life values, an increased openness to living with ambiguities and uncertainties. For example, changes in physical health may mean that the range of activities of daily living that the person can engage in without assistance may change radically. Further, adjustment to the decrements of an ageing body require decisions and the setting of priorities for living effectively. This is often a struggle for frail elderly people, and sensitive care from family and all who are engaged in aged care is of primary importance.

Summary

- *Meaning is almost synonymous with hope.*

- *In spiritual care it is important to meet the person at their place of meaning.*

- *In multicultural and multifaith societies there are varieties of sources of life-meaning.*

- *Different images are held of God even within one faith and it is important to know what a particular person's image of God is.*

- *Sudden changes in physical well-being may displace life-meaning, for example following a stroke. Spiritual and pastoral care should seek to support people facing such spiritual crises.*

Note

1   It is noted that in the coming decades, there will be a much larger proportion of Asian elderly in the Australian population and further studies of spirituality in later life will need a focus on other major religions; it just happened that the majority of residents in the nursing homes used for this study were from an Anglo-Celtic background.

CHAPTER 5

Wisdom, Final Meaning, the Spiritual Journey and Frail Older People

Erikson, Erikson and Kivnick (1986) wrote that in the final stage of psycho-social development the task was to come to a sense of integrity and should this not occur, the person may come to a sense of despair. The outcome of finding integrity is wisdom. Through the earlier years of the life cycle the meanings we assign to events are provisional ones, subject to review and reframing. It is only as we become conscious of our impending mortality that we begin to form final meanings. This chapter focuses on the process of finding final meanings.

Wisdom viewed in a spiritual perspective is part of the deeply human potential for being. Wisdom is living and dealing with ambiguity and un-certainty, and in later life, is involved in transcending the physical and psychosocial losses and tensions that are so frequently part of the life experi-ence. Wisdom is not something that can be ordered up, rather wisdom comes with grace. Wisdom is intricately bound up in spiritual integrity. Randall and Kenyon (2001) write that life should be seen as both story and as journey. Further, they say that 'wisdom is fundamentally a spiritual phenomenon, since it has to do with meaning: meaning of life, of relationships, of ourselves, of the cosmos' (p.29). It is in that vein that this chapter is written; with the focus of journey, how ageing affects frail older people and how these older people respond to the opportunities and challenges of the fourth age of life.

Assumptions for the journey using a developmental approach to understanding spirituality

The meaning of each and every situation of our lives is understood, sometimes even unconsciously at the time, as provisional meaning. It is only later in life, and more likely as we become aware of our own approaching death, that we begin to see the final meaning and purpose of our life. Then our sense of life meaning may change as we reframe earlier experiences, and review and affirm our values and world views. Ultimate meaning points to something beyond this world, a sense of the other, something greater that cannot be analysed scientifically. There is mystery and a sense of otherness that defies quantification of the spiritual dimension, and this remains throughout the lifespan.

A developmental approach is used in this chapter, based on a number of assumptions. First, older adults may be at different points in their personal spiritual journey. Fowler (1981) has set out a framework of faith development across the lifespan. Fowler defined faith as:

> The process of constitutive-knowing underlying a person's composition and maintenance of a comprehensive frame (or frames) of meaning. Generated from the person's attachments or commitments to centers of supraordinate value which have power to unify his or her experiences of the world, thereby endowing the relationships, contexts, and patterns of everyday life, past and future, with significance. (Fowler 1986, p.26)

The way Fowler has defined 'faith' is similar to the way I have defined spirituality (see Chapter 1), acknowledging that everything has a spiritual dimension. Meaning, relationships and a sense of otherness, which he calls the 'supraordinate values', are at the centre of his frame of 'faith'. This framework assumes the possibility of progression through a number of stages of faith development. Not all people will progress through all stages; according to Fowler (1986), older people are more likely to be at stages three to five of his seven-stage model.[1]

- *Stage III: Synthetic-conventional faith* is a faith stance of late childhood but, says Fowler, it may remain through life, where the judgments and expectations of others are important and it is accepted without question and is conformist.

- *Stage IV: Individuative-reflective faith* sees a relocation of authority in the self, with a critical distancing from previously held value systems. Again, this may be a final stage for some.

- *Stage V: Paradoxical-consolidative or conjunctive faith* is described as 'balanced faith, inclusive faith, a both /and faith' (Astley and Francis 1992, p.viii).

- *Stage VI: Universalizing faith*, the final stage of faith or spiritual development, is described as a selfless faith and involves relinquishing and transcending of the self. It is seen by Fowler (1981) as being rare. It is noted, however, that this stage of spiritual development is seen in numbers of frail elderly people in the studies reported in this book.

Fowler did not interview people in the fourth age of life and this may account for his view that this final stage of faith or spiritual development is rare. Thus it can be said there may be changes in spirituality right across the lifespan, and there is the potential to continue to develop spiritually across the lifespan until the point of death (and perhaps beyond).

Second, spiritual development is a dynamic process. Individuals respond to the deep stirrings of spirit; they respond to life-meaning and make choices in their spiritual lives. In the Christian context, there is a response between the person's spirit or soul and the Holy Spirit. Julian of Norwich (in Hide 2001) writes of 'oneing', that possibility of spiritual unity between the individual and God.

Third, there may be blockages to continued spiritual development. These may be identified by effective spiritual assessment. Blockages may include such things as a sense of meaninglessness or hopelessness in life, resentment, anger, unforgiveness or unresolved grief. Conversely, these factors may also serve as triggers for spiritual growth.

Spirituality is both generic and specific (MacKinlay 2001a). That is, each person has a spiritual dimension (generic: meaning, transcendence, relationship), but how each person develops their spirituality is very individual (specific: practice of religion, music, art, response to environment). All of these aspects of spirituality should be taken into account when assessing the spiritual dimension.

Finally, a developmental approach allows for the possibility of continued spiritual development in ageing. It opens up possibilities, even in the face of loss and disabilities, and perhaps even more so as people acknowledge loss and grief in their lives. It acknowledges the place of spiritual and psychosocial dimensions in interaction with the biological dimension in ageing. A spiritual approach also acknowledges the Buddhist quest in ageing, to find love and meaning in the face of frailty and death.

What is wisdom?

There are a number of perspectives taken on wisdom, ranging from Baltes and Baltes' (1990) concentration on the measurement of cognitive constructs of wisdom to the broader definitions of Csikzentmihalyi and Rathunde (1990) and Randall and Kenyon (2001). Chandler and Holliday (1990) suggest that we do not clearly understand what wisdom is. Csikzentmihalyi and Rathunde (1990, p.28) suggest three major dimensions of the concept of wisdom: first, wisdom as a cognitive process, that is, a way of obtaining and processing information; second, wisdom as a virtue, as a socially valued pattern of behaviour and finally, wisdom as a good, or a personality state or condition. Randall and Kenyon (2001) in their book *Ordinary Wisdom* identify six dimensions of wisdom: cognitive, practical–experiential, interpersonal, ethical–moral, idiosyncratic expression and spiritual–mystical.

Erikson *et al.* (1986) take a developmental view of the final psychosocial stage of life and they write, in relation to the rest of life: 'It is through this last stage that the life cycle weaves back on itself in its entirety, ultimately integrating maturing forms of hope, will, purpose, competence, fidelity, love, and care, into a comprehensive sense of wisdom' (pp.55–56).

In Blanchard-Fields and Norris' study of wisdom, a consistent theme emerges: 'the personal quest for meaning of life or finding meaning and purpose in life in order to become whole' (1995, p.114). That is of course the very domain of the spiritual dimension. Blanchard-Fields and Norris note a 'sizeable portion of the population does not necessarily exhibit' the qualities of wisdom that characterizes adult development and ageing (p.115). They say that many of this older age group, lacking the skills for appropriate spiritual growth in ageing, may have adapted to the society by way of the *socially expected and imposed certainties of life*, thus retarding the potential for wholeness of development.

The model of spiritual tasks of ageing: growing in spiritual integrity and wisdom in later life

The model of spiritual tasks of ageing, developed from the in-depth interviews of older independent living people, identified the spiritual task of moving from provisional meaning of life to final meanings. This stage of spiritual development became apparent, for the most part, as people became more aware of their approaching mortality. This task was also related to growth of wisdom in ageing after the final stage of psychosocial development identified by Erikson *et al.* (1986). They saw wisdom as the outcome of effective negotiating of the final developmental stage of integrity versus despair. In earlier studies (MacKinlay 2001a) I defined spiritual integrity in later life as:

> A state where an individual shows by their life example and attitudes, a sense of peace within themselves and others, and development of wholeness of being. The search for meaning and a degree of transcendence is evident. (p.180)

While I wrote then of independent living older people, I noted 'true wholeness and integrity is probably only possible at the point of death, however, many may approach it in the later stages of life' (MacKinlay 2001a, p.180). In this book I am exploring the spiritual life journey of older and more frail people, who may be in need of residential care. These older people are in the fourth age of life. The informants in this study demonstrated this process. In effect, they were further along the ageing journey than most of those interviewed in the earlier study (MacKinlay 1998). The data recorded here supports and reinforces the model of spiritual tasks of ageing that was designed from the earlier study.

Seeking to understand the spiritual journey, finding final meaning and the getting of wisdom, raise a number of questions. First, is the increased interiority seen in some older people a response to an increasing awareness of their own mortality, and the shortness of time until death? Second, is the more intentional search for meaning a desire for connection with God or ultimate life-meaning? Third, how important are the life events that may present crises of meaning for that person in their journey, for example a life-threatening illness or the loss of a loved one through death? And, finally, how important are other factors such as personality, stage of faith development or spiritual crises over the life journey, in the meaning/spiritual search in later life?

Listening to life stories provides anecdotal evidence of these possible influences on the deepening of the life journey. Certainly, sometimes tellers of life stories are able to point to events and changes in their own life journeys where they have been aware of healing and spiritual growth.

For whatever reasons, increased awareness of the search for meaning is often seen in later life. Sometimes this may be forced by increasing bodily disabilities and decreasing energy levels; these older people were more likely to be attending to the third of Frankl's three tasks: facing a fate that we cannot change and making a stand (Frankl 1984). Growing awareness of one's own mortality provides a stimulus to finding final life purpose and meaning; the question 'Has my life been worthwhile?' becomes increasingly important for numbers of older people. It is also noted that some older people do not want to discuss issues of final meaning and may deny their impending death.

Wisdom as a construct is very similar to spiritual integrity as I have just defined it. Wisdom may be understood from a psychological perspective as mainly a cognitive construct, or it may be understood, as defined here, as a spiritual construct. Wisdom is:

> An increased tolerance to uncertainty, a deepening search for meaning in life, including an awareness of the paradoxical and contradictory nature of reality; it involves transcendence of uncertainty and a move from external to internal

regulation. (MacKinlay 2001a, p.153, based on Blanchard-Fields and Norris 1995)

One of the strategies used in the process of finding life-meaning, and sometimes called a 'task' of ageing, is reminiscence. This was widely employed by the informants in this study, with 75 per cent of them using reminiscence. What is needed for fourth age people, both in the community and in aged care settings, are opportunities to tell the story and process meaning. This is explored more thoroughly in Chapter 6 on reminiscence.

Being on a journey

Of the frail elderly study participants, Violet is very aware of her changing spiritual journey over her life. She first became aware of the presence of God when she was about three years of age. She had a convent education, but this seemed to have little impact on her. I asked her if there was a time in her life that she came to a conscious acceptance of faith for herself, and she responded: 'Well actually, to tell you the truth, not till I came in here [the nursing home]... Well I don't think I ever thought of religion in any respects till I came in here, and like I say I thank God every night that I'm still alive, you know.' I asked: 'So what happened when you came in here, that you became aware of God like this?' Violet thought for a few moments and replied:

> Oh that I don't know, I can't remember how it came about in my mind other than the two assistants in nursing used to stand here and talk to me...I wouldn't even know what they were talking about, because I suppose after a while some of that stuck, you know. [One of the assistants in nursing was also a priest.]

I asked Violet what her image of God is now and she responded:

> It's funny you ask me that because some nights when I lay here, that light out there is always on and I'm in the dark in here and I'm sort of talking to, I don't know who, and I can see a vision in my mind, you know, and I think it's between my eyes and my glasses [pointing to her face]. I can't place the face or the figure but it's just there and I often think, whether He's there talking to me and helping me you know. Because although I'm talking to, feel that I'm talking to that little vision in the centre of my eyes sort of thing.
>
> It's a silly thing to say but... It's not any of my family or anything it's just this little vision that seems to come in between on my nose here and I'm sort of and I can feel myself bowing my head talking, and after when I go back to sort of try and get back to sleep, I think you stupid... who was I talking to, who was I thinking about, you know. But I often think, wonder if it is God that's helping,

'cause it is helping me. I would be a lot worse if He wasn't helping me, you know.

Violet paused, then she said: 'I couldn't share that with just anyone.' Statements like this were common in these in-depth interviews.

Violet has a sense of not being good enough: 'I'm quite certain God's talking to me or helping me in some way, you know, or picking me up all the time. I'll never get upstairs because it would never have time to correct all I've done.' Then she asked: 'I don't know whether you'd know what happens to us when we die, what happens to us is, …it's just a shell when you die, your spirit is gone?' I replied: 'Yes, your spirit does go when you die but where exactly I don't know, but certainly St Paul talked about that in his letter to the Corinthians and he talked about having a resurrection body, a new body which is different to what we are.'

This question is one that many over the centuries have grappled with; perhaps the most significant of these being Paul in 1 Corinthians, where he explains the resurrection of Christ and links that to an explanation of our own deaths. Paul explains that in planting a seed, it does not come to life unless it first dies. Then, Paul writes: 'So it will be with the resurrection of the dead. The body that is sown is perishable, it is raised imperishable; …it is sown a natural body, it is raised a spiritual body' (1 Corinth. 15: 42–44). There is mystery associated with death, and, for each of us, this is a journey into the unknown. A journey that we may make with fear and uncertainty. Violet went on to ask: 'We come back as people not animals?' My response in the Christian context was: 'I don't think we come back, reincarnation is not part of the Christian way of life, because Jesus said that he had gone ahead to prepare a place for us.'

How can we share with Violet, or others like her, in ways that they can understand? It is far from appropriate to present deep theological answers to questions from these frail residents, what is important is to meet them at their point of need. I responded to her in words that I felt she would understand, in her context of Christianity, and I offered to discuss any further questions with her. Residents from different faith backgrounds need explanations that will be relevant for them. For example, for Buddhists, reincarnation is certainly part of their belief system, and ultimate release from suffering is found in *nirvana* (Scotton 1998).

I have found that a number of people have little idea of even the possibilities of an afterlife. In my earlier work with registered nurses working in aged care, one of the nurses reported back to me that a resident she was caring for told her that she did not believe in life after death, but she would not want her minister to know that. She was able to talk about her beliefs with the nurse, but not the minister. It would therefore be possible to miss these questions altogether if elderly residents do not feel they can talk to those who provide pastoral care.

Violet has trouble with breathing sometimes and is scared. Sometimes staff will just come and hold her hand and be with her until she settles again. A number of factors seem to have been involved in Violet's spiritual journey, as she has struggled with events, including loss and disability, to come to a sense of meaning in her life. Despite the multiple physical health problems she faces, she is finding meaning. She has come to faith only since being in an aged care facility. Like a number of other older women, she had been married to a man who did not welcome religion and, faithful to him, she had not attended church again until quite a while after she was widowed and already in a nursing home.

Charlie says that being religious gives his life meaning now, although it has not always been so. Prayer was an important part of this. Charlie did not like to reminisce and he expressed a fear of death.

On the other hand, Bert, a farmer, seemed to talk of God naturally. He said his earliest memories of God were: 'I was about four. Of course it was in the home, the old Irish nun, you know, blood and guts and frighten you…since I've grown up I've become broadminded.' Bert says that now he sees God

> More in the spiritual way, I never ever quite grasped onto that I must admit, I've tried, I've never grasped the same thing well, there's plenty of denominations and you've only got a different slant of mine. I don't know if it's because I didn't understand the Irish traditional religion or…it was sort of a blind faith but this is now more of a spiritual kind.

Bert said that sometimes he felt closer to God these days. When I asked him to give me an example, he replied: 'I suppose you'd be closer to God when you've lost a son, he was accidentally shot.' Bert acknowledged having spiritual needs and said: 'I mean things have happened to me in my lifetime that I didn't really expect to happen. I haven't settled down to the problems of this year finishing up in a nursing home.' He said that he was still dealing with being in the nursing home. Bert had Parkinson's disease and found talking difficult, until we had met on several occasions and he knew that he could take his time and that I would wait for him to speak. He also knew that if he got too tired, he could rest; I would come back another day.

In the conversations I had with Bert he was speaking of his spiritual journey, and moving from provisional to final meanings, Bert was still struggling with the meaning of his life; there were still a number of unknowns in his life. He was in the process of working through these. As I was visiting him as a researcher, and not as a pastoral carer or counsellor, I asked him if he would like to talk to someone about some of these things he was dealing with; his response was that it would have to be someone he felt comfortable with. I took this to mean someone who would respect him and his life story, who could give him time and space, and allow him to be in control of the meetings. Listening to his story was a central aspect of his care.

A woman, living independently, Win, aged 78 years, says she experiences lower energy levels these days and she had found that she is resting more in God, with an acceptance that she can't do all she wants to. The ability to accept the changes of ageing is an important aspect of wisdom, and Randall and Kenyon (2001) differentiate between acceptance and resignation in later life. In coming to acceptance, Win takes an active part in the changing; she is listening to her body and prayerfully working to discern what God wants her to do at each part of the changing journey. For her the process is almost sacramental. In all of this process, she is, to use New Testament terminology, growing into Christ. Overall there is a growing sense of wisdom apparent here in this woman's spiritual journey, with a complex interplay, continually testing between abilities and disabilities. The process for Win is empowering and life-affirming and this is far from a state of resignation.

A sense of growing confidence in mid to later life

Some older people find that as they grow into mid and later life, they experience a growing sense of confidence. Bonnie spoke, as a number of women in the studies of independent living older women in an earlier study had done (MacKinlay 1998), of lacking in self-confidence until she was about 49 or 50 years of age. She described this:

> But, I thought [of] a period in my married life, when my husband was always putting me down, [saying] you're stupid, you're this, you're that. I stopped short and thought you're not stupid, you've got a damn good brain, you play a very good game of golf, you play a good game of bridge, you're a good player, you're not stupid. So I began to let [it] just wash over me, just wash over my head and I felt a lot better.

Bonnie suggested that mid life was the usual time in life for people to start questioning. This is certainly consistent with the findings of Neugarten (1968). Bonnie said she had regrets but no sense of guilt, she said: 'I've realized my weaknesses and my strengths and so you can't dwell on guilt, it's too negative, it's too negative.' Bonnie seems to have continued to grow in her self-confidence into her later life, supported by a continuing searching and exploration of various spiritual perspectives.

Bonnie lived with chronic obstructive pulmonary disease that greatly restricted her daily activities. Reflecting back on her spiritual journey Bonnie said:

> Every step had its reason, you know what I mean, I started off with sort of Bible banging and then realized that that wasn't enough, that wasn't enough! It had to be something that reached people's hearts not just their minds, but reached their hearts and that was I think was really why I explored as far as I did. But I don't think there's any more I can explore as far as that sort of journey is concerned. I can only enjoy which is rather nice, enjoy the fact of…it is…it is…just enjoy the knowledge that He's there, right there!

Bonnie's journey was a very individual one, she had explored many avenues of spirituality and spiritualism, and her spirituality at the time of the interview was uniquely hers. She had no community of faith and her only connection with others in her spiritual journey was through her reading. Yet among this variety of things spiritual there were some aspects of a Christian journey into faith. There was an openness to the possibility of continued spiritual development in this older woman.

Bob, who was recovering from a stroke, spoke at length about his faith and its meaning for him:

> Oh not that just, see that and [I] mean not if God's not just going to come into existence, just because I believe in Him. But as I tried through with my beliefs I found it necessary to vet everything that I go through and I can put some things down and cross them all off. Anyway I haven't found any difficulty in believing fully in the God-like Christian that we're supposed to with whoever it might be and whether…just completely as I said before, that's the basis for all our thoughts, well the basis of thought that's needed it certainly is that we need to have a world wide religion but not like the present religion.

These stories are *works in progress*, as the story tellers continue their life journey. They are very individual, and at the same time some share part of the life journey of their communities. Each of these people is at a different place in their journey, and even their spiritual or faith journeys are different. Relating to these people spiritually means listening and journeying with them. Chapter 6 takes up the process of reminiscence and ways of using spiritual reminiscence with individuals and small groups.

Conclusion: the spiritual journey in later life

Fowler (1981) writes of the possibility of moving from one stage of faith development to another through the lifespan; he also raises the possibility of conversion to faith in later life. These frail older people are still on a journey that will continue until they die. Some have experienced conversion in later life, even in the nursing home, while others have remained at an earlier stage of faith or spiritual development.

Spiritual care will include journeying with these frail older people, supporting and encouraging them, while affirming them in their continuing journey. The frail older people whose stories are related here were mostly residents in aged care, however, increasingly more frail older people will be living at home. These people also need the presence of a person to support and care for them in the journey. Sometimes there may be times of darkness for these people, times when they feel very alone, at other times, some will experience that deep sense of hope and joy that passes human understanding.

Summary

- *Spiritual development potentially continues until death.*

- *Fowler (1981) outlines stages of faith development across the lifespan; these stages are very similar to spiritual development.*

- *Wisdom is intricately related to the spiritual journey: 'wisdom is fundamentally a spiritual phenomenon, since it has to do with meaning: meaning of life, of relationships, of ourselves, of the cosmos' (Randall and Kenyon 2001).*

- *Wisdom is more than a cognitive construct, there are six dimensions of wisdom: cognitive, practical–experiential, interpersonal, ethical–moral, idiosyncratic expression and spiritual–mystical.*

- *Wisdom includes increased tolerance to uncertainty, a deepening search for meaning in life, including an awareness of the paradoxical and contradictory nature of reality (MacKinlay 2001a).*

- *Listening to an elderly person's story is both a privilege for the listener and empowering for the story teller.*

- *Being present to and journeying with the fourth age person are important aspects of the roles of health professionals and pastoral carers.*

Note

1   Fowler (1986) wrote that few older people reached the final stage of his faith development model, that of universalizing faith. In my studies I have interviewed numbers of older people whose faith perspective fits into this stage. I thus disagree with Fowler's writings, and suggest that his studies perhaps contained too few older people to draw this assumption.

CHAPTER 6

Spiritual Reminiscence

Provisional and Final Meanings in Frail Older People

In Chapters 4 and 5, *ultimate meaning* and *moving from provisional to final meanings*, *growing in wisdom* and the *spiritual journey*, as these concepts apply to fourth age people, were described. This chapter extends the journey of spirituality in the fourth age of life by focusing on understandings of narrative in later life before providing guidelines for conducting reminiscence sessions.

Owning our stories

Our story is one of the greatest gifts that each of us has to share. Yet some older people have said to me, 'but I have nothing to tell, I haven't ever done anything worth telling'. Yet each person's story is unique and special, including the stories of people with dementia. Our story is part of our identity; it is an expression of the sum of our being. Each individual is the expert of their own story.

Recognition of the central place of story in the lives of human beings is one of the important developments being seen in the early years of the twenty-first century. Reminiscence, life review, autobiography, narrative gerontology, spiritual reminiscence and spiritual autobiography, reminiscence therapy, spiritual reminiscence work – call it what you will, there is growing interest in human story.

Richness of too often untold stories abounds among older people, and no less among those who reside in aged care facilities. Both being 'listened to' and 'listening' are vital components of our life stories. In the current busyness of work and social spheres of western societies, story has been neglected until relatively recently. Without these connections of story between generations we are lessened in our humanity and in our communities. However, in current western societies it seems each generation has to find its own way and to make its own links within the meaning of being human. We need to be connected with loved ones and within communities by story.

Kenyon (2003) notes that a basic assumption of narrative gerontology 'is that storytelling and story listening are not just things we do occasionally, rather they constitute the process by which we create and discover our personal identity as human beings' (p.30). In other words, we *are* stories, and 'the processes of storytelling and story listening take on a spiritual quality in the sense that our stories express what is meaningful (or meaningless) to us in life' (p.30). Kenyon enlarges on this to include the function of story telling and listening not only to ideas, but emotions and behaviour. Additionally, we are each a part of the larger stories of our families, our faith, our communities and our nation and our own story is interwoven with each of these larger stories.

In many ways it has been a privilege to be able to listen to the life stories of older people; they have shared much and I have learnt much. The telling of stories can both contribute to healing of the past and help to provide hope for the person for the future. Coleman (1999) describes the characteristics of a 'successful' story as being one that bears on the subject of reconciliation or harmony between the past, present and future.

Connecting through story

Telling one's life story is a way of connecting with others, but it is also a means of finding meaning from within the story. People find meaning in the process of telling their story. If they are not able to tell their story, their life's meaning may not become apparent to them. As I have listened to more than one hundred older people tell their stories for research purposes, I have often been privileged to be present for the 'Aha!' where the person suddenly saw the meaning of a particular episode of their life. Often this has opened up new vistas for them, and brought a sense of affirmation to them. This is part of what Erikson *et al.* (1986) had identified as the integrity of ageing; it is only once one has arrived at that point oneself, that it is possible to 'know' for the first time what this actually means.

The terms used in story telling

A number of terms have been used in recent decades to describe the use of story, particularly in later life. These terms are: reminiscence, life review, autobiography, narrative gerontology, spiritual reminiscence, spiritual autobiography, reminiscence therapy and spiritual reminiscence work.

The term *reminiscence* may be used very generally, simply to talk about past experiences; however, this is not only an activity to pass the time for older people, even children engage in 'remember when...' stories of past holidays or special events in their lives. Perhaps older people reminisce more often because they have more to remember and they are beginning to be more reflective and introspective, as Neugarten found (1968). Older people are becoming more conscious of their own mortality and they are now searching for personal life-meaning. Thus there is a change in focus of the reminiscence of older people. Part of this change is reflected in the move from living with *provisional meanings* towards finding *final life-meanings* that resonate for that individual. Reminiscence is thus the general term that refers to remembering events from the past and it is a naturally occurring event (Butler 1995). An individual may simply go over past life events in their own mind, or they may talk about these events with others. Sometimes this is simply a time of mutual remembering and enjoyment.

Life review is a term used to describe a more focused and deliberate process of remembering and going back over life events. Moberg (2001) has provided a valuable chapter on spiritual life review, outlining the process of preparing for the review and factors to include. The term *autobiography* is used where the story is written.

Narrative gerontology has been developed as a special area of study in ageing, and is the study of the use of story by older people. *Spiritual reminiscence* is reminiscence that focuses on life-meaning in remembering and, in particular, this strategy seeks to consider the person's story in relation to their spiritual life journey, that is, their life journey as an individual, with their family and community, and with God. In *spiritual autobiography* the person writes their spiritual journey and usually this involves reflection and review of their life journey. The term spiritual autobiography is used by authors such as Birren and Cochran (2001) and, as the term suggests, a central part of this work is through the writing of the life story and using this to explore meaning.

Finally we examine the terms *reminiscence therapy* and *spiritual reminiscence work*. The term *therapy* means that reminiscence is used as a therapy by a pastoral counsellor or a diversional therapist or nurse trained in reminiscence therapy. Using the term spiritual reminiscence *work* (Gibson 1998) acknowledges that the reminiscer works with their past life experiences and events to come to some sense of purpose and meaning. Gibson (2004) differentiates between oral history and reminiscence, noting that although some similarities exist, the focus of oral history is on preserving and transmitting knowledge, while reminiscence work focuses on benefiting the individual in specific ways, in particular through the social construction of reality and celebration of story.

The emergence of reminiscence as a strategy in aged care in recent decades

In recent decades reminiscence has been used more extensively in aged care facilities. In some circumstances the purpose has been to entertain and it has been regarded as an activity, and in other situations it can be used to assist older people to connect with their life-meaning (Gibson 2004; Haight and Webster 1995). Reminiscence has recently been developed as a therapy by Haight and Webster; courses are available and moves are being taken towards certification in reminiscence therapy (Webster and Haight 2002). Faith Gibson (1998; 2004) has tended to use the term reminiscence work in her study and research. This view of reminiscence is a valuable one as it places reminiscence as a process for engagement by older adults. In our work (MacKinlay *et al.* 2002–2005) with people who have dementia, we have chosen to use the term reminiscence work as it seems to more accurately reflect the interaction with the participants in the study; the participants do *work* with their memories. In fact we have further refined the term to focus on spiritual reminiscence work; in that perspective we are examining issues of meaning in later life, including relationship with others and/or God.

Narrative gerontology

It is not possible to write about ageing and spirituality without including at least some reference to narrative gerontology. *Narrative Gerontology* is the title of a book by Kenyon, Clark and de Vries (2001); the term meaning both story and ageing. This is a growing field of study and as their book suggests there is theory, research and practice within the field already. They note that this term was first used by Ruth in 1994. The authors suggest that narrative gerontology presupposes five basic assumptions:

1. 'Story telling is a fundamental aspect of being human' (p.4), that is, we don't just *have* a story, rather it can better be explained that we *are* story. Further, they suggest, human beings are not just biological entities or social constructions, but also biographical beings, aesthetic compositions, and at least at some level, a work of art, a work in progress with ourselves as the artist.

2.   Our lives as stories are composed of both facts and possibilities. Human stories are open to change and review. It is the way we understand our story that is important.

3.   The 'meaning and nature of time are connected to our lives as stories' (p.4). They talk of the difference between clock time and story time. Clock time progresses in an ordered fashion, always future orientated, while story time allows the person to reflect on earlier life experiences, to return to the past and explore meanings.

4.   Our lives as stories involve four interrelated dimensions: our personal story and the larger story in which we live. These dimensions are first, the *structural dimension*, issues of social policies, power relations and economic realities of the particular society. Second is the *socio-cultural dimension* that includes cultural, ethnic and gender stories of that society. The third is the *interpersonal dimension*, that is relationships, family and friends, while the fourth dimension they term the *personal dimension* as it entails discovery of our own meaning and purpose in life.

5.   'As fundamentally interpersonal beings, we are, paradoxically, creating our personal story in a context that is larger than our individual selves'... The authors see the paradox as being at the same time, bringing a 'potentially liberating realization of the distinctly inner, spiritual quality' and being 'an intensely personal experience' while at the same time having strong connections with the wider community. As they say, our stories have both a 'fundamentally social and/or interpersonal context' (p.8).

The self and otherness in story

Kuhl and Westwood (2001) found in a study of people living with terminal illness that transcendence was experienced by most of their participants and they spoke of a 'power beyond themselves' (p.322). Kuhl and Westwood noted the importance to these people of realizing their connectedness with 'the spiritual dimension within'. This connectedness, 'the spiritual dimension within', was met for some people through relationship with others, and for still others, nature became part of the 'other in story'. The fifth assumption of Kenyon, Clark and de Vries (2001) is very much tied to the fourth; the whole is larger than the sum of its parts and this is part of the paradoxical wonder of the human being, both individual and feeling connections to the wider picture.

Against these five assumptions Coleman describes four characteristics of story: the need for coherence; assimilation of life events into the story; a convincing structure and a 'truth value', that is, the story has an ethical dimension (Coleman 1999). These five assumptions and the four characteristics fit well into a spiritual understanding of being human and ageing.

First, to say that we *are* story is to acknowledge that story connects us to our deepest points of being, to our souls. Story is deeply tied to our individual identity, to the core of our being. Second, stories being composed of both facts and possibilities leave open the possibility of spiritual journey through the lifespan. Conversion, change and renewal of being may occur; the future is open and remains so as long as we live. Third, the meaning and nature of time can also be considered at a spiritual level. At the spiritual level it is suggested that story time becomes more relevant than clock time, again, there is an air of openness to the future and the possibility of connection to our past. Fourth, the interrelated dimensions of both the personal and the larger story link very well to the spiritual dimension. We are individuals but we are part of a larger whole, and we yearn for connections with others, with the stories of others and with God, or a sense of otherness, however perceived by the person.

Thus reminiscence or narrative gerontology is a central component of being human, and part of the spiritual journey in life. Increasingly this is being recognized in our ageing society and in residential aged care. A biomedical model for ageing simply does not paint the whole picture; story lies at the centre of what it means to be human and growing older.

Use of story

Story telling is part of being human. There are multiple uses of story. First, it is simply a communication from one person to one or more others, about one or more aspects of one's life. Telling one's life story helps others see the connections between individuals and community. It is a connection to the past and a bridge to the future, because the story is never finished. It is always being added to and refined. What about the authenticity of story? Stories are always told from the perspective of meaning for the teller. It is in connecting meaning with events that the story becomes real. It is sometimes asked whether reminiscence can be relied on for veracity of past events. To ask that question, it seems, is to miss the point of story. The point is the coming together of meaning with the events as perceived by the teller of the story. In that sense the story is unique for each person. This raises the issue of the degree of importance that is placed on memory and its accuracy in story telling. Take people with dementia, for example; these people still have a story to tell, and difficulties of memory do not render story telling impossible for these people. Telling one's whole story in later life can be enlightening, affirming and healing.

Robert Butler first presented the concept of life review in 1961 (Butler in Haight and Webster 1995) and he continued to develop this over several years. Butler was the first person to see reminiscence as part of the normal life review process that occurs at all ages but is accentuated in later life as older adults become more aware of approaching mortality. Butler notes that in later life people tend to have a particularly 'vivid imagination and memory for the past and can recall with sudden and remarkable clarity early life events' (p.xvii). He writes that the personal myths of invulnerability and immortality are no longer satisfying and this results in reassessment of past life that may result in depression, acceptance or satisfaction. Butler contends that this process occurs in all older people in their final years, although Coleman (1986) found in some of his research that some older people did not appear to engage in reminiscence. There may be various reasons for this: perhaps they have already processed their life story, perhaps very privately, or perhaps they feel unable to deal with some aspects of their story and a blockage to reminiscence may be experienced. However, Butler's assumption of the universal nature of reminiscence seems now to be well accepted.

Butler also notes that it is often difficult for younger people to listen to the stories of older people, as they may see this as a living in the past and a preoccupation with the self, and it is often seen as 'boring, meaningless, and time-consuming chatter' (Butler in Haight and Webster 1995, p.xviii). He counters these attitudes towards reminiscence in elderly people by saying that life review is a necessary and healthy process in both daily life and in mental health care. Butler ends his foreword with:

> As one's life nears an end, the opportunity to confront lifetime conflicts and acts of omission and commission, which warrant guilt as well as opportunities for atonement, resolution, and reconciliation, is precious because this is the last opportunity one had.' (p.xxi)

With a growing literature available on reminiscence some debate has focused on whether reminiscence is best used to assist older people to enjoy times of positive remembering, and whether it may be inadvisable to encourage the reminiscence of negative aspects of earlier life. If we consider Erikson *et al.*'s stages of psychosocial development, it seems pertinent to include all life experiences, and the struggle that occurs in the final stage of life development between integrity and despair may enable the person to review and reframe earlier life experiences. In fact the remembering and reprocessing of earlier negative memories may enable the person to move towards ego-integrity in later life.

To deny the existence of disturbing or negative memories may move the person towards a blockage of psychosocial and spiritual growth in later life. Taking this perspective, Coleman investigated the task of reconciliation for older people, noting that normally reminiscence is rewarding for both the speaker and the listener, however, this is obviously not so with painful memories (1999). Coleman notes that the healing and reconciling activity of life review has been neglected, despite Butler's early work in the 1960s. In a study of older people and their memories of the Second World War Coleman noted that where disturbing memories remained unintegrated it was necessary to make the original experience explicit 'by categorizing and understanding it, for it to lose its power to haunt us' (1999, p.136). The techniques needed to do this may be found in 'reframing'. Birren has developed a process of guided autobiography over the past 25 years that is valuable in this process (Birren and Cochran 2001). His method includes individual preparation for a series of workshops where participants are guided through a range of life topics and questions to tap into the richness of their life stories.

Reframing the story

It may be useful to note that the term 'reframing' commonly used in counselling and now in pastoral care assumes a perspective where the counsellee is guided to see the situation from within a different frame. This is based on the assumption that it is possible to change the frame of an event and thus change the way the event is perceived (Capps 1990, p.11). It seems in this counselling technique that the onus is more often with the counsellor to get the client to think about events differently. In contrast, in reminiscence work, the responsibility to reframe lies with the reminiscer, the one telling the story. This may become a powerful means of healing and reconciliation of earlier life events. Rather than the counsellor suggesting the frame, in reminiscence work it is the reminiscer who knows the story intimately and is thus able to reframe the event themselves. The reframing is done in the light of subsequent life experiences and events, for example, Edith at 76 years described how she had felt bitter and hated what was going on in her life. She had a cardiac arrest, was resuscitated and found that her life turned around. She said: 'I hated people. And that was one of the things in my life that was very wrong... But [now] I was looking at it and I wasn't condemning like I did...I [found I] still had a purpose in life.'

Reminiscence as therapy

Reminiscence can be used therapeutically for the reminiscer to re-journey to earlier life episodes, re-examine chapters of the story and, with the benefit of hindsight, to realize they had acted the best way they knew at that time. Reminiscence allows the person now to shed new light upon that long-past time. The person may see the event for the first time in a new light, with fresh insight, where the pain, guilt and regrets may be finally laid to rest, and the event can be reframed in this new knowledge of the event. This can be a powerful and freeing experience for the individual, who has perhaps been burdened for many years by guilt, regrets or a sense of unforgiveness related to the event. This may be valuable in various matters such as divorce, grief or memories of child abuse.

The role of the pastoral carer or other listener is to journey with the reminiscer, to be present to them, and to be supportive. In some circumstances the reminiscer may uncover memories that are difficult to deal with, perhaps memories that they are not able to reframe themselves, or that are so painful they may deny them. Referral (with permission of the person) to skilled pastoral counsellors or other qualified counsellors may be needed.

The power of story to heal is based on story being present now. The story is always told from the perspective of today, and thus it is always open and changing. We can come to new meanings for our stories but, as Kenyon cautions (2003, p.31), we must be authentic and our story must be based on fact. We, after all, have to live with our story, and we carry a responsibility for our story, being simultaneously narrator, editor, protagonist and reader. Kenyon notes importantly, however, that we are not sole author but only co-author. It is possible, according to Kenyon (p.31), to create a wisdom environment for story telling. This environment is one in which the 'desire of the story listener calls forth the words of the storyteller'. Here Kenyon is saying that the attitudes of the listener and the way in which the listener engages with the story teller are crucial in setting an environment where the story teller may even unmake and remake the story. In using story telling in this way, it is also possible to work with people who have dementia. As Kenyon says, story telling is an art (p.32) and a deeply ethical activity.

Reasons for engaging in reminiscence work

Gibson (1998) gives ten reasons for doing reminiscence work. (The term 'work' seems an appropriate one, and we have found it very relevant in our small group reminiscence work with people who have dementia. It is not therapy as such, but a work that the members of the group mutually engage in.)

Reminiscence:

- makes connections between a person's past, present and future
- encourages sociability and opens up new relationships
- confirms a sense of unique identity and encourages feelings of self-worth
- assists the process of life review
- changes the nature of relationships
- alters others' perceptions and understanding
- aids assessment of present functioning and informs care plans
- reverses the gift of relationship
- preserves and transmits the cultural heritage.

And, finally, most people 'enjoy' reminiscence (Gibson 1998, pp.20–21).

Reminiscence is, therefore, extremely valuable if used appropriately, both as naturally occurring reminiscence and as therapy in residential aged care.

Obstacles to story telling

There are obstacles to story telling. First, having no one to listen; in aged care facilities busyness of staff seems to deter residents from sharing. Coleman (1999) in a study of older people in a hospital found that 30 per cent would like to speak about their life story but feel that they have no one willing to listen. Some older residents seem to have forgotten their story, perhaps through the lack of opportunities for sharing. Perhaps some think their lives are not worth remembering, or they have not valued what they have done through their lives, while others may not see a connection between the past and now, and still others have traumatic experiences they wish to shut out of consciousness. According to Coleman refusal to reminisce may be a sign of deep grief. But now, as Coleman says, 'they may feel they the need to tell the whole story, and require support in doing so' (1999, p.134).

Ways of using reminiscence or life review

Individual or small group?

Some would argue that reminiscence therapy/work must be conducted on a one-on-one basis, and that people will not share with others due to the very personal nature of the story. Others, such as Birren and Cochran (2001) and

Morgan (2003), have actually developed group activities for life review and promote group work on the basis of building relationships and reducing isolation among older people. This has certainly been our experience (MacKinlay and Trevitt 2002–2005) with participants in small groups who trust each other and share at a deep level. In the case of elderly residents, new friendships may emerge from these small groups. Among the participants with dementia, the support of other group members is invaluable. This is an important aspect of reducing social isolation among aged care residents. We have found that participants with dementia in small groups have expressed their enjoyment of these groups and appreciate the regular chance to talk with others.

Making and keeping a story

A number of strategies have been used in aged care facilities for some years now to assist the resident to piece together their life story and to assist staff to get to know this unique person. These include use of photograph albums, scrap books, life story books and memory boxes. Tape and CD recordings, and perhaps videos, may also be kept. These may contain valuable aspects of the person's life. Working with people to review a life lived, drawing a family tree or using a time line may be helpful. Faith Gibson suggests that a life story book should be thought of as a 'living' working document, that can still be changed, modified and expanded (1998, p.84). She suggests that a form of loose leaf binder, that can easily be changed, modified and added to, is used. The inclusion of pockets for clippings from papers, for photos and work to be done is helpful. Personal writing may be preserved, and records of important milestones through life collected. Of course, where personal details are recorded, the book becomes a very individual and personal record that must be valued and treated with due respect. It may be that the person will not wish their book to be openly available to others, but perhaps the author may agree to lend it on occasion.

Thus, some means of telling and recording the person's story is valuable. It connects the significant events of life for the individual and sometimes helps their family to see the meaning of the older person's life too. It also assists staff to gain a greater knowledge of who this person is and this knowledge will colour and enrich the resident's care. As some of the registered nurses remarked, once they had sat and listened to the life stories of their residents, they felt they came to know them for the first time (MacKinlay 2001e). Seventy-five per cent of the sample of older people in residential care said they used reminiscence and found it something that they both liked doing and was useful (MacKinlay 2001b).

Skills needed for effective leading and facilitation of reminiscence groups

An essential beginning for group work is respect by the group facilitator for the group members and a willingness to meet them where they are in their life journeys. The skills used in small groups are those used by the helping professions, active listening and being really present with the participants. Effective facilitation of group participation includes using appropriate and open ended questions and then allowing space and silence while the individual reflects. It includes the use of paraphrasing, unconditional acceptance and the skills of focusing and summarizing.

It is important that the leader allows time for the group members to share, is respectful of each person's contribution and encourages quieter group members to contribute. The group time is for the group members to share, not for entertainment by the group leader. The skill of the leader is to draw the participants into deeper sharing, at the same time maintaining a level of comfort within the group.

Katie spoke of her need to reminisce:

> You miss your family, you've got no one to talk to about them, you know. I just lay there, well last night I think I must have been there, it must have been easy 12 o'clock before I went to sleep because I kept going over the years, what happened this year, what happened that year, I wonder how so and so is, you know and then I went off to sleep.

Then Katie asked if she was giving the 'right' answers. I responded: 'It's not right and wrong answers, it's your story and your story is the important thing, it's not a test.' She seemed relieved, and went on with her reminiscence. Each story is unique to that person; each story teller has a right to be heard. Telling one's story is part of the healing process in itself, it is part of the coming to final meanings in life. In current society too often there is no time, and no listeners for the stories. We have lost the art of former times.

Simply having someone to listen is affirming. Many of those we have listened to have said that this was the first time they had been able to share their life story. We have conducted in-depth interviews one-on-one with all our participants prior to assigning them to a small group. This approach has several advantages. First, it is a non-threatening first encounter with the new resident. Second, it gives the resident an opportunity to speak freely and to share their story. Further, some residents may feel apprehensive of first sharing in a group situation with people they do not know well. Small reminiscence groups can be led by diversional therapists, pastoral carers, trained volunteers or other aged care staff.

Using reminiscence work with people living with dementia

A number of people with dementia may have found communicating difficult. Now, in the aged care facility, in an environment of support, reminiscence therapy may affirm the participants and meet them at their point of interest and concern. During this process their ability to communicate may improve (see Chapter 8 on dementia).

How to apply spiritual reminiscence work: using the topics in small group work

It is important to have potential small group facilitators first experience the process of life review; it is only by engaging in life review that individuals will come to an appreciation of the value of the process. In spiritual reminiscence it is best to focus on the meaning of events and experiences in the lives of the participants rather than simply on the description of the events remembered. This moves the conversation to a deeper level and enables review of life meaning.

The process of small group spiritual reminiscence

A facilitator can work effectively with up to eight residents, but if any participants have hearing deficits, cognitive difficulties or diminished concentration span, the groups should be smaller. We have found that with groups of people who have dementia, it works best to assign group participants who have similar levels of cognitive ability to the same group; it may work well to use the Mini Mental State Examination (MMSE) to assess cognitive levels. With people who have communication difficulties, working with two to three people in the group may be sufficient.

Depending on the topic chosen for the day, the group session may vary in length from 30 minutes to an hour. We have also found in sessions that explore the participants' faith and relationship with God, that it is important for the group facilitator to be comfortable in talking about issues of faith; if the facilitator is uncomfortable, this will readily be communicated to the participants, especially if the group members have dementia.

The meeting place

A quiet place where interruptions are kept to a minimum is required for the groups. It is helpful to have a designated meeting place so that participants become comfortable with that environment. Aged care facilities can sometimes be very noisy, and it is therefore hard for residents to concentrate and to hear the other members speaking. Do make sure that participants with hearing deficits have their hearing aids on and working.

Memory prompters and vehicles of story

Kunz (2002) notes the importance of using all the senses in prompting reminiscence. Participants with fewer cognitive deficits may be encouraged to bring their own memory prompts – photos, craft work, flowers – the possibilities are limited only by imagination. The facilitator may know of particular memory prompts that work for various of the group members or for people with dementia. Some life events may have been significant in the participant's life formation, for example, birth order, places they lived, who they married, their children, their work, their hobbies, their faith, their relation with God or other spiritual experiences. Memories of holidays and other significant life events may also be triggers for discussion. The suggested questions also focus on the hard things of ageing; coping with an ageing body, grief and losses they have experienced, disappointments and regrets in life. Each week a different topic is the focus of discussion and questions. Suggested topics and questions are in Appendix 3.

Conclusion

Reminiscence is now widely accepted as a natural part of ageing. Further, spiritual reminiscence is becoming more widely recognized as having an important part in the process of ageing and coming to final meanings in life. Many older people will use reminiscence; however, in current western societies, many have not had the opportunity to tell their story, nor have they had someone to listen to them should they wish to tell it.

Spiritual reminiscence involves the telling of the individual person's story; finding the linkages between their story and God's story, and connecting with the story of their family and wider community. Reminiscence can be used effectively with older people to assist them to reflect and reframe aspects of their life journey in the process of moving from provisional meaning to final meanings in life. Reminiscence can be used in individual and group work as a process involving the spiritual tasks of ageing. It may be used by diversional therapists and pastoral carers as well as other aged care professionals working with older people, both in the community and aged care.

Summary

- *Through research and practice, story is now acknowledged as being a naturally occurring component of ageing.*

- *Story is used in everyday life as a means of connecting between friends and family in simple reminiscence.*

- *Story is used in exploring one's life to find purpose and meaning.*

- *Story is not only for social occasions, but may be used therapeutically to deal with past grief, guilt and the need for forgiveness.*

- *Reframing is a technique that assists in revisiting memories and, in the light of more recent knowledge and experience, the story teller is able to see the earlier events in a new way. Final meanings of events may be found.*

- *Group and individual sessions may be used to review the life story.*

- *The pastoral carer or pastoral counsellor may work with the older people in reminiscence work.*

- *Spiritual reminiscence occurs where the content of reminiscence includes the person's life journey, its relationship with family, their community of faith and their story linked with God.*

- *The use of story can be a powerful healing and growth tool.*

Further reading

Gibson, F. (2004) *The Past in the Present: Using Reminiscence in Health and Social Care.* Baltimore: Health Professions Press.

Jamieson, D. (2005) *Exploring and Affirming my Life.* Canberra: Centre for Ageing and Pastoral Studies.

Morgan, R.L. (1996) *Remembering Your Story: A Guide to Spiritual Autobiography.* Nashville: Upper Room Books.

Webster, J.D. and Haight, B.K. (eds) (2002) *Critical Advances in Reminiscence Work: From Theory to Application.* New York: Springer Publishing Company.

CHAPTER 7

The Spiritual Journey and Mental Health among Older Adults in Need of Care

Mental health is associated with an absence of mental disease and the presence of psychological, emotional and spiritual well-being. To be mentally healthy infers the presence of effective coping strategies and a functioning personality. In later life it seems that there is greater interaction between mental and spiritual functioning (MacKinlay 2001a). Thus to be mentally healthy, the person also needs to be spiritually healthy. Spiritual distress may be related to mental illness such as depression. McNamara (2002) notes that finding meaning in life sustains mental health.

Early research into connections between religion and mental health showed conflicting results; however, over recent decades more research has shown positive relationships between religion and mental health. One reason for this could be changing research methods that now more often take account of intrinsic religion, or non-organizational religiosity, rather than simply measuring church attendance. Koenig and associates (1992) in a prospective study found that religious coping was the only predictor of fewer depressive symptoms. Considering this study and a subsequent study of his, Koenig states that the findings 'suggest that religious involvement exhibits both preventive and therapeutic effects on mental health status.' (Koenig 1998, p.36). However, a study by Strawbridge *et al.* (1998) found a buffering effect of organizational religiosity on non-family stressors and depression, but not for family stressors, suggesting that the relationship between religion and depression may be complex. Yet another study (Murphy *et al.* 2000) found it was religious belief not religious behaviour that was a significant predictor of lower levels of hopelessness and depression. These studies were all North American studies, and in some other western countries such as the UK and Australia, where lower levels of church attendance are commonly found, it may be more useful to consider concepts of spirituality rather than religion in relation to mental health.

This chapter focuses on mental health and common departures from it, such as later life depression, suicide risk and recognizing delirium. Other factors that may predispose to mental health problems such as social isolation are dealt with in Chapter 12 on relationship and intimacy needs.

Depression in later life

What is it like to have depression? An elderly woman in hospital remarked: 'How can I see the sun shine, when I don't feel the sun shining inside me?' Surely this remark indicates the devastating effect of depression and the burden of living under it.

Mental health problems that occur in later life, as at any point in the life cycle, may impair quality of life, as in the case of depression. Depression is not part of the ageing process. However, in later life, depression is more likely to be written off as merely part of growing older, and later life depression is often under-diagnosed and consequently under-treated. Yet for those who experience it, it can be a devastating condition. Snowdon (1998, p.58) reported that only 25–50 per cent of depressed outpatients were recognized as being depressed by interns and, further, that general practitioners detect only a minority of potentially treatable depression.

Estimates of the prevalence of depression in older people vary, Koenig (1995) claiming that more than 25 per cent of community dwelling people have depressive symptoms, rising to more than 40 per cent of older people in hospital. In some studies of community prevalence of depression in people over 65 years in the UK levels range from 4–6 per cent rising to 20 per cent in those over 80 (Minardi and Blanchard 2004). These researchers also reported that 57 per cent of those identified as having depression were not treated. In a study of depression among aged care residents in Australia, 40–60 per cent of residents were found to be depressed and approximately 50 per cent were depressed at the time of admission to aged care (Fleming 2001).

Depression adversely affects quality of life, and it is contended that should it be possible to lower levels of depression among older community dwelling people, there may be less need for residential care. At a very basic level finding meaning in life is protective against depression and mental ill health (MacKinlay 2002). Further, Butler (1995) had said that some people with chronic illnesses may first show signs of depression, for instance cardiovascular conditions including stroke. Butler also reported that depression rates were higher among those who had Alzheimer's disease, Parkinson's disease, diabetes, thyroid disorders, cancer, chronic obstructive pulmonary disease, rheumatoid arthritis, deafness, chronic pain, renal dialysis and chronic constipation. It may be difficult to diagnose dementia in a person who is also depressed, and both conditions may coexist in the same person.

Some recent studies have shown that older people have a 40 per cent greater likelihood of developing coronary heart disease and a 60 per cent increased risk of death than those who have lower mean depression scores (Ariyo and Haan 2000). Minardi and Blanchard note that the prevalence of depression in older people is associated with age, gender, family history, physical illness/disability, life events, change in living patterns, social and interpersonal support, financial and educational status, urbanicity, loneliness and personality (2004, p.22). They suggest that such a range of associations points to a multifactorial etiology of depression in older people, but they also note that depression is not an automatic response to these factors. However, it is likely that depression may be more common in certain circumstances, and Goldsmith (2004) notes a significant association of depression and anxiety for females over the age of 65 years who are also co-resident and next of kin caring for people with dementia.

In a pilot study in London of a day care centre, Minardi and Blanchard (2004) set out to identify levels of depression in attendees and describe associations that depression had with perceptions of handicap, loneliness, social support networks and satisfaction and, finally, life satisfaction. They also examined possible roles for Community Mental Health Nurses (CMHN) in offering psychosocial intervention for these people. It was assumed that attendees would have been referred to the day care centre for social support, however, the high level of depression (41%) in the group would indicate that these people would benefit not just from social support but from therapeutic interventions as well, which, Minardi and Blanchard note, day cay centre staff are generally not trained to provide (2004, p.27). They found loneliness positively associated, and satisfaction with life negatively associated with depression. They further found that handicap and social support were not associated with depression. While these findings conflict with previous studies, it is noted that the sample size was small, and further study into this vulnerable population with high levels of depression is warranted. However, it does show that there are likely to be multiple reasons for occurrence of depression.

THE SPIRITUAL JOURNEY AND MENTAL HEALTH AMONG OLDER ADULTS / 99

A psychotheological perspective on depression

Depression has traditionally been classified, diagnosed and treated from medical assumptions of biochemical and genetic etiology. However, an alternative view is proposed by Close (2000). Close combined the perspectives of Frankl (1984) of the noogenic (meaning) dimension and Tillich's (1963) perspective of the onto-logical dimension (anxiety and the threat of nonbeing) as a basis for reconsidering depression. This perspective may have important implications for treating de-pression in later life and follows Buckwalter's (1999) assertion that no one theory adequately explains the occurrence of depression in later life.

The model of spiritual tasks and process of ageing and depression

I have developed a model of spiritual tasks and process of ageing that seeks to describe spiritual development in later life at a generic level and also applied to different faith groups. For the Abrahamic faiths (Christianity, Judaism and Islamic faiths) the model of a God-centred approach holds. This model (MacKinlay 2001a, and illustrated in Chapter 1, Figure 1.2) considers that each person seeks to find ultimate life-meaning and in these faith traditions the person would move toward a life centred in God, so that life-meaning would be centred in God. In a real sense, this quest for life centred in God is a journey which may not be completed in this life.

It is from what lies at the centre of life that meaning is found. Thus, holding a life-giving image of God will be a source of hope for a person. On the other hand, having an image of a judgmental God or a distant God will colour the person's response to the whole of life and may result in a sense of hopelessness and meaninglessness. Thus hope and meaning are closely related to mental well-being.

A lack in life-meaning may be a major factor in the onset of depression. Further, suicide is related to profound meaninglessness. A person who finds nothing to hope for will not be mentally healthy, and will not be able to flourish and thrive; indeed, this person will merely exist. Without hope the soul lacks nourishment and failure to thrive may occur, and the person may become hopeless. Depression may be a feature of the physiological changes that occur near the time of death, and this can be part of a failure to thrive.

There is a complex interaction where grief from a relationship loss can result in a loss of life-meaning; this would be especially so if the person who had died was the centre of meaning for the bereaved person. Thus, as all major theorists in loss and grief acknowledge, depression is a commonly expected part of the grief experience (Kubler-Ross 1970; Raphael 1990; Stroebe *et al.* 2001; Worden 1997). In these situations, the person needs support through the work of grieving and the associated depression.

Management of late life depression

Identifying depression

Depression is the most readily treated of all mental health problems in later life (Butler 1995). A first step in dealing with depression is recognizing it. Snowdon (1998) recommends using a simple screening test for depression, such as the Geriatric Depression Scale (GDS) (Yesavage, Brink and Rose 1983) on all older people who have physical, cognitive or psychiatric disorders, unless they are *not* obviously depressed. The classical clinical diagnostic test for depression is the DSM-IV (American Psychiatric Association 1994) that sets out diagnostic criteria for depression.

A person is said to have a major depression should they exhibit over a two-week period five or more of the following: depressed mood; markedly diminished interest in most activities; significant weight loss or gain; insomnia or hypersomnia; psychomotor agitation or retardation; fatigue or loss of energy; feelings of worthlessness or inappropriate guilt; diminished ability to concentrate and recurrent thoughts about death or suicide. It is noted, however, that older people are more likely to exhibit depressive symptoms than to have a major depression (Gatz and Fiske 2003). They note a particular constellation of symptoms that occur more frequently in older people: loss of interest, loss of energy, hopelessness, helplessness and psychomotor retardation. This is called depletion syndrome (p.5); it could also be termed failure to thrive.

Considering prevention of further depressive symptoms in older adults, Alexopoulos *et al.* (2005) found that longitudinal assessment of older depressed primary care patients for depression, hopelessness, anxiety and physical and emotional functional limitations is critical. They strongly recommended continuing case management and care for those with prominent symptoms or impairment in these areas.

Treating late life depression

Once depression is diagnosed, it is readily treated (Butler 1995). Best outcomes result from accurate identification of clinical depression followed by pharmacological treatment supported by psychotherapy, including cognitive-behavioural therapy. While the effectiveness of psychotherapy with elderly depressed patients is well supported, Alexopoulos *et al.* (2005) found that too few older people are being offered this means of treatment, and Raymond (2002) suggests that medications are too often used alone.

Treatment may range through antidepressant medications, psychotherapy, pastoral care, and if other forms of treatment fail, ECT (electroconvulsive therapy). In this chapter pastoral care is suggested as another means of care that may be effective in the care of older people who have depression. Gatz and Fiske (2003) describe spirituality as a coping strategy to buffer the effects of stressful life events on depression.

Pastoral possibilities in residential aged care

In a study of aged care facility residents Baker (2000) used pastoral care with three groups of residents:

- a depressed treatment group taking antidepressive medications
- a group of people identified as at risk of depression not taking medications
- a control group of subjects without depression.

The study used 30-minute weekly pastoral care visits to each treatment subject over a six-month period. The control subjects received only minimum pastoral care. Baker found pastoral care to be equally effective in both treatment groups.

The study supported the hypothesis that intentional pastoral care, nurturing the spiritual dimension, may reduce the prevalence and degree of depression. Baker found that pastoral care was equally effective with people taking antidepressants and those not taking antidepressants. Analysis of scores on the non-depressed treatment group showed greater existential well-being and self-transcendence than depressed participants; however, depressed participants reported greater reduction in depression than those not depressed. Pastoral care interventions that were shown to be significantly associated with reduction of depression scores and enhanced scores of spiritual well-being were: prayer, counselling for issues raised, grief work, the provision of blessings, active listening and life review.

However, an increase in depression levels after the study was completed highlights the need to examine ways of implementing long-term support, after a period of support from a chaplain. Trained volunteers may have an important role in providing follow-up pastoral and spiritual care.

Another project reported by Koenig and Lawson (2004, p.186) involved teaming older residents in joint activities with young volunteers through the Faith in Action organization, thus, say the authors, providing a sense of purpose and meaning in the lives of both groups and thus preventing depression. The high school volunteers in this programme are academically underachieving and disadvantaged students. The Faith in Action programmes in the US serve both independent older people and people in residential aged care. A word of caution is given here, that while involvement in activities that bring purpose to life do work to prevent depression, these strategies will fail to assist people who are already depressed.

Awareness of residents' spiritual care needs should be everyone's business: chaplains, nurses, social workers and other aged care workers, including ancillary staff. Baker (2000) describes pastoral care in health settings as having four functions: healing, sustaining, guiding and reconciling. He also notes the importance of providing spiritual care equally to people who regard themselves as religious and those who do not. The development of a spiritually aware environment may do much to lower rates of depression among older adults, especially those who reside in aged care facilities.

Delirium

Delirium is a rapidly debilitating condition that may occur in older adults. It is included here because it is frequently misdiagnosed and prompt recognition of it will have important effects on positive outcomes for the elderly person. The key factors in its recognition are:

- a rapid onset of confusion, hallucinations
- association with some other condition such as an infection, commonly urinary or respiratory
- a possible relationship to drug toxicity, or to electrolyte imbalance
- a rapid return to pre-delirium state if correctly treated
- it is easily confused with dementia
- dementia and delirium may be present at the same time in the same person, so a rapid change of mental state in a person with dementia should always be investigated.

Treatment of delirium

Prompt diagnosis is always important. This condition may be a frightening experience for both the resident and their family. Treatment of the underlying cause will in most instances result in a rapid return to normal function.

Elder abuse

Lang (2005) cites elder abuse as an urgent problem, stating that 2–10 per cent of elderly people are physically or mentally abused and that mistreated older people are three times more likely to die within three years than those who are not abused, adjusting for comorbidity and other factors associated with mortality. After 13 years, 41 per cent of non-abused elders were still alive, but only 9 per cent of those who were abused (Lachs and Pillemer 2004, p.1270). There seems to be general agreement that elder abuse may include physical, psychological, emotional, sexual, financial abuse and neglect (Lachs and Pillemer 2004). Gray-Vickrey (2004) found that approximately 70 per cent of abuse was associated with neglect of older people, emotional abuse 35 per cent, financial abuse 30 per cent, while physical (including sexual abuse) made up about 25 per cent of cases. (Obviously from these percentages, more than one type of abuse was perpetrated in numbers of cases.)

Abuse may occur within the family, the community and within aged care facilities. A study in the Australian Capital Territory (ACT) in 2004 (related to ACT 2001) found a low level of public awareness of elder abuse, and that elder abuse was mostly seen as acts of commission rather than of neglect. Few people in the study mentioned sexual abuse as one type of abuse of elders. As a result, a taskforce was set up to raise public awareness of elder abuse, a help line was established for phone contact, and an education programme for health providers and the public was established.

Hardin and Khan-Hudson (2005) writing of the situation in the US, where legislation on elder abuse has now been passed in all states, note that abusers tend to be family members and care providers, and that it may be difficult to identify cases of abuse due to the isolation and vulnerability of the victims. Family stresses may be a factor in abuse occurring. They also report numbers of cases of institutional elder abuse. Teaster and Roberto (2004) in a study of sexual abuse in older adults, found that in aged care facilities, those abused were likely to be older and female, often they also had cognitive disabilities and were frail. Most abusers were either other residents or staff.

Incidents of abuse are often perceived to be physical and sexual abuse. However, in everyday life, when working with frail and vulnerable people, seemingly trivial events may be demeaning to residents, and in this way, constitute abuse. Small instances can prove to be disempowering to these people, and some of those I talked with shared their concerns. We need to ask the question, when does an action or omission of an action become abuse, or neglect?

Sonya, a resident in an aged care facility said: 'Life's one big fear for me.' When I asked her why, she replied:

> I'm even an old softie you know about wanting things of the night time, you know, it's the night's staff are entirely different to the day girls and if I can avoid it I don't like buzzing them at all, because if they're cranky they upset me, I don't want to… I don't want to say anything much about them.

Staff attitudes can have marked effects on residents, both those who are cognitively competent and those who have dementia (Bird 2002). Because of the vulnerability and high level of need of these frail elderly people they are at increased risk of abuse. Veronica was another vulnerable resident, she had been wheelchair bound for four to five years now and she has an electric chair. Veronica is anxious about being lifted in the slings they use to transfer her from bed to chair. She says that some staff don't seem to know how to use the equipment and she feels apprehensive when they try to lift her; she is obese and lifting must be done in a particular way. She says sometimes new staff don't seem to like to be told how to do it:

> And I mean we get the new ones in you know, some haven't seen a sling lifted before, it's a bit hard that way and trying to tell them. They don't take notice what you tell them sometimes, it's a bit hard that way… Because I've got to depend on them you know and can't stand and walk you know.

Veronica has reason to be apprehensive as she fell when living at another nursing home and sustained a leg fracture. Sometimes aged care facilities find it hard to attract qualified staff, and some rely on agency staff who may not be adequately trained in the use of specific equipment, including lifting machines. Adequate orientation of new staff and continuing education and monitoring of staff practices are all important responsibilities of aged care management.

Prevention of elder abuse

Aged care professionals having contact with elderly clients are well placed to identify signs of elder abuse, however, a high level of suspicion is needed to detect signs of abuse. A number of authors suggest that general practitioners may be so busy that they fail to see elder abuse as a priority and therefore miss identifying cases.

Good assessment skills are needed, and one elder abuse and neglect assessment is the Elder Assessment Instrument (EAI: available at www.hartfordign.org). Fulmer (2005) critiques the instrument saying its strengths are rapid assessment capacity and its ability to sensitize the clinician to screening for abuse. Its weaknesses lie in lack of a scoring system and weak specificity. An evaluation of elder abuse assessment instruments by Meeks-Sjostrom (2004) found the EAI instrument to be the best of the three tested, but recommended that further work is needed to enable accurate assessment of abuse.

Elderly people who are abused may be reluctant to admit to the abuse due to their vulnerability, and because of feelings of shame, guilt and fear, or because of being socially, mentally or physically isolated (Meeks-Sjostrom 2004). Family relationships may be complex, with the elderly person relying on care from the abuser. Aged care organizations need to maintain a high level of vigilance for the possibility of staff abuse of residents and complaints of residents need to be taken seriously and acted upon. Continuing education is a vital component for prevention of abuse.

Suicide in later life

Currently, suicide rates for males over 85 years of age in the US and Australia are higher than most other groups. In Australia, rates increased from 37 to 50 per 100,000 in the ten years to 1990 (Hassan 1995). Hassan writes that preliminary evidence from South Australia suggests that for older people, particularly men, suicide is often planned and rational. Further: 'Suicide for many of them means not an unwillingness to live or inability to live but a willingness to die' (p.67). The fact that they have survived to old age demonstrates their will to live to an old age; but Hassan suggests that the economic, psychosocial and health problems of old age 'become unbearable' (p.66). Leenaars (2003) studied suicide notes from older people, both with terminal illness and without, and although Leenaars says the wish to die does seem very strong in older people and that unbearable pain certainly features highly in the notes, suicide in older people is seen as a complex phenomenon requiring further research.

Suicide in later life has consistently been shown to be higher among males. Gatz and Fiske (2003, p.5) report that older men who committed suicide were more likely to have had financial problems, while older women were more likely to be depressed. Gatz and Fiske note that a large proportion of older adults who commit suicide had visited a medical practitioner a short time prior to their suicide. They suggest that one reason that signs of suicidal ideation were not identified may be that physicians tend to normalize depression and suicidal ideation in older adults. While older women engage in fewer acts of overt suicide than older men, they may be at greater risk of indirect suicide behaviour in aged care facilities. Gatz and Fiske (2003) cite a study of indirect suicide in 463 facilities in the US, where 80 per cent of suicidal behaviour was indirect, 'most commonly a conscious, persistent refusal to eat, drink, or take medication' (p.6). Koenig (1998) reports that 50 per cent of suicides may be preventable if helpers, including clergy, are properly trained. Perhaps these problems in turn become spiritual distress in the older person. It would seem that the spiritual dimension is also important in the decisions of such older people to commit suicide (MacKinlay 2001a). Issues of meaninglessness must also figure in decisions to commit suicide.

Mental health in later life

This chapter has not addressed personality issues or psychotic illnesses in later life. Information on these may be found in the literature on psychology, mental health and psychiatry. The chapter does, however, recommend strategies for spiritual well-being.

Finding meaning in later life

To be human is to search for life meaning. Older people are often confronted with events that shake their sense of meaning, for example, the death of a partner of more than 40 years, loss of health, loss of friends through death, loss of home. Lifetime coping strategies will be important in working through each of these situations. Life experience, personality, attitudes and spirituality will all be involved in the search for meaning after such losses. Psychological counselling and pastoral counselling may be important means of assisting an elderly person to work through grief and come to new life-meaning.

Spiritual strategies

In recent years the term spiritual hardiness (Carson and Green 1992) or spiritual resilience (Ramsey and Bleisner 2000) have been used. Spiritual resilience is a concept that describes the ability of a person to survive and to thrive in adverse situations, often when facing tremendous challenges in life. It has now been widely accepted that there are differences in the survival rates of different people that cannot be explained by the disease process alone. Is spiritual resilience an inbuilt attribute or can it be developed as a coping strategy? Having recently described these concepts, we are only now beginning to consider these questions.

Spiritual portfolio

One factor that seems to be associated with spiritual well-being and resilience is having a spiritual portfolio, or a number of spiritual strategies that are used as ways of living effectively and can be drawn on in times of crisis and grief. Examples of this include for Christians, Muslims and Jews, a God-centred life and for Buddhists and Hindus, an ability to find *nirvana*, and to lose oneself. Other strategies include prayer, appropriate liturgies and rituals, the use of scripture, meditation and contemplation, and having a community of faith and support and involvement in meaningful social interactions. Having a confidante was important for some of the participants in the study of independent living older people (MacKinlay 2001a). Long-term membership of a small group provided for the well-being of several of the participants.

Spiritual health is an important factor in mental health and well-being in later life. This chapter has provided an overview of major mental health issues in later life, means of identifying issues, and ways of preventing mental health issues, from a spiritual perspective. Pastoral and wholistic strategies for mental and spiritual well-being have been suggested.

Conclusion

Depression and dementia are common conditions in later life, but neither are part of the normal ageing process. Dementia is specifically addressed in Chapter 8. A raised community and aged care provider awareness of mental health issues will do much to increase the chances of early identification of departures from mental health. Adequate access to appropriate treatment for these conditions is needed, so that with treatment these older people may enjoy a greater quality of life.

Pastoral and spiritual care, in combination with antidepressant medications and psychotherapy, make important contributions to the effective treatment of depression in older people. Depression is a risk factor for suicide and may be associated with elder abuse. Having a spiritual portfolio may be protective against depression.

Summary

- *Mental health problems may be the cause of decreased quality of life in older adults.*

- *Depression is commonly under-diagnosed and thus under-treated in older people.*

- *Depression is the most treatable of all mental health conditions of older people.*

- *Depression is best treated by antidepressants and psychotherapy and/or pastoral care.*

- *Delirium involving acute confusion requires urgent treatment. It is always associated with other factors such as infections, exacerbation of other chronic illnesses, falls or drug toxicity.*

- *Delirium may be present in a person who has dementia.*

- *Suicide rates rise among older men and there are higher rates of completed suicide than in younger people.*

CHAPTER 8

Meeting the Challenge

Older People with Memory Loss and Dementia

Corinne Trevitt

Dementia is a condition feared by many older people. Even diseases such as cancer and disabilities such as stroke or arthritis do not strike the same fears as dementia. In a study of older independent living people, it was identified as a fear by one third of participants (MacKinlay 1998) with one participant describing that she did not want to be 'off her legs and out of her mind'. Relatives often describe their loved one as 'having already gone' or that they experience death twice – once as a result of memory loss and then again when the person truly dies.

Dementia is responsible for progressive cognitive and functional impairment over a period of years, with great cost to individuals, families and the community. In an ageing society dementia is a significant issue with prevalence expected to double every 5.1 years after age 65, affecting 24 per cent of those over the age of 85 (Henderson and Jorm 1998). In residential aged care facilities only 20 per cent of residents are identified as not having dementia (Australian Institute of Health and Welfare 2004). While there is continuing research into both the causes of dementia and pharmacological cures, the greatest need presently is to find ways to enhance quality of life for those diagnosed with dementia. This means there needs to be an emphasis on understanding the world of the person with dementia; on communication that can tap into the 'inner core of being' of the person with dementia; and, thoughtful strategies to manage the most disturbing behavioural challenges in a setting that is caring, secure and meaningful.

The aim of this chapter is to provide carers (either in pastoral care, personal care or relatives and friends) with an overview of dementia and the major challenges faced on a daily basis when undertaking to enhance the quality of life of those with dementia.

What is dementia?

Dementia is a complex syndrome that results in the loss of intellectual capacity. The intellectual losses are severe enough to cause the person considerable social, occupational and physical deterioration. We are all familiar with the characteristic memory loss, but this is just one part of the deterioration in cognitive abilities that comes with dementia. Other brain functions such as language, perception, problem solving, abstract thinking and judgment are all affected. Personality characteristics may be maintained or exaggerated in some people or altered in others. This may be evident as social withdrawal, anxiety and fearfulness. Irritability, agitation, paranoia and delusions can occur as well as physical and verbal aggression towards family and carers. Many of these traits are more obvious as the person with dementia loses control over his or her environment (Davies 1999).

We tend to think about those with dementia as being all the same with memory loss being the predominant problem. But each person with dementia experiences the changes brought about by dementia in a different way, thus care always needs to be individualized. Practices that work for one person may cause agitation and discomfort in another. For this reason, dementia remains one of the most challenging syndromes affecting older people.

In the research project 'The search for meaning: Quality of life for the person with dementia' (MacKinlay, Trevitt and Hobart 2002), the consent form asked for participants with dementia. This resulted in very few participants. However, when we described the project being for older people with memory loss there were no problems attracting participants. This seemed to indicate that having dementia was something carers and older people alike were reluctant to admit.

There is still stigma attached to mental illness and dementia is often included in this category. Goldsmith (2004) describes how a person is treated differently, both consciously and unconsciously, once the diagnosis of dementia is made. People are on the look-out for lapses and personality changes which increases the pressure on the person with the diagnosis of dementia. The person is supposedly unable to remember, therefore unable to understand, and they have no insight, and therefore cannot contribute to decision making about their care or future (Bryden 2005). Kitwood (1997) described this as malignant psychology. He says that those diagnosed with dementia suffer by being stigmatized, intimidated, labelled, banished and objectified. To name an issue is so often to allow a difficult topic to be spoken about openly. Dementia is one such topic. We still, in some settings, find that people don't want to talk about it, at least not to the person who has dementia. The assumption seems to be that the person will not understand. Or can it be fear within those who do not have dementia?

Christine Bryden (2005) describes how the diagnosis of dementia affected her life. Being just 46 years old, she was not a typical person with dementia. It took her two years before she was able to 'come out' and declare that she had dementia. During the first period of her disease she felt that she was sliding into depression and living the 'medical model' view of dementia – gradual and inexorable decline. Then, two years after the diagnosis, she decided to embrace life – to reject the model of what was supposed to happen and make things happen for herself. She wrote her first book and enrolled in a degree – not the activities we expect for someone with 'dementia'. She describes the stigma she felt as she ceased to be a person and became a person with dementia. In her second book she records the continuing journey into dementia.

Types of dementia

When we speak of dementia, we often immediately think of Alzheimer's disease. But dementia is just a symptom of a number of different diseases. There are about 60 causes of dementia. Each has its own attributes and differences and the course of the disease is dependent on the type of dementia the older person is experiencing. All the dementias have the effect of increasing disability and reducing life expectancy (Kirshner 2005). Some of the more common dementias are described here.

Alzheimer's disease has a specific course or progression beginning with memory lapses, difficulty learning new information and altered attention span and leading to total physical and cognitive decline. In the brain there are specific changes causing 'tangles' of neurones leading to deterioration over time of all aspects of cognition including memory, language, perception and personality. In the final stages of the disease, the person has severely reduced cognition and language skills, and is generally bed-ridden. The disease may have a course of as little as 18 months up to 27 years, while the average length of the condition is 10–12 years (Davies 1999). About 60 per cent of people diagnosed with dementia have Alzheimer's disease.

Vascular dementia is the next most common cause of dementia. This type of dementia is caused by small emboli (or infarcts or 'mini strokes') affecting the blood supply to different parts of the brain. The types of behaviour seen are directly related to the area of the brain affected. Where Alzheimer's disease is progressive and relatively predictable, the course of dementia caused by vascular problems is characterized by dips and plateaus over time. However, both types of dementia may be present in the one person.

Lewy body dementia is characterized by the presence of 'Lewy body' changes in the neurones of the brain. It is a progressive degenerative dementia that has some differences from Alzheimer's disease. In Lewy body dementia, there are more fluctuations in cognitive function with varying levels of alertness and attention; and visual hallucinations and tremors (similar to Parkinson's disease) (Crystal 2004). The disease progresses more rapidly than Alzheimer's disease (Australian Institute of Health and Welfare 2004).

Other, less common, causes of dementia include Pick's disease or frontal lobe dementia. In this dementia, the average age of onset is younger than that of Alzheimer's disease. Some people experience only aphasia (language difficulty) for periods exceeding 10 years, while others progress to dementia within a few years. In frontal lobe dementia, presenting symptoms often involve alterations in personality and social conduct including: becoming disinhibited; neglecting personal hygiene and being 'tactless'. Conversely, they could also become withdrawn and 'mute' or suffer from perserveration (repetitive word phrases) (Kirshner 2005).

Huntington's disease, Parkinson's disease, alcoholism and infections are other causes of dementia. Each has specific signs and symptoms but all are characterized by deterioration in cognitive abilities (Miller 2004).

Admission to residential aged care

Management of dementia is both costly and complex, with a current focus on maintaining those affected at home for as long as possible. For most, institutional care is required during the later stages. Admission to aged care facilities usually occurs because of unmanageable behaviour such as aggression, incontinence or being unable to live alone for a range of safety issues. For the person living alone, this could mean that their ability to manage stoves, electricity and hygiene have become compromised. For the person living with their spouse or another carer, other behaviours such as wandering, paranoia, aggression or increasing frailty can result in admission to an aged care facility.

Frequently, the need to move to an aged care facility comes after a crisis and there is much stress for both the family and the older person. Family members may argue over the necessity of residential care, the costs involved and who is to take the major responsibility for care management. In families where there is a history of stressful communication, this event can lead to family crisis. Many people, older and younger, have a deep fear and aversion to aged care facilities. There may also be the situation where one family member has promised never to send their mother/father to a nursing home, increasing feelings of grief and guilt (Davies 1999).

An older person entering an aged care facility faces significant losses. There can be loss of community and friends, possessions, their own home, pets, independence and privacy. Although relieved of the burden of the day-to-day management of a home, the person has no control over the types of food provided and the people caring for them. It may be impossible to have a single room and a person who has valued their independence and privacy can be in the situation of having to rely on others for basic human needs. These losses lead to considerable grief reactions and can include anger, anxiety and fearfulness, mental disorganization and feelings of being overwhelmed. For an older person already managing memory loss, these feelings can create further confusion leading to aggression, paranoia and depression. Older people have to choose carefully the few items they can take into an aged care facility. But even these few personal possessions can enhance the adaptation to residential care – thus lessening some of the stresses of loss (McCracken 1987, in Powers 2003).

For family members there can be feelings of loss, grief and guilt. Despite their greatest efforts, the decision has had to be made to place their relative in care. Fountain (2003) describes measures that families take to become involved in the day-to-day care of their relative. Things like getting to know as many staff as possible personally; developing a relationship with the director of nursing; visiting regularly and frequently and providing clothing that survives the industrial laundry. She describes the pleasure she had from those staff who took extra care to ensure that her mother, a fastidious dresser, was always looking smart in well-matched clothing.

Types of challenging behaviours

Up to 90 per cent of people with dementia will exhibit challenging behaviours (Cohen-Mansfield, Marx and Rosenthal 1989, in Richards and Beck 2004). These can cause significant problems for carers and in some cases may lead to placement in a residential facility. They are also in many cases cyclic and have a 'life'. Behaviours come and go as the person moves through various stages of the disease. A person experiencing aggressive behaviour may pass through this stage into one that is more accommodating of family, carers and others. For this reason, it is essential that carers accommodate the behaviour, not force the person with dementia to change. Increases in problem behaviours are a good predictor of depression and care-giver burden in carers and can result in early admission to aged care facilities. Giving those caring at home more support to manage difficult behaviour may lead to delay in admission to residential care (Gauger *et al.* 2005).

The significant attribute of problem behaviours is that they are repetitive and may result in personal injury or injury to others. The person may display lack of concern for others or potentially violate their rights. Problem behaviours should be regarded as symptoms of an unmet need rather than as a final diagnosis. Unmet needs could arise from loss of personal space and personal time; poor communication skills (on the part of the carer as well as the person with dementia); loss of self-esteem, personal identity and autonomy; discomfort; lack of meaningful activity and reduced cognitive understanding leading to fear and uncertainty (Richards Hall and Gerdner 1999).

There are a number of difficult behaviours identified in the literature. These include disruptive behaviour, aggression, wandering, agitation, anxiety and sleeplessness (Richards Hall and Gerdner 1999; Stanley and Gauntlet Beare 1999).

Problem behaviours arise for a number of reasons. Many studies have tried to define problem behaviours, but these suggest that problem behaviours are difficult to define and determined by the perceptions of the care provider (Richards Hall and Gerdner 1999). One of the issues present in all reporting is that there is a 'one size fits all' approach to aged care and dementia care, when in reality everyone has different needs. Frequently, professional outside help to solve disruptive behaviour is requested only when the behaviour has escalated to an intolerable level.

The first step to minimize problem behaviour is to assess and describe the behaviour. Questions to ask (Richards Hall and Gerdner 1999) include:

- What does the behaviour mean to the individual?
- Who is involved when the behaviour occurs?
- Where does the behaviour occur?
- What is the timing of the behaviour?
- What is the antecedent or trigger to the behaviour?
- How are the care-givers or family members currently interpreting the behaviour?
- What are the consequences of the behaviour?

Once the assessment measures are undertaken there are three ways to plan behaviour change:

1. Reframe the meaning of the behaviour to the caregiver.

2. Modify the situations that trigger the behaviour.

or

3. Alter the responses to the behaviour.

Frequently, reframing the behaviour for the care-giver can reduce the problem. Gaining an understanding of the person's previous life can help the carer to understand the behaviour and thus reframe the meaning of that behaviour. Good assessment leading to modifications to care routines can alter the behaviour enough for the carer to manage. Identifying and modifying triggers can eliminate the behaviour. Changing responses to the behaviour can also significantly impact the behaviour. All these interventions depend on carers all having one goal in mind – to improve the quality of life for the resident.

Bird (2002) described in his paper 'Dementia and suffering in nursing homes' how relatively simple changes in care management can have significant effects on behaviours – although these may take several months to occur. He describes how suffering on the part of both residents and carers can be minimized by simple interventions embraced by all carers. Three assessment questions he proposes are:

1. What is the cause of the suffering of which the behaviour is the outward expression?

2. What causal factors are contributing to the distress others feel about this resident and his or her behaviour?

3. Which of these causes is fixable?

There is good evidence to suggest that behaviour of residents is influenced and guided by carers and vice versa. Bird believes that difficult behaviour occurs for reasons other than or in addition to cognitive impairment. Carers may say the behaviour is because the older person has dementia, frontal-lobe syndrome or cerebral irritation, or that the person is attention seeking, manipulative or naughty. Often, however, the behaviour is because of the attitudes of carers, not the disease. It is difficult to imagine an 89-year-old person with dementia planning how to be manipulative or aggressive, but frequently this is how carers regard this type of behaviour (2002, p.57). To manage difficult behaviours, carers, together with relatives, need to plan a care framework which everyone follows. Care needs to be consistent and compassionate, putting the needs of the older person first.

Much behaviour may arise as a result of environmental stressors and can be reduced or relieved with some simple steps (Stanley and Gauntlet Beare 1999):

- Decrease environmental press.
- Carefully attend to primary-self needs.
- Balance active times with rest.
- Always seek to determine triggers to the behaviour.

Environmental press is the demand character of an environment (Stanley and Gauntlet Beare 1999). It is the noise of television, chatter, calling-out, call bells, phones ringing and other background noises. People with dementia do not just have memory and cognitive loss, they also experience other visuo-perceptual changes in smell, taste, balance and gait. Accompanying these are the usual changes related to ageing, such as loss of hearing and depth perception. A sunlit room with activities may become for the older person a frightening, glare-filled environment with a cacophony of background noise. They may wander aimlessly looking for a way out, or become frightened, agitated and angry.

I have experienced this background noise with the *Into Ageing* game (Dempsey-Lyle and Hoffman 1991) – an experiential learning process for aged care workers to experience the world of the aged care resident. An audio-tape of 'typical background' noise in an aged care facility that we have used with this simulation game is enough to cause even the most patient person to scream in frustration. This could be the everyday surrounding sound for many older persons – a truly frightening prospect!

Regardless of the cause of the behaviour, all authors agree that good assessment of the behaviour and a calm, sustained and consistent approach to managing the behaviour will, in most cases, result in improvement for the resident and staff. Some tips for common behaviours follow – keeping in mind that assessment and asking questions as already described, is the first part of dealing with a challenging behaviour.

Aggressive behaviour

Malcolm Goldsmith cites Martin Luther King who said 'violence is the voice of the unheard' (2004, p.43). For many older people with dementia, being violent may be their only way of asserting their rights and maintaining some degree of autonomy or of letting us know about pain, both physical and emotional. If we as carers thought first 'what is this person trying to tell me' rather than responding in a defensive way to the aggression, then perhaps aggression would cease to be 'problem' behaviour.

If a person becomes aggressive the carer should back off and ask the following (Jackson and MacDonald 2004):

- Does this need to be done now?
- Is there someone else who can do it more easily (other carer or relative)?
- Is there another way of doing this?
- Are others safe?

Development of respect and trust is essential to manage aggression. Jackson and MacDonald (2004, p.190) describe a number of approaches to take to reduce aggression and instill confidence in the older person. These include:

- Approaching the person from the front.
- Using the person's preferred mode of address.
- Introducing themselves.
- Adopting a non-threatening pose.
- Using eye-contact.
- Being calm and unhurried in manner.
- Speaking in a clear, gentle voice.
- Explaining what they are going to do *for* the person not *to* the person.
- Keeping instructions simple.
- Offering alternatives.
- Respecting the person's right to refuse.
- Being consistent.
- Coming back later.

Medication intervention is sometimes required to manage aggression but, this needs to be used with caution. The side-effects of these drugs often produce problems that are more difficult to manage and frequently contribute to more complications. Behaviour modification can take time and effort but in many cases will eliminate the need for medication (Bird 2002). Jackson and MacDonald

(2004, p.187) state this well: 'Football hooligans are not sedated in anticipation of the possibility that they *might* harm others. Is it right to do so in dementia care?'

Wandering

Wandering can be one of the most dangerous behaviours to manage. If still at home or in an aged care facility the carer is always worried that the older person with dementia will wander onto a road, go into other residents' rooms and trigger an aggressive response, fall and be injured or get lost. All of these cause increased anxiety for carers. Even in secure environments wanderers can 'escape'. I have seen an 80-year-old man with dementia use a kitchen stool to scale a 3 metre (10 foot) wall to leave a 'secure' environment. As it was in winter, just on dusk, with a rapidly falling outside temperature, there was considerable anxiety as to his safety. He was finally found, two very anxious hours later, some distance from the facility.

There is no general 'cure' for wandering. Behaviour modification has been shown to produce a slight improvement but this was rapidly lost if rewards were not continued for an extended period of time (Heard and Watson 1999, in Lai and Arthur 2004). An enhanced environment with different scenes can help. Establishing a home-like environment with flowers, furniture, running water (fountains) and gardens has been shown to reduce wandering. If an older person frequently wanders into another person's room, perhaps that room has better amenities or view. These types of changes have been shown to help reduce wandering (Lai and Arthur 2004).

Wandering is not always a disadvantage. Provided an assessment has been undertaken and the wandering behaviour is not the result of an unmet need, then wandering can be an effective exercise. Exercise maintains mobility, fitness and interactions with a variety of people and may result in better sleep patterns. Some ways to manage wandering (Lai and Arthur 2004, pp.79–81) are to:

- promote social interactions through planned programmes
- maintain a safe environment designed to allow wanderers
- use music and other relaxation techniques
- promote group activities and personal contact
- try to understand what the person wants to do
- promote meaningful activities and a sense of completion.

Anxiety and agitation

Older people with dementia face a new world every day. When they look for their parents to give them guidance they cannot find them. They try to find their spouse, siblings or old friends – all of whom they remember from 50 years ago. When they ask for things they are reassured: 'Don't worry about that,' say carers. Of course they worry – for many years they have been trying to earn enough money for their family's needs, or been juggling a household budget to feed everyone. They worry constantly about who will be preparing meals, who will help them shop, cook and clean. What kind of a world is this for them? Certainly, a very frightening world. Aggression and wandering are frequently caused by anxiety. Within an aged care facility many personal articles are lost. Carers may assume that a handkerchief or a singlet has no or little value, but for an older person with dementia, this loss may represent another aspect of a world in which they have little or no control. Few possessions are allowed in an aged care facility – so any loss is precious (Powers 2003).

This anxiety is especially evident when the person is moved from their usual environment. One of my friends' mothers was admitted to hospital for a series of investigations. She was scared and anxious by everything around her. She was even scared by the tympanic membrane (ear drum) thermometer. But when it was explained what it was and we gave her time to take that in, she settled and allowed the nurse to take her temperature. It's so simple in many ways, but often busy staff do not stop to explain, maybe working from an assumption that the person will not understand, after all they have dementia, don't they? We still have so much to learn.

Anxiety and agitation can be reduced by going back to the assessment questions in the first part of this section. Use all the tips to manage aggression and wandering. Look ahead and use the simple communication strategies. Some ways to reduce anxiety and agitation are:

- Approach in an open friendly manner.
- Validate the person's concerns meaningfully; do not dismiss these with 'don't worry'.
- Take time to listen to the person's concerns.
- Help the other person feel at home.

It is always important to remember that 'even if the anxiety or fear is quite unfounded, this does not make the emotions any less real or painful' (Crisp 2003, p.100).

Sleeplessness

Carers can find that trying to manage sleeplessness can cause significant strain on the care-giving relationship. One older person with dementia I knew used to roam through the house at night switching on the lights and overfilling the bath with hot water. This behaviour led to increased stress for his wife. She had her own health problems but found it impossible to sleep at night because of her husband's nocturnal wanderings. In an aged care facility, nocturnal sleeplessness can increase stress on carers. There are reduced numbers of staff at night and the wanderers frequently wake others who are sleeping.

In people with dementia, there could be a number of reasons for sleeplessness. Depression is frequently found in this age group and can contribute to insomnia (Arthur and Lai 2003). Pain, lack of daytime stimulation and napping, incontinence, reduced exercise and evening stimulation can also cause sleeplessness.

As with any other challenging behaviour, good assessment is the first step in managing sleeplessness. Once a comprehensive assessment has been done, then steps can be taken to treat health problems contributing to sleeplessness and plans implemented. Some tips for managing sleeplessness include:

- Treat depression and pain if these are the cause.
- Reduce evening stimulation and provide routine.
- Reduce drinks with caffeine during the late afternoon and evening.
- Maintain a peaceful quiet environment at night.
- Manage incontinence with appropriate pads.
- Increase daily exercise and prevent frequent napping.

As with other challenging behaviours consistency is the key to management.

Creating a caring environment

A caring environment enhances the quality of life for older people with dementia, whether at home with relatives and friends or in an aged care facility. Providing a caring environment includes using good communication skills, treating pain, maintaining personhood and providing meaningful activities to encourage the continued use of abilities.

Communication

Commonly held views about dementia assume that the person with dementia is unaware of and unable to communicate with others. Work by both Kitwood

(1997) and Goldsmith (1996; 2004) challenge this view. Frequently communication with those with dementia is superficial, trivial and patronizing. Little emphasis is given to meaningful questions that allow the older person to pose considered answers about things that interest them. This comes about for a number of reasons, including lack of time on the part of staff, feeling ill-equipped to deal with the responses, and thinking that the person would be unable to communicate adequately to respond. Frequently, it is felt that this is the role of the pastoral carer and that staff may be embarrassed by asking these 'touchy' questions. It is obviously easier to discuss the action of bowels rather than meaning in life.

David Snowden describes an amusing incident when an older man with dementia, who had almost ceased to speak to his wife, was very talkative when asked about his 'feelings' in a study interview: 'Imagine his wife's surprise when she suddenly heard her husband's voice from the other room. One of the things he said to Danner (researcher): "I don't talk anymore because no-one listens anymore"' (Snowden 2001, p.195). Killick and Allan (2001) describe the importance of communication skills when interacting with those with dementia. Issues such as knowledge of the person's life story, listening and not interrupting, taking risks and asking questions we might not feel comfortable about are all important when communicating with this group of older people.

There are a number of strategies to use when communicating with people with dementia (Emick-Herring 2001). Some of these are:

- Minimize fatigue.

- Learn about the person's past experiences and relationships.

- Combine verbal clues such as actions and facial expressions to enhance understanding.

- Keep communication simple and allow time to respond.

Many of these guidelines sound to me like 'good manners' or simple communication techniques. It is interesting to note that when we speak to older people with dementia we need to be reminded of these guidelines. Carers should 'always assume that whatever is being said or done by those in their care does have meaning – whether or not it is immediately understandable' (Crisp 2003, p.102). Often, it takes extra time to grasp this meaning, but if we treated the older person as a 'person' rather than a 'dementia' the meaning would quickly be more obvious.

It has been shown that communication, even with people with severe dementia, can be significant and meaningful (Goldsmith 2004; Killick and Allan 2001; Normann, Norberg and Asplund 2002). Goldsmith (2004) contends that frequently the communication problems when interacting with an older person with dementia are to do with the carer not the older person. From our studies into spiritual reminiscence (Trevitt and MacKinlay 2004), we have seen that communication strategies aimed at allowing the person with dementia time to consider answers in a small supportive group can greatly enhance their ability to talk of meaningful issues. In small groups, discussing issues of spiritual reminiscence, we often observe thoughtful answers and considerable insight into their situation. The ability of the person to respond, however, is frequently linked to the quality of the facilitation of the group. Listening to transcripts, we can hear instances of not allowing the person time to respond, putting words into the person's mouth or answering for them. Some of these communication styles match with Kitwood's (1997) claim of 'malignant social psychology'.

Personhood

When considering issues related to communication, our notions of personhood become very important. When we speak of a person with dementia, families, friends and carers often talk about the person who is 'no longer there'. This poses some significant problems. If the person is no longer 'there' why spend time with that person? Why take trouble to communicate, work with and assist that person? If the person is 'no longer there' where is the value in caring for that person? If you are a carer (paid or unpaid) where is the respect from others and for yourself? In our community, older people are frequently regarded with less respect than younger ones. If the older person also has dementia, where on society's pecking order does that person come?

Kitwood (1997, p.8) describes personhood as 'a standing or status bestowed upon one human being by others in the context of relationship and social being. It implies recognition, respect and trust.' All interactions with older people with dementia need to be based on this notion of personhood. If we dismiss what the older person with dementia is telling us as having no value then we refuse to acknowledge them as a person. The poems written by John Killick (1997) illustrate what we can hear from people with dementia if we take the time to listen to what is being said and relate back to Crisp's (2003) notion that we should always assume there is meaning in what is being said.

How often have you heard it said of someone who has dementia 'she didn't know me'? Usually that means that the person with dementia cannot put a name on the person. Calling a person by name actually has to do with honouring the person. So highly do we regard this that we treat people differently if they cannot name a person. Yet Christine Bryden (1998) has said that she still knows who people are, even when she can't access the name. She describes it as being like a computer file that is inaccessible. She may not remember the name, but she still has a sense of who that person is.

Many residential facilities encourage relatives to prepare a memory (achievement) book of the person with dementia to help carers get a picture of the person. This book can also assist carers to 'reframe' behaviour and help to reinforce the notions of personhood. The book can be a communication trigger to enhance meaningful conversation with the older person.

Managing pain

Older people experience pain more frequently than younger people because of the increased incidence of progressive chronic conditions. Although there is an increased incidence of pain in older people, this is not a usual ageing change. Older people tend to under-report their pain. Many have an underlying belief that increasing pain is a usual occurrence in ageing, that pain medications are addictive or that taking pain medications will reduce their effectiveness when they really have pain (Snow, Rapp and Kunik 2005). Frequently they will refer to chronic pain as discomfort and save the 'p' word for acute pain (Davies *et al.* 2004).

If there is under-reporting and under-treatment of pain in cognitively intact older people, it is not difficult to imagine the difficulties associated with pain treatment in people with dementia. Assessment of pain relies heavily on the person being able to describe the quality and quantity of pain experienced. The person with dementia is unable to accomplish this.

Snow *et al.* (2005, p.24) propose the following mnemonic to assist carers describe the impact of pain in people with dementia:

B – What **B**ehaviours did you see?

O – How **O**ften did the behaviours occur?

D – What was the **D**uration of the behaviours?

I – How **I**ntense were the behaviours?

E – How **E**ffective was the treatment, if given?

S – What made the behaviours **S**tart/**S**top?

Many of the challenging behaviours discussed in the previous section are caused by or exacerbated by pain. Appropriate treatment can reduce or eliminate the behaviour.

Pain assessment for people with dementia requires a multidimensional approach. Pain can be expressed by the older person as sensory, behavioural, emotional or cognitive distress. The external signs of pain could be verbal, non-verbal or physiological. Carers then need to observe these signs and then interpret these as the result of pain in order to ensure that pain treatment will occur (Snow *et al.* 2005). Adequate treatment of pain is one more way of providing a caring environment.

Meaningful activities

Dementia care is about fostering 'creative partnerships' with carers, relatives and volunteers to provide wholistic flexible care that meets the needs of a large number of individuals – not a one-size-fits-all approach (Bowen and Hudson 2003). Some activities for creative care are:

- sharing recitation of a poem by carer and resident
- providing a resident with art or writing materials
- dancing with a resident who prefers this to structured exercise
- provision of aromas of the resident's choice
- singing along in the shower
- reminiscing during all care routines
- creating opportunities for visiting pets
- inviting a restless resident to sit in a quiet place with a calm ambience.

(Bowen and Hudson 2003, p.252).

The suggestions can be incorporated into an everyday environment by encouraging an active approach between carers and those with dementia. A creative work environment has been described by Ekvall *et al.* (1983) (in Norberg *et al.* 2002) as one in which members (staff and residents) feel able to:

- challenge and change goals
- have new ideas supported
- trust and have confidence in the organization
- be dynamic and lively
- demonstrate playfulness and humour
- debate issues and settle disagreements
- recognize and solve conflicts

- take risks and tolerate uncertainty
- have time to work out new ideas.

In one study, residents spent almost twice the amount of time with staff in a 'creative environment' than in the less creative environment. In the less creative environment, residents showed more behavioural disturbances. Whether this led to a decrease in 'creative' care because of staff workload or whether the less creative environment caused the behaviour is not clearly understood and deserves further investigation (Norberg *et al.* 2002).

Fostering creative partnerships in care can help staff to relate to the person with dementia more effectively. Creative care comes about when there is an attitude in the organization that this type of care is important and should be nurtured. It is interesting to note that in the Norberg *et al.* (2002) study, there was no difference in the psychosocial-spiritual care given to residents between the creative and non-creative environments. Emphasizing this type of care needs to be a clearly stated priority in the organization. It does not occur accidentally.

Spiritual reminiscence

There have been a number of different types of reminiscence identified. Gibson (1998) discusses the use of reminiscence with people who have dementia, particularly focusing on issues of personhood and quality of life. Gibson carefully distinguishes between 'general' and 'specific' reminiscence in working with people who have dementia. Her work was conducted with people who have severe dementia and she found that 'specific' work was more effective for these people, and easier to do on a one-to-one basis. The term general reminiscence covers 'well-prepared work that uses a variety of multi-sensory triggers to stimulate shared conversation on an agreed topic or theme which relates loosely to the known background and interests of the participants'. Specific reminiscence consisted of 'carefully selected, highly focused, con-centrated consistent efforts to stimulate recall and conversation using carefully selected triggers known to closely approximate the detailed life-history of the participant' (Gibson 1998, p.16).

Spiritual reminiscence is a particular way of communicating with older people. Rather than general reminiscence when a life story may be discussed, spiritual reminiscence asks questions about meaning in life, joy, sadness, grief and regrets. Within spiritual reminiscence we speak of hopes and fears for the future, what people want from the last years of their lives, who they can share deep concerns with and whether they feel that their spiritual needs are being met. We ask questions about a person's relationship with God or other deity, whether they pray, meditate or engage in other spiritual practices. Sometimes people cry or become upset as they speak of difficult or sad times. There is a feeling in aged care that people should be happy all the time or be jollied out of feeling sad. By continually demeaning the older person's feelings or not taking these seriously, we encourage lack of communication and a similar situation to that encountered by David Snowden above. Often carers are afraid to ask significant questions for fear of what might happen.

The spiritual reminiscence project has included 113 participants – all with a diagnosis of dementia. Even asking 'difficult' questions has elicited many responses. When we ask about meaning in life, most people talk about their family – their parents, siblings or children. They make excuses for why their children do not visit regularly. They remember the meeting times for the small groups and are ready to form the group prior to the meeting time. Following the groups, some of the participants have been noted to be animatedly chatting as they go to the dining room. Once separated from the reminiscence group they attempt to engage the people on each side of them at dinner, but soon give up as they receive no response. Again, they become listless, quiet and uninterested in what is going on around them. What is it about the spiritual reminiscence group that encourages this interaction? On the conclusion of one group meeting one participant said: 'Thank you for this. We do not get to talk about these things usually.'

Other activities

There are a number of activities that have been introduced into aged care facilities to help to maintain interest among the residents. For those with dementia, these activities can assist behaviour difficulties and increase social interaction. Activities such as music therapy, art and drawing, poetry, reminiscence, craft, exercise and indoor sports have been used in aged care facilities. There has been criticism that these activities have not been demonstrated through research to improve quality of life or impact on difficult behaviours. A literature review by Marshall and Hutchinson (2001) identified methodological and sampling difficulties in a number of published studies on different activities. However, if we return to the idea of creative care, then different activities should be considered as part of usual care. There are many instances described in the literature and I have had personal experience of how connections can be made through these activities. As researchers in aged care we need to concentrate on sound research projects that can demonstrate how these activities can impact on the person's life and well-being. Only by providing sound data can structural changes be made that encourage 'creative care' to become the normal approach to dementia care.

Conclusion

Dementia is a significant issue in aged care for the person involved, their relatives and friends, our society and policy makers. The way we treat symptoms and manage day-to-day care of those with dementia is a reflection on the type of society we inhabit. Recognizing the person and interacting in a compassionate, caring and consistent way can ensure that those with dementia enjoy the quality of life the rest of us expect as normal. Identifying ways to connect, exploring ways to enhance meaning, assisting relatives and friends to communicate and providing a safe, creative environment are ways we can help those with dementia enjoy their last years. Older people with dementia are among the most vulnerable in our society. How we care for these people reflects on our society in general.

Summary

- *Dementia is responsible for progressive cognitive and functional impairment including language, perception, problem solving, abstract thinking and judgment over a period of years, with great cost to individuals, families and the community.*

- *Personality characteristics may be maintained or exaggerated or altered. This may be evident as social withdrawal, anxiety and fearfulness. Irritability, agitation, paranoia and delusions can occur as well as physical and verbal aggression towards family and carers.*

- *In residential aged care facilities only 20 per cent of residents are identified as not having dementia.*

- *Management is costly and complex, with a current focus on maintaining those affected at home for as long as possible. For most, institutional care is required during the later stages.*

- *A caring environment enhances the quality of life for older people with dementia.*

- *Providing a caring environment includes:*
  - ° *managing challenging behaviours in a compassionate and consistent way*
  - ° *using good communication skills*
  - ° *treating pain*
  - ° *maintaining personhood*
  - ° *providing meaningful activities to encourage the continued use of abilities.*

CHAPTER 9

Worship and Use of Ritual among Older People

Working in Multifaith and Multicultural Societies

Ageing in multicultural and multifaith western societies requires a broad perspective of understanding of the practices of the major faiths, as for numbers of older people, their faith journey becomes more important in later life. During recent decades even societies that have been traditionally mono-faith have changed markedly. There are growing numbers of older Muslims, Buddhists and Hindus, as well as older Jews in most western countries, and while Christianity remains the religion with the largest number of adherents in western countries, numbers of older people do not practise any faith. Thus workers in aged care need to be aware of the needs for use of ritual, symbols and religious practices of people from a wide range of backgrounds.

The model of spiritual tasks of ageing (MacKinlay 1998) describes response to meaning as the second task, after the search for ultimate meaning itself. The way that people respond to meaning will depend on where they find ultimate meaning, and thus their response to meaning will be modified by this. For members of a religious faith, response to meaning will be worked out through various rituals and liturgies and the use and understanding of symbols.

Response to ultimate meaning forms one of the spiritual tasks of ageing (MacKinlay 2001a). It is apparent that whatever lies at the core or heart of one's being provides the focus of response to ultimate life meaning. If God is at the centre of one's being, the response to ultimate meaning will be to reach out to connect with that God. The desire to connect with God leads the person to desire to worship. Some people have other centres of meaning, and it is out of these centres that they will respond to life and ultimate meaning. We all make choices, some more consciously than others, as to where we find meaning and how we respond to meaning.

How important is worship to the health of older adults? Research on religion and church attendance

Much of the earlier research conducted in the field of religion and spirituality examined church attendance and its relationship to well-being and health in later life. These studies tapped into the religious practices or religiosity of older people. This was an obvious place to begin, as it is relatively simple to measure the number of times people attend church, or read religious materials and books, or pray. There have been mixed findings from such studies. Based on the findings of Koenig *et al.* (1994; 1997) and Musick, Blazer and Hays (2000), it was reported that in fact 'cumulative exposure to religious social support' (Hays *et al.* 2001, p.247) was more strongly associated with health behaviours and may be a more important predictor of health than later life organizational religion. It may be that the meaning or social component of the worship experience is the most important aspect of worship associated with health and positive well-being. However, it is difficult to isolate variables that account for this phenomenon. At one level, searching for causality of well-being related to religiousness is to ask the wrong question.

If we are to understand more about the relationship between health, ageing, well-being and religion, we need to study it from the perspective of the older person, and the questions we ask need to be of a qualitative nature. Essentially, we should ask: What does the person's practice of faith mean to them? And, what does it mean for older people to attend religious services?

More recent approaches to the study of religion and spirituality (McFadden, Brennan and Patrick 2003) have included a move to conduct studies that provide a greater understanding of the complexity of the phenomena of religion, spirituality and ageing. They have included an increased tolerance of diverse forms of inquiry and there has been a greater openness to the variety of religious and spiritual experiences and practices of older people, and finally more recent studies have considered a wider array of life circumstances that may be affected by religiousness and spirituality in later life.

In addition to these pillars of the faith, purification (both spiritual and physical) is an important part of the faith. Staff may need to be aware of the need for physical purity, as a Muslim cannot handle the Qur'an or be involved in various of the rites unless ritually purified (Denny 1994, p.113).

Spiritual therapies in Islam utilize faith and trust in God, charity and prayer, repentance and seeking God's forgiveness, doing good to others and helping the weak and vulnerable. Muslims believe that death is the start of life thereafter.

Fasting may be difficult for frail elderly people, and great sensitivity is needed to assist the person to meet their religious needs and not to become dehydrated. Routines may need adjustment where there are Muslims in residential care so that they may pray and observe the faith without being compromised. This will require adjustment within an aged care facility for times of prayer, a place to pray, the availability of appropriate food and sensitivity to these requirements.

Hindu ritual and practices

Hindu religion is rich in ritual. There are four paths to attain spiritual liberation: devotion, ethical action, knowledge or mental concentration (Tarakeshwar, Pargament and Mahoney 2003). For individuals, the Hindu manuals of moral conduct and social law prescribe 16 rituals that span an individual's life. The most prominent daily ritual is *puja* (religious ceremonies), which enacts the individual's relationship with the Absolute and connection with the Divine. Daily prayer and a range of ceremonies are involved, including listening to religious music, chanting hymns and reading religious scriptures. Many rituals may be conducted by lay folk, but some rituals, for example, life cycle rituals, may require Brahmans (Hodge 2004). Idol worship forms part of the religious rituals of Hinduism, with many Hindus having idols in their homes. Idols in modern India may include pictures or idols of Jesus and Mary.

Hindu meditation is also important, and has been found to relieve depression and hypertension (Hodge 2004). Fasting forms an important part of the Hindu practices. Religious festivals can be important occasions for reordering of life priorities and social support.

Buddhist ritual and practices

It is important to know something of the background and culture of the particular Buddhist, as the practice of Buddhism may differ between Tibetan Buddhists, Theravadan Buddhists and Zen Buddhists.

Meditation or mindfulness is an important practice for Buddhists. All traditions of Buddhism encourage the observance of the Five Precepts for laity that assists in developing both character and mind towards a state of mindfulness. Following the Noble Eightfold Path is seen as the way that leads to *nibbana*. Spiritual development is nurtured through looking closely and repeatedly at 'all conditions of embodied life until no longer perturbed by them'. It is suggested that to achieve *nibbana* is to come to an end of suffering, and at the same time, to the end of ageing as a problem (Thursby 2000, p.171). The Noble Eightfold Path entails having right understanding, right thoughts, right speech, right actions, right livelihood, right effort, right mindfulness and right concentration. Thus morality, concentration and wisdom could be said to be the basis for the life of any Buddhist.[1]

Cultural differences and ageing

Culture is important in worship and ritual. Kanitsaki describes culture 'as an inherited 'lens' through which individuals perceive and understand the world that they inhabit, and learn how to live within' (2002, p.22). What we have grown up with is both familiar and will be the vehicle of meaning for us. To be deprived of this may be particularly distressing.

Cultural differences and worship

Even within one faith tradition, cultural differences may influence the way worship is done. Thus the one form of worship may not hold meaning for older people from different cultural groups. In addition, numbers of aged care facilities provide care for people from a range of cultural backgrounds. Some older people, particularly those who experience dementia, may revert to their primary language and become very isolated within a large organization where they cannot understand or communicate effectively with other residents or staff. The participants of one of the small groups of people with dementia doing spiritual reminiscence work (MacKinlay *et al.* 2002–2005) all came from the same Eastern European country where they had experienced many hard times during the Second World War. In this small group, they were able to share their common background and to deal with some of these experiences from so long ago, experiences that had little chance of being spoken of in their earlier lives.

It would be desirable to arrange for numbers of older people of a particular cultural and religious group to live together in the same complex, where they may share common rituals and cultural practices may be more readily upheld.

Where this is not possible, staff should do all they can to facilitate the meeting of religious practices.

Rituals as orienting anchors

As well as the specific rituals of religious groups, rituals form an important aspect of life within any community. In aged care, we come back to consider the more intimate scene of the group of older people within a single aged care facility, or within a small group within that facility, and the needs for symbols and rituals that will anchor meaning for these people in the latter years of their lives. Friedman (2003) describes ritual as 'an orienting anchor' (p. 135). She uses Myerhoff's definition of ritual 'as an act or actions intentionally conducted by an individual or group employing one or more symbols in a repetitive formal, precise, and highly stylized fashion' (p.135). Ritual can become an orienting anchor for people who are experiencing confusing and alienating losses, changes and stresses in their lives. Thus ritual is important within an environment of aged care.

Functions of ritual

Ritual:

- serves as an anchor or grounding in times of crisis
- connects with a sense of 'otherness' and the environment; the sense of otherness is particularly enhanced in religious rituals (that have meaning for the people)
- reduces isolation and builds community
- affirms and reaffirms meaning – so rituals may be repeated
- provides security in times of uncertainty
- marks milestones in the life journey.

(Friedman 2003, p.135)

Constructing rituals of transition

Almost any experience, positive or negative, can be marked by ritual. Often later life is marked more by closures than by celebrations. Both closures and celebrations are important in life.

Rituals do not have to be pre-constructed; they can be designed by the pastoral carer or aged care professional working with the individual and with their families. Examples of positive experiences of later life include becoming a great-grandparent, making new friends, taking on a new role, entering a new romantic relationship, recovering from a serious illness. Negative life experiences or closures also need to be marked, for example moving from the family home, giving up one's driving licence, adapting to a disability, entering a nursing home.

Effective rituals capture the meaning of events and help us to celebrate and/or grieve. So it is important to explore the meaning of the particular event with all those involved and construct the ritual so that they will feel included. Memorial services are important for residents and staff of aged care facilities, as these can help celebrate the memory of those who have died and also facilitate the grieving process. Friedman (2003) writes that effective ritual needs to reflect the transition it is marking, and it needs to be credible, asking what is the guiding metaphor that has emotional resonance and will anchor those involved. Further, the ritual should involve doing something that will increase the impact without needing explanation. Finally, Friedman writes that ritual should be relevant to the individual and community through use of symbols, words or actions (p.141).

Religion and attendance at religious services

When I have asked older people in aged care about attending church services, a high proportion of them have said that they enjoy attending church. There are a number of factors involved in why older people attend church services, first, the familiar gathering together of a number of people may simply provide a feeling of comfort and memories from early life for some older people. Second, being at a church service may connect them with traditions and rituals that have been part of their religious and/or cultural background throughout life. Third, music and singing are important for many, and it is well known that people who have dementia and find it hard to speak will often be able to sing a hymn or old song and obviously enjoy doing so. Finally, it may be some other part of the liturgy that is important and holds meaning, for instance, the prayers, the reading of scripture, the sacrament of Communion.

Some have said that they go to every church service that is on, regardless of any denominational background. It is noted that for many of these older people a faith or denomination is not as significant as being with others at a service. So it can also be said that attending a service is an event where residents can feel a sense of being with others, and being part of community, thus reducing the sense of isolation that many aged care residents express. This will feed importantly into the need for intimacy with others.

In the independent living group studied in MacKinlay (1998), 45.8 per cent attended church regularly. In this study of elderly nursing home residents 75 per cent regularly attend services in the nursing home. Some are dependent on being taken to the services, while others will have Holy Communion brought to their rooms. Some attend every church service that is held, regardless of the denomination. Seventy-five per cent say that religion or the spiritual dimension is important to them, however, not all of these people attend church, and not all of those who do attend church say it is important to them. Some of these elderly people said they attended church because they could be with others, so social reasons for attendance may well be important too.

Agnes finds her spiritual supports through going to Mass on Sundays and having visits from the chaplain every day. Agnes also has an interest in craft and reads a lot. She watches news and documentary programmes on TV. She says of her prayer life: 'But if I feel something going wrong or I'm waiting too long, I always pray and He sends someone along [laughs]'.

The 75 per cent of frail elderly participants in this study who attended church services did not seem to have concerns about which denomination service they attended. What part does attendance at religious services play in the well-being of these people? Boff (1985, p.105) speaks of encounter with God as being at the core of religion and he notes the person who seeks ceremonies and rituals primarily, rather than God, may lose the purpose of religion, which is to lead the individual to the divine. This may serve to explain what is occurring with those who have been regular church attenders for many years, but who do not find comfort and hope in their religious practices. Perhaps it has been the rituals and ceremonies that they have used as an end in themselves, and perhaps some of these people have never found God through religious ceremonies. Those whose primary purpose of worship is to bring one's heart and soul into the divine will find that worship is a means to strengthen their faith.

Church services: what the older people said

Dora enjoys the church services in the nursing home. Elaine goes to all the church services at the nursing home, no matter which denomination they are; usually this is every Saturday and Sunday. She adds realistically: 'A person couldn't get to church at all if they didn't have it here.' Spiritual support for Sonya is from the priest; she loves to receive the Mass. She expresses sadness in listening to tapes and reflecting on memories, wishing she was home. Margaret says: 'If I'm taken to Mass I join in and I feel God's really with me.'

Rebecca attends the church services at the nursing home when someone takes her, but says she prefers her own religion (Christian Science) more. Rebecca is somewhat isolated from her own belief system in residential aged care, but she does have tapes and quite a bit of literature from her church.

Katie had always had some contact with church. Like a number of nursing home residents she said: 'Well I was going to Pentecostal, until I came here, until I got sick of course, but I go to all their churches, religions [are] all the same to me, we're all going on the one road but whether we reach the other end of it remains to be seen.' Katie remembered and missed her church community in Sydney:

> It used to be church there four times a day, 100 at each service, and you only had to say if you wanted anything and with a lot of people like that, there was always someone to help you. And I learnt more, and understood religion more when I was with them because it was such a simple attitude I suppose you'd say they took. But I was very happy with it, and I miss them all. There were about eight of us who were very good friends, and there was a couple of us always used to go down to church on Tuesday nights. I used to have my 'own' church, I used to hold in my flat but Sundays [they] always used to send the bus to pick us up and it was a happy time for me.

The importance of that small group Katie spoke of was found in previous studies also (MacKinlay 2001a). Membership of a long-term small group seemed to provide for some of the needs for intimacy of widows and other single older people, where it is necessary to build new friendships in later life.

Violet has Holy Communion every week, and it is brought to her in her room, 'Well the priest comes every week and gives me Communion and I sort of feel a great help from that. Sometimes two of them come and I'm a bit greedy, I'll have it one day and I'll have it another day.' Violet spoke of the importance of the Holy Communion every week, and she described the visits:

> They hold my hands and they said the Lord's Prayer with me and that. While they're here it's a great comfort and I often think when they've gone out well I'm pleased that happened, you know. I didn't want to be silly about it but I really do, I wouldn't say that to anyone else but I really feel pleased when they've done that with me, you know.

She has both the Roman Catholic and Anglican communions, and says: 'Well I mean what's the difference? We've all got to go up to God or down to the devil haven't we? You know, and I don't think anyone's God is anything different to anybody else's.' Of the support the chaplains give her she said: 'No I don't think anybody could give me more help than the ministers that come, you know, and on Saturday, they'll sit and talk to me before I have Communion and that.'

Veronica does go to church sometimes in the nursing home. She had not been associated with religion at all during her marriage. But now, since being widowed and in the nursing home she feels that going to church is helpful to her. It is important to leave open the possibility that people's needs for spirituality may change over the life journey, and that someone who has not been interested in spirituality in earlier life may become interested in later life. It is also possible that some older people will choose not to want to be involved with anything of a spiritual nature, or more likely, a religious nature.

Prayer

Seventy-five per cent of the participants in this study pray, with 55 per cent saying that they pray daily or more often. Five per cent pray more often than they used to and 15 per cent pray when they have a need. On the other hand, 15 per cent do not pray at all, and 10 per cent said they prayed less often than they used to.

Alice described her life-long habits of prayer and said: 'As soon as I get into bed before I go to sleep I always say my prayers and I go on and on in little ones as well as big ones. It's funny how they stay in your memory.'

Alice reflected: 'I've always [prayed]… when I get into bed, but when we were growing up we had to kneel down beside the bed and then Mum was with us.' Alice did not change her prayer patterns over the years and drew comfort from the prayers of her childhood. Dora prays every day, sometimes she falls asleep while praying and feels this ought not to happen. Heidi prays to God nightly. Bonnie, who had constructed a faith of her own, found for the first time, when she was going into a nursing home, that prayer was answered. She had never got on with her mother, and now she prayed to be able to love her mother, and she found herself changing. Charlie says he draws comfort from praying. Katie also finds comfort from prayer, and prays for others. Katie described her prayer life:

> Well, I often pray to Him and particularly at night and I ask for help, and I tell Him I know that I'll get it when I pray through His Son. Prayers will help us through our troubles and that sort of thing. Help not only me, but others in the hospital here, I pray for them, that He's with them and giving them the comfort that they really need. Because there's times that you do need comfort. You know, you don't know how about getting it unless you pray and that doesn't

always come easy. Depending on what you want to pray for of course. No, I think on the whole I'm happy. I do thank God for all He has done for me in the time that I've been with Him. Sometimes it seems hard that you should be left on your own then I think well there's a reason for it, because I think He has a reason for us all. I do really! It mightn't suit us always.

As at other times while Katie spoke with me, she talked of both her need to pray and her sense that God would answer her prayers. At the same time she expressed her sense of loneliness in the nursing home.

Bob spoke of his spiritual life and response to this:

I think it's to be light of the flame or the fear, that makes my life get the most meaning is the ability to love, I don't mean by that anything sort of phoney or…I often thought about it and I think if I say it, a prayer. I've got to be saying look thank you for giving me the ability to love, because if I didn't have that I wouldn't have…you see.

He said: 'My day's full of that, this and bits and I've got to thank my friends and I've got to thank the God that gives me this feeling and that's where and that's where the prayers must go for these things, yes.' Bob found prayer an important part of his life now, and he seemed to centre his prayer on a sense of gratitude and love.

Nurse role in prayer

I would argue that it is just as serious an omission of care to neglect to pray with a person who wants prayer, as it is to neglect physical care, such as assisting with showering and providing adequate skin care for someone at risk of pressure ulcers. The person who needs prayer support and does not receive it, is at risk of neglect of the soul. However, there are obviously some important components of how to provide and support people in prayer.

While it is acknowledged that many older people do pray, the question of the ethics of praying with and for residents is raised by some authors and practitioners. Winslow and Winslow, taking a nursing focus, examined the ethics of praying with patients (2003). They suggest that prayer as an intervention with patients is part of the 'broader spectrum of spiritual care' provided by nurses (p.170).

Ethical considerations in providing prayer support for patients and elderly residents

Winslow and Winslow (2003) raise the important issues of ethical practice related to spiritual care, specifically praying with patients. They note that many patients are vulnerable, and this is so certainly for frail elderly people in residential care. They state that spiritual care is sufficiently well accepted nowadays that the ethical questions do not rest on whether or not patients/ residents should be asked about their spiritual and religious preferences and practices. Now the focus should be on whether and how to include prayer in appropriate ways in clinical settings for those who want prayer. However, nurses who do not feel comfortable praying with residents, are advised to, with the resident's consent, refer the resident to someone who can pray with them.

Questions arise from both a practice perspective and from recent research on beneficence of prayer to patient and resident well-being. Koenig and Lawson (2004) claim that prayer may have a beneficial effect on the immune system. Further, they claim, in a study of religious affiliation and religious attendance and use of acute hospital care at Duke University by older people, that active practice of one's religion shields against stress and depression.

Bible reading

Elaine said: 'I think [pause] it's good to be able to pray and ask for help, the likes of that [pause] as I say it's a bit hard for me reading the Bible and things like that without the education.' She had grown up in a poor family and could not read, so she was dependent on having the Bible read to her. In an affluent society it is easy to assume that everyone can read, often those who can't feel too embarrassed to admit to this. I asked Elaine if she would like to listen to the Bible on tape, but she said no, she would simply continue to attend church services.

Bible study groups are used in some aged care facilities, and these are important to provide further learning and dialogue of the person's faith, and also these groups can provide means for social interaction and support. For older people with cognitive difficulties, who can no longer concentrate and take part in discussions, Bible reading groups may bring comfort.

Meditation

In this study 30 per cent of informants practised meditation, higher than in the independent groups. Fifteen per cent practised Christian meditation and 15 per cent practised other types of meditation. Sixty per cent seemed not to know much about meditation. Those who did meditate found it helped them to relax and feel less anxious. Meditation groups are used effectively in some aged care settings.

Difficulties of worship within an aged care facility

Busyness of the facility and lack of staff to get residents ready for church services was an issue for some residents. This is overcome in some places by the use of volunteers to assist in bringing people to church services.

A lack of appreciation of the importance of liturgy for older people is found in some places. Different cultural background of staff members, age differences of some staff and a lack of knowledge and understanding of the need for connecting with ritual and liturgy make it more difficult to appreciate the needs of residents. Traditions that are observed within rituals come both from culture and religions. Traditions form an important part of connecting people within a particular culture and society. In the nursing home, an individual's traditions may not be observed, simply because they are unfamiliar to the staff. Changes from a familiar tradition that has helped to anchor an individual may produce feelings of insecurity.

Concentration span may be shortened for a high proportion of residents through cognitive disabilities and rituals should be only long enough to be appropriate for their needs.

Physical disabilities, eg. post-stroke, mobility problems, inability to sit in one place for too long, may mean that some residents will feel anxious about attending a service, in case it is too long for them. Frailty may mean the person may be too tired to attend a service, once they have been showered and dressed and perhaps attended some other activity.

Hearing and sight deficits make it hard to take in the stimuli from the sight, sound, touch and smell of a religious service.

Conclusion: enhancing meaning through the use of symbol and ritual in aged care

Using symbols that carry meaning for the residents will help to connect these people with a sense of identity and meaning. Understanding the culture of the residents is a critical starting point. Too often in multicultural societies people are lacking in awareness of the culture and associated rituals and use of symbols by particular cultural groups. Facilitating the use of ritual involves knowing the people and their history, their cultural heritage and preferences. It involves being sensitive to sensory loss.

In the case of church services, ask the older people what they are comfortable with; discuss with them what kinds of services they want, how long they can sit for, and ways that we can make worship a meaningful experience for them.

Good ritual will provide stimuli for the senses of sight, smell, hearing, touch and speech. Ritual will be rich, using prompts such as flowers, familiar music (but don't make assumptions about what music older people will like), candles, poetry, reading of scripture, stimulation through touch of different textures, the touch of human hands and movement. Memorabilia that has been chosen by the residents will speak much more powerfully to the residents.

Summary

- *Ritual and symbol are important conveyors of meaning and can help connect older people with life in residential aged care.*

- *Staff need to be aware of their own spirituality and aware of the particular needs of those they care for.*

- *Awareness of cultural differences and needs is needed, so that appropriate care may be given.*

- *Multifaith communities require understanding of the particular faith needs and a willingness to provide for these in sensitive ways.*

Note

1   Notes from Ruwan Palapathwala.

CHAPTER 10

Vulnerability
and Transcendence

Some years ago I was struck by the comments of some undergraduate nursing students who said that one of the good things about ageing would be to get Alzheimer's disease because you wouldn't know you were getting older. None of those students had any personal experience of being with older people, except for sick and elderly patients they had cared for in acute health care settings; perhaps that explains the apparent desire not to know that one was getting older. It does raise questions of ageing and consequent losses that come with growing older: the physical decrements, disabilities and pain, perhaps even suffering, psychosocial problems, social isolation, depression and dementia. How does an older person deal with such challenges? This chapter examines increasing frailty and vulnerability and the relationship with transcendence in the fourth age of life.

Responses vary tremendously, with some older people seeming to deny their ageing while others embrace theirs. Is ageing to be endured, or is it a time, as some seem to think, of new freedoms and coming to a deeper peace and joy. Levin (2003, p.408) writes of the possibilities of wider life experience in ageing 'to an awakening from the trance of everyday life into consciousness of the higher spiritual reality in which all human life is embedded'. He notes that chronic or functionally limiting conditions and awareness of one's approaching death may be powerful triggers to becoming fully conscious. This is a way into transcendence, to which a necessary beginning is the concept of self-forgetting described by Frankl (1984).

Jones (2001, p.102) grapples with the issue of how we age, as he notes that three marks of 'success' of western societies are exactly what the ageing process threatens to remove from us: power, status and security. As older people lose these marks of 'success' they are increasingly avoided according to Jones, as a form of 'symbolization-avoidance', that is, they are a discomforting reminder of our own approaching death, best to be avoided. These attitudes fly in the face of Christian beliefs of 'success': to side with the poor, the weak and the vulnerable of society, to love and be loved simply because one exists, not because of what one does. Even 'successful' and 'positive' ageing have a focus on keeping active at all costs and maintaining a mid-life focus. Often people are only seen to be valued as long as they can still make a contribution towards society. Therefore, those who have physical and/or mental disabilities cannot be seen as engaging in successful ageing, and those who require residential aged care are regarded by some standards at least, as having failed in their ageing.

In many ways the churches mirror secular society attitudes towards ageing and older people. There is value in 'being' as well as in 'doing'. Jones writes of the 'desert' experience of being cast into a place where one can no longer 'do', suggesting that as in the ageing process we are forced to pull back from engagement with society, it is then that 'spiritual conversion' can take place. The challenge is to revalue life, so that *being* is valued as much as *doing*. One does not have to justify one's being, and this kind of living is called 'grace'. As Jones says, real meaning 'resides neither in doing nor in having, but in the integrity of life drunk deeply, intrinsically, thankfully' (2001, p.106). It is to this kind of living, without being anxious about anything (Philippians 4:6) that we are called to be. The transition may be hard. After a lifetime of performing to produce evidence of outcomes and production, suddenly this may no longer be important, and there opens up the possibility of newness of being. This is a hard journey of transition for many older people in our society, a journey that might not be really begun until they become residents in aged care facilities. However, for those older people who do travel this journey into frailty, and do move from 'doing' to 'being', or are on a journey of 'becoming', there are gifts of peace and joy that are hard to explain. Will we allow ourselves, including the older people of our society, the joy of growing older and being affirmed for what we are, loved by God?

The beginnings of self-transcendence

Frankl wrote of the need to move beyond oneself, of being able to self-forget, in the process of self-transcendence. According to Frankl, humans are not concerned with any inner condition:

> be it pleasure or homeostasis, man is oriented towards the world out there, and within this world, he is interested in meanings to fulfil, and in other human beings... [Through] the pre-reflective ontological self-understanding, he knows

that he is actualizing himself precisely to the extent to which he is forgetting himself, and he is forgetting himself by giving himself, be it through serving a cause higher than himself, or loving a person other than himself. Truly, self-transcendence is the essence of human existence. (Frankl 1997, p.138)

It is suggested here that self-transcendence is foremost, about self-forgetting, and that involves reaching out to others and placing others before oneself. At the very least it means other-focused. And yet, at the same time, self-transcendence is also located in the ability of the person to move beyond the physical decrements and disabilities that so often accompany ageing (Peck 1968). It is also acknowledging that it is alright to simply 'be'.

In many ways self-transcendence is not encouraged in western societies. Perhaps we have lost the skills and the desire to affirm people for their intrinsic worth, rather than for their doing. And, as Jones (2001) has pointed out, the fear of impending death results in a denial of anything that might remind us of the inevitability of dying in this life on earth. There is also a sense in which transcendence is grace, and not something that can be forced. In the model of spiritual tasks of ageing (MacKinlay 2001a), dying to self is the beginning of self-transcendence. The focus of life changes from a focus on me and my body to a focus on otherness and others. This is not, however, a splitting off of body from spirit; it is not a denial of the physical. Rather it is a process in which otherness takes on greater importance than self; it is to see, perhaps for the first time, that there is more, and thus it is an enlarging of perception and the beginning of a new world view. It is a letting go of material and physical aspects of life; a letting go that holds lightly to the material, yet still embraces life in all its uncertainties and ambiguities and all its blessings.

The transcendent, and the mystery of otherness, remains as an extra component beyond the self; the ultimate that lies beyond human understanding. According to Bellah (1969, p.85), in traditional theological terms: 'Transcendence is an attribute of God that indicates he is outside and independent of the world.' This interpretation of transcendence may be an appreciation of a reality that is independent of ourselves, our societies and our cultures. Bellah notes that the main 'inner' dimension of transcendent reality has always been an inner experience of fulfilment, rather than of need. The feelings that accompany it are of wholeness, rightness and well-being. The experience is often acknowledged to be a conventional religious phenomenon, but it seems that many people experience such things in a secular sense as well. Perhaps, in a secular sense, this is what Maslow (1970) meant by self-actualization, and it would seem self-actualization is only possible as a part of self-transcendence. Frankl (1984) described this process of self-transcendence, remarking it is not 'an attainable aim at all, …the more one would strive for it, the more he would miss it' (p.133).

Frankl (1984) explains transcendence in the mode of the human need to search for meaning, to take responsibility to reach outwards from oneself, to connect with others and with one's environment. He says that human beings are incomplete in themselves, and in need of relationship with others. Self-transcendence requires that an individual 'forgets' themself and directs their interest towards another. He says the more one is able to self-forget, the more human one becomes. From a Christian perspective, this ultimate other is God; the term transcendence is used in this context to refer to God being more than, and outside, the created world (Stott 1992). Self-transcendence may be regarded as part of the development tasks of ageing. Various authors including Bellah (1969) and Fowler (1981) have referred to what Maslow has termed 'peak experiences' as examples of such transcendent experiences.

Self-transcendence as a spiritual concept compared with gerotranscendence

While the discussion to this point has focused on self-transcendence as a spiritual construct, it is important to acknowledge the concept of gero-transcendence, as developed by Tornstam (1999/2000). Tornstam began by requestioning disengagement theory (Cumming and Henry 1961), suggesting that there might, after all, be some truth in that theory. He suggests that engagement in activity might not be the only way to age 'successfully'. Tornstam's research over the last decade has been used to develop the theory of gerotranscendence as a new way of looking at ageing. He espouses a new and different reality in ageing, compared with the commonly held mid-life view of continued activity and human 'doing'. Gerotranscendence, he says, includes 'a new feeling of cosmic communion with the spirit of the universe, a redefinition of time, space, life, and death, and a redefinition of the self' (p.10). He compares gerotranscendence with Erikson *et al.*'s (1986) stages of psychosocial develop-ment, noting that from Erikson *et al.*'s perspective the person comes to an understanding of who they are and a sense of integrity through looking back at their life lived, whereas his theory of gerotranscendence 'implies more of looking forward and outward, with a view of the self and the world' (p.10). It is argued that both are needed, the first approach is to grapple with the life one has lived and its meaning, and the second to look forward and outward. To this end, the spiritual tasks of ageing (MacKinlay 2001a) use Erikson *et al.*'s stages of psychosocial development as a starting point to move towards spiritual integrity, which is defined as:

> A state where an individual shows by their life example and attitudes, a sense of peace with themselves and others, and development of wholeness of being. The search for meaning and a degree of transcendence is evident. (MacKinlay 2001a, p.180)

This definition of spiritual integrity shows a wholistic move towards wisdom and final meanings. It includes both the concept of gerotranscendence and integrity. The concept of gerotranscendence, it is suggested, is a description of spiritual development that occurs in ageing. It is argued in the concept of spiritual integrity that transcendence is part of the change that is occurring in many older people, but that this change is also associated with the search for meaning and purpose. There are also parallels between gerotranscendence and Fowler's (1981) description of faith stages, which recognizes, quite clearly, the universalizing stage that some older people move towards and into. The whole of this spiritual development is a dynamic process that may continue until death, and as Tornstam (1999/2000) notes, it may be blocked or accelerated by various factors, such as life crises.

Factors in the development of self-transcendence

Within a society that sets such store in retaining independence, anxiety about future dependence may be expressed by many. This was so in the study of independent older people, where autonomy and self-control were set as high values (MacKinlay 1998). The theme, based on the data, was self-sufficiency versus vulnerability, presenting a continuum on the life journey. Perceived future vulnerability was a fear for 100 per cent of those interviewed who were older and living independently (MacKinlay 2001a). The people interviewed in this more recent study were all residents of nursing homes, living with more than one chronic illness and already frail and vulnerable, in fact these participants were all sufficiently vulnerable to have been assessed as in need of residential aged care. Of this group 45 per cent expressed some fears, a much lower proportion than those living independently. In fact, 55 per cent said they had no fears. Yet the people in this study are much more frail and require assistance in several of the activities of daily living. They were much further along the continuum from self-sufficiency to vulnerability.

They are in fact, experiencing the very things that those living in the community held as future fears. In spite of this, they have lower reports of fear, in other words, the reality is not as hard as was expected and they did not feel so fearful. Another question asked was, 'Is life still worth living?' to which 90 per cent emphatically said 'Yes!' Even those experiencing many disabilities expressed a sense that life is worth living. It is noted that physical health alone does not account for the expressed perception of these frail older people that life is worth living. In fact, some of these frail elderly people were working, either consciously or unconsciously, on the spiritual task of ageing, transcendence of loss and disabilities, that is drawn from the theme: self-sufficiency versus vulnerability. A number of reasons for these findings will be explored in this chapter.

As with the independent living group, I asked all the informants how healthy they regarded themselves to be, their responses were: fairly healthy 45 per cent; 15 per cent in good health, and 20 per cent claimed to be in very good to excellent health. Twenty per cent stated they were in poor health. As with the other sample, these people did not seem to be rating their health status in line with their medical diagnoses, but at a higher level than would be accounted for by medical examination and diagnosis. It is suggested that this is indicative of transcendence of physical disabilities and difficulties of ageing. It is probably also true that transcendence of psychological difficulties is encountered in ageing.

When I can no longer actively engage with life – What is quality of life?

So, how do we access this thing called 'quality of life'? What does it look like? About four years ago I was in Melbourne, where my mother had been admitted to hospital. She has dementia (vascular dementia), resulting from a series of small strokes and multiple other health problems. On one visit she was sitting going through the motions of doing needlework, something she had done almost constantly for years, while she was still able. I watched amazed as I saw her pick up a part of the blanket, thread an imaginary needle, and begin sewing. I noticed the look of concentration on her face, the skilled movements of her hands, hands that had not held sewing for a few years now. As she did this she was smiling. I was deeply touched by this, and later shared it with an elderly friend of mine. Her quick response was, 'I don't want to live to be like that.' I have a sense that my mother, at that time, was connecting with something that has been a special part of her life. Her facial expression was one of both concentration and I think, happiness, so was that experience not a good one? How can we tell from the outside? How can we gauge what the quality of life is for someone else? Whose standards are we using?

Decreasing energy levels

Seventy-five per cent of informants in this study of frail elderly people stated they had experienced lowered energy levels in recent months or years. It is well known that in frail ageing, energy levels do decrease. It seems that this decrease in energy is associated with the move from *doing* to *being* that is a part of the psychosocial and spiritual ageing process. For some people at least, the increasing lack of energy forced the move from *doing* to *being*, because they no longer had enough energy to continue to do the activities they had been used to engaging in. Some older adults find this very difficult and experience a real sense of loss of the person they had been, and a loss of their identity. This may be threatening for some older people, particularly if their identity has been drawn from their abilities to remain active and retain earlier life roles. Clements (1990) wrote that, as these roles are stripped away, they may be found naked at the core. Others, however, seem to accept energy loss and become more reflective and may go on to develop that deeper sense of joy, in spite of their lack of ability to continue to 'do' things.

Transcendence among the residents of the study

Joyce was certainly a person who had to learn to live within increasing and obvious boundaries of inability to 'do'. Joyce spoke about her future; she has had muscular dystrophy for 39 years and has been confined to a wheelchair for the past eight years. Joyce said:

> My main worry is getting to a point where I can't feed myself and I don't mind being helped with showering and dressing and that sort of thing but I mean that's my main worry. I've got so used to being in a wheelchair now that I don't even give it a second thought.

She said that the condition has progressed slowly over the years: 'So I've had lots of years to live with it.' She compared her condition with that of someone who had a stroke: 'My lifestyle is very fortunate though because I've seen those who have had a stroke, like today they're really well and tomorrow they can't feel a whole side or their voice is gone or something.' She felt this would be much more difficult to cope with. Joyce says she has many things to be thankful for:

> I cherish all memories, you know, because I had so many good years and I think it's what really keeps you going, is looking back on all the happy things that happened to you. When each of my children was born that was wonderful and then when each of my grandchildren came along. And now they do so much for me that I've got so much to be thankful for.

In spite of all the difficulties of physical disability, Joyce has a very positive outlook on life. So how does she cope?

Well it's the only way I can really smile and make every day a winner! You see, so I read and I crochet and I write letters and I like watching a few shows on the TV. I'm not into the soapies and things like that I mean they're so boring and in the afternoon I love watching the quiz shows because I like to use my brain and see if I can answer them.

Joyce is showing many signs of transcendence as she travels this slow and difficult journey into increasing disablement. She has arrived at a stage where she has let go of the need to control her environment, and admits and accepts her need for assistance with most of the activities of daily living. One of the practical difficulties for Joyce in the nursing home is toileting. Because she can't stand she has to wait for a second nurse to come and help, sometimes she says that she has to wait a long time. Even though she understands that sometimes the staff can't come straight away, it is still hard for her, and there is the fear that she might not be able to wait.

I asked Violet if she worries about anything and she replied: 'Actually I've given up worrying about anything, because I can't do anything about it.' Violet has come to an acceptance of her life. With all the problems Violet experiences in her life, she seemed to have transcended these to move beyond, in the manner written about by Frankl, and as described by Tillich (1963) as sanctification. This could also be described as spiritual hardiness (Carson and Green 1992), or spiritual resilience (Ramsey and Bleisner 2000). While Violet needed analgesia for pain each day before her leg ulcers on both legs were dressed, she was able to reach out to those who attended the dressings and provided other care for her, so that in the process of caring for her, they would feel cared for by her. Thus Violet has come to a point of self-forgetting.

Vulnerability in ageing and the move towards transcendence

The spiritual tasks of ageing support this change from *doing* to *being*, which is a part of transcendence of loss and difficulties in ageing. It is only since the late twentieth century and early twenty-first century that we can see sufficient numbers of people living longer, and examine the processes of psychosocial and spiritual ageing to identify patterns of development in these dimensions. The changes described by these informants are consistent with and support the model of spiritual tasks of ageing (MacKinlay 2001a).

Frailty in ageing

The term 'frailty' is poorly defined in the ageing literature (Stone, Wyman and Salisbury 1999) although the term is used frequently. Most definitions of frailty agree that frail older adults are vulnerable and 'have the highest risk of adverse health outcomes' (Stone *et al.* 1999, p.315). Frailty is associated with underlying physiological changes of ageing that are evidenced by weakness, lowered energy levels, poor appetite, dehydration and weight loss. This frailty often leads to falls, injuries, increasing disability and associated dependency, being admitted to an aged care facility or hospital, and death. According to Strawbridge *et al.* (1998) a frail person is someone who has evidence of deficiencies in more than one area or domain of functioning, thus rendering the person vulnerable but not necessarily disabled. They define frailty as 'a syndrome involving deficiencies in two or more domains involving physical, nutritive, cognitive, and sensory capabilities' (p.S10).

Kirby, Coleman and Daley (2004) examined the relationship between psychological well-being (PWB), its relation to frail and non-frail older people and spirituality. This British study found that after controlling for covariates, frailty had a significant negative effect on total PWB, meaning that as frailty increased, so psychological well-being decreased. However, they also found that spirituality was a weak but significant predictor of total PWB. Further, and importantly, spirituality was found to moderate the negative effect of frailty on PWB. Thus spirituality can be seen as a resource for elderly frail people and this study of PWB shows that spiritual beliefs predict the subscales of personal growth and positive relations with others (Kirby *et al.* 2004, p.127).

It is considered that increasing frailty is also associated with an increased perception of approaching death and a move towards transcendence and the search for final meanings. Increasing frailty may act, in at least some older people, as an impetus to further spiritual development and transcendence. It would seem that reduced energy levels that are experienced by many older people may be associated with the personal awareness of one's own mortality. Also, importantly, a part of this phenomenon is the move from *doing* to *being.* In a society that is so firmly tied to affirmation of people through their ability to contribute to society, this stage of being that occurs in the frailty of ageing is confronting to family and carers; it may also be confronting for some of those frail older people. If those who care for frail elderly people fail to understand the changes that are taking place in them, it is hard to provide appropriate care. Attitudes of ageism do unfortunately occur in some aged care facilities and residents may be valued as 'good residents' if they do not cause extra work for staff, for example, those who can wait to be taken to the toilet, and those who do not call out. Others who do 'make extra work' for staff are all too often labelled, at least in the minds of some carers, as being 'difficult'.

Frailty and failure to thrive

Failure to thrive is now widely accepted as a reality that may occur in later life, particularly among those who are frail. This concept was first identified among babies in orphanages who were deprived of contact and love and failed to thrive; adequate food was not sufficient to keep the babies developing normally.

Hildebrand, Joos and Lee (1997) concluded from their study of pre-dominantly male older veterans that failure to thrive may constitute a discrete syndrome; however, there is a large degree of subjective variation in the way the term is applied. Many physicians apply the term to elderly people with unexplained weight loss and/or functional decline. In Hildebrand *et al.*'s study of 132 patients 34 per cent were admitted to nursing homes. Fifty-seven per cent of the participants died within a year of the study. Thus the syndrome could be described as a group of symptoms that begin to appear as the person is moving toward dying and death. However, there are times when the individual has simply lost hope, and finding hope could turn the syndrome around.

It is contended that failure to thrive in frail older adults may be related to a lack of nourishment for the soul. Applying the model of spiritual tasks of ageing (MacKinlay 2001a), it can be seen there is a connection between lack of intimacy, loss of meaning in life and failure to thrive. Human beings need love in order to thrive.

Experiences of frailty among the participants of this study

In this study of frail older people, resident in aged care facilities, all participants lived with multiple and chronic diseases and disabilities. One of the participants, Elaine, said that it was a real relief to be in the nursing home: 'They're a wonderful mob here. I always thought it'd be terrible to have to go to a home, but anyone out there that's gotta go to a home it's not as bad as we think it is before we get in.' This was echoed by many of those interviewed in the nursing homes. It is interesting that all those who were living independently (MacKinlay 2001a) were fearful of future perceived vulnerability, whereas these frail elderly people who were already in nursing homes did not have this same fear. Margaret has a chronic illness and disability and the only thing she can do for herself is read. She said: 'I get used to it. God helped me, true.' She has no fears now.

Alice has Parkinson's disease. She too says she has no worries living in a nursing home. She enjoys activities in the home. 'There's a lot of friendly people and especially if I go down to the dining room, downstairs, the big one, they often have things on. And really I think, no worries! See I've got nothing to worry about.' Alice reflected about her experience of Parkinson's disease, a disease not unknown to her. Alice said: 'My father died in 1966 and he had Parkinson's in the hands, and his hands used to shake.' I asked her: 'How do you feel about having Parkinson's?' Alice said: 'Well it wouldn't be so bad, only I've got it in the feet and legs and when I stand up I'm a bit wobbly and feels as if I'm gonna fall backwards, so I go somewhere when someone comes with me.' This has made Alice more dependent on others, even for getting about in the aged care residence. Even so, she seems to accept her circumstances very well and has adapted to the restrictions on her life.

Bert also has Parkinson's disease and has increasing physical frailty, and he spoke about his need to be in residential care and his wife's struggles to care for him before he was admitted to residential care:

> Well it was the only practical move because my wife wouldn't have been able to handle it. Like she couldn't pick me up off the floor or something. I haven't had any falls since I've been here, oh only minor ones but there's always someone around to pick you up.

I asked him: 'And how do you feel on the inside with your disabilities, you were saying you don't like your friends to come into the institution, but how do you *feel* about your disabilities at the moment?' Bert responded:

> Well I don't think much about them I, if I can get up and get myself dressed. I haven't been able to dress myself as well as I used to or as easily as I used to. I was much better when I first came in here, matter of fact I didn't know I deteriorated (as) much as apparently I did.

Bert responded to my use of the word 'feel' with 'think', but then he acknowledged his physical deterioration. He seemed to be reflecting on what was happening to him physically.

Bert found the good things about being in a nursing home included: 'I don't have to worry about, well just my everyday needs, I mean they're cared for.' However, he did have other concerns, about how his wife could manage financially: 'Well we're worse since financially, our standard, our at least, our ability to obtain money as you pay. Any extra accounts or that or anything extra it's worse because of the demand of the health scheme the way it works.' It is unclear whether some of his concerns may have been because of recent changes to health care funding in aged care, and how these are understood by residents.

Bert has troubles with sleeping at times, he has been experiencing 'dreaming or hallucinating' a couple of times 'almost every night'. He said:

Well I didn't know that it happened so often till they tell me next day. Of course, they push so many drugs into you, they claim they're not but there's one, some for pain and some for this, but I haven't had a natural sleep for months.

This has only been a problem since he has been in a nursing home. As my role there was that of researcher and Bert did not want me to speak to the nursing staff about his concerns with sleeping and medications, I did not follow up on that. His problems with sleep could have been associated with ageing, the medications he was taking, Parkinson's disease, or a combination of these.

Certainly these are important issues for aged care residents. They are issues that should be addressed in the individual care plans. Residents should feel free to discuss their health problems with staff. It seems at times residents feel that staff do not have time to listen to them: the staff are seen to be too busy. Dealing effectively with Bert's sleeping troubles would possibly make marked differences to his overall sense of well-being. Obviously the staff did know about Bert's problems sleeping as he was being given sedation. Other strategies besides sedation could be used, in discussion with the resident. Such strategies could include appropriate physical activities and exercise, relaxation and meditation sessions, and assessment to see if there are any other matters of concern for the resident.

Bert was too tired to complete the interview in one session, so I returned at another time. The first time I met Bert he had seemed to have little to say. It was hard to get him to talk about anything of a deep nature. On my subsequent meetings with him, four in all, he became more able to communicate effectively, and at a deep level. It would seem that he did not talk very much with anyone in the nursing home. One reason may be that it took him some time to start talking, so that by the time he got going, the staff member would have moved to another task.

I asked Bert how hard it was for him to cope with the increasing health problems he has now and this started a long account of what it was like to have Parkinson's disease. This was an instance of being and meeting in sacred space with this man:

I've got a problem with the bones and it hasn't held me up till now really. Early in the piece after it was diagnosed, I will have to say it sort of took me quite while, probably 12 months or so, but oh yes, it's still going and performing alright…I suppose it was the one thing that I found, it affected me when I dam well couldn't, I couldn't put up a strainer post and a stay. My arms weren't strong enough. Then I realized that I had a problem! But I didn't know [then] what it was, but I knew it was a problem. I called in to see a mate of mine one day, I was up there and by chance his wife had a brother who had, who had found he'd been ill and there was something wrong with him and it was Parkinson's. After I had spent about half an hour with him well, I said, well I have it, and it scared hell out of me. But I tried to talk myself that it wasn't that, because well I didn't know for sure. But I ended up at the farm about three years I was there with [wife] and then suddenly hit me then that I couldn't perform the functions that I'd have to do, if I wanted to load the wood for the Raeburn heater or something, once I go out with the chainsaw and get the ute, go over the hill and then bring it home and that was that. But I couldn't do these small jobs and I always remember when I came over.

I think it's probably in this part, I decided that night. I said to my wife, I'm going over to the hospital in the morning and find out what's all this about. And then it took him about half a minute flat with this little GP fellow. From then on they put me into hospital, it seemed to be the procedure those days. Put me into hospital for about a fortnight and gradually put me on these drugs and I didn't come out of it too badly in the finish but I lasted about three years without any trouble and then I, I knew I was too tired, just couldn't, I couldn't keep going. So that's how it affected my life, it sort of snuck up on me and I sort of held it at bay for as long as I could, but it didn't affect me directly, not really from what I can remember, it made it a bit, I didn't know what. I didn't read a lot about it, I suppose mainly, well, because I didn't really want to know.

I have summarized his story here. I was left with a sense of wonder that this man, who seemed to have so little ability to communicate with anyone, could be so articulate. I had seen him about the nursing home on a number of occasions, apart from my interviews. He would be so hard to hear when he did speak as he spoke so softly, and would only answer questions about, for instance, what he wanted to drink. Here he told a story, deeply meaningful, of his journey into Parkinson's disease, expressing openly his fears and how he had handled coping with the diagnosis and his responsibilities as a farmer and husband. This was indeed a special time of sharing. Bert subsequently offered to lend me his written story of the family's early pioneering days as farmers. It was a very special story that brought me into a still greater regard for this normally quiet and gentle man.

Bert had engaged in his own narrative and knew who he was, and he knew his roots; he grappled with challenges in his life, weighing up priorities and considering others. Bert was moving into transcendence in his life journey, it can be assumed that his health problems have a part in this journey. He was no longer able to keep his role as farmer, a role that had been a central part of his life and identity for most of his life, yet he was finding meaning, even in the tough times. The story that he had written was an important part of his search for meaning and identity.

He was a person of courage and he faced his future with great dignity and with hope. How can Bert find peace and joy in his present state? Nothing can take away or replace his loss of health, or the fact that he can no longer live at home and is separated from his wife (apart from home visits on occasion). But pastoral care can help him to transcend the difficulties and to find meaning in these last days. Pastoral care can help him to know he is loved by God.

Bert shared deeply with me and months later I was surprised and delighted to receive an assignment from one of my nursing students, and although she had not used his real name and did not know that I had interviewed him, it was easy to see that Bert had shared deeply with another person. He was a very special person. So are many who live in aged care residences. Too often, because of staffing and funding restrictions, staff do not connect deeply with residents. Even chaplains may have far too little time to spend with residents. These frail elderly people may draw further into themselves and communicate little with others, becoming quite isolated within an aged care facility. Activities are often difficult for these people, and they tend to not participate, particularly in large groups.

The importance of listening

In a busy aged care facility it seems there is so much to do, and so little time to listen to residents. Yet listening is as essential as any other care for these people. Listening is important therapy; it is an opportunity to affirm the residents as people of worth. Listening to a person's story is a great privilege and both the listener and the one listened to are affirmed in the telling (see Chapter 6).

Another resident with decreased energy levels was Bonnie; she still struggled with her increasing disabilities. She described her breathing problems and the effect these problems had on her quality of life, raising for her a sense of vulnerability and helplessness as she needed to depend on others for so much of her care:

> Well, of course, it means that wherever I go, somebody has to bring this thing [oxygen cylinder] with me, I've got to have two people to go in the wheelchair, I can walk in and out of the toilet but that's as far and to the door if need be. So that is restricting and that's aggravating when I see other people just being taken out in their wheelchairs, I think it'd be nice just to do that.

And yet, Bonnie says she accepts the limitations and appears at peace and more involved in her spiritual journey than in her physical limitations. She has in a sense been engaging in what Frankl (1984) termed 'self-forgetting' and transcending her physical difficulties. The struggle to transcend physical disabilities will be explored further in the following chapter.

Financial vulnerability

While energy loss seems a natural stimulus to moving from human *doing* to human *being* and *becoming*, issues of financial concern seemed to weigh heavily with some of the older people in this study. In a way, financial concerns seemed harder to let go of, and could even be a blockage to continued spiritual growth and transcendence. A number of these older adults were concerned or anxious about financial matters. Some of these anxieties could be a result of government changes in aged care funding that were made not long before the time of the interviews. Dora's only fears are associated with a need to sell her house:

> The only fears I've had are selling the home and getting all that off the plate and knowing where I'm going to stand financially because I'm not a wealthy woman, I'm just living from week to week, and ah to get that all fixed, I'm just waiting for a letter from the government now to tell you it's gotta be sold.

Elaine had a tough up-bringing, in the depression years. She said that she had to walk three and a half miles to school, and she did not go for long. Now Elaine's main concerns seemed centred on her house:

> Before I came in here [nursing home] I was very worried, I didn't think I'd settle like I did. But I'm still paying my house, you know, heck of a struggle but things worked out, that I got a friend that gives me just enough to pay my house and land rates and, and keep the house in good nick and gardens and things like that, just to cover that. And my pension covers it here and gives me enough to, to sort of get what I want [pause]. So that's brought that up to square one. It did worry me for a long time because they'd reckon I'd have to sell my home, I didn't have it paid for and all this was getting me down.

Grace was another of the residents who worried about not having enough money for her needs. Even though these women possibly had no need to worry about their ability to pay for their care in the aged care facility, they still worried about financial matters. It could be related to earlier life experiences where they had always struggled financially. This was part of the collective life experience of this cohort of older people that included memories of the great depression and living through two world wars. Money was still a concern for them. Staff should be ready to listen to concerns and to take action to make referrals where residents perhaps need information, or counselling, and support with financial matters. Subsequent cohorts of older people will have lived through different times of history and will have experienced different social conditions and times; these must be taken account of and included in awareness of the personal life experiences of these people.

Conclusion

This chapter has examined the ageing processes of increasing vulnerability and the consequent changes from *doing* to *being*. All of the people in the study of aged care residents lived with multiple chronic conditions. Different people handle the decreasing energy levels in different ways, some continue to deny their ageing, while others actively engage with the changes and adjust, continue to do what they can, or find different ways of engaging with life. It seems that the move towards self-transcendence, or gerotranscendence, is a natural and important part of the process of ageing in the fourth age. Those who are able to move towards self-transcendence appear to be more at peace, and to experience a better quality of life, even while they live with multiple disabilities.

Summary

- *An important change of ageing is the move from living actively, from doing, to being.*

- *Often this is associated with decrements of the body and decreasing energy levels, and the loss of important relationships.*

- *Tornstam (1999/2000) has coined the term 'gerotranscendence' to describe this apparent disengagement from society and a move to a more reflective life.*

- *Frailty and associated failure to thrive are seen in fourth age people.*

- *Failure to thrive may be associated with a lack of nourishment for the soul.*

- *The model of spiritual tasks of ageing may be used to identify the coping strategies that these people are using in transcending the losses and difficulties they are experiencing.*

Further reading

Jamieson, D. (2004) *Walking with Forgotten People: Some Aspects of Pastoral Care with Older People.* Canberra: Centre for Ageing and Pastoral Studies.

CHAPTER 11

Living with Chronic Physical Health Problems

Chronic physical health problems

This chapter explores the relationship between physical decrements and disabilities and transcendence. In the previous chapter energy loss was suggested as a means of triggering the move from human *doing* to human *being*. In this chapter another trigger for the development of transcendence is explored. Some older people seem to transcend their multiple physical conditions to a large extent, while others seem to be overwhelmed by them. Peck (1968), based on Erikson *et al.*'s stages of psychosocial development, described one of three psychosocial developmental stages of ageing as *body transcendence versus body preoccupation*. In this stage he said that the elderly person may resist the ageing process, and become preoccupied with bodily complaints and issues. He noted that for people who had up until mid-life relied on their physical health for a sense of well-being, loss of physical health may be the 'gravest insult'.

Another perspective of this, which is becoming more apparent now than when Peck wrote in the 1960s, is the industry building up around maintaining a youthful body including an increasing use of plastic surgery to remove any evidence of physical ageing. Peck saw the task of *body transcendence versus body preoccupation* to be able to self-forget and move beyond the inevitable physical decrements of ageing. The person who faces their signs of physical ageing will also see the questions of life-meaning, and these lead into the spiritual dimension of growing older.

Many of the residents in the study of frail elderly people on which this book is based lived with physical health problems. Elaine said she has had leg ulcers for 51 years. The ulcers on both legs were healed for a short time but, more recently, one leg has an ulcer again. She described her condition as 'brittle bones', having osteoarthritis and gout, and having had two fractures she is now confined to a wheelchair. She says she takes 25 tablets each day. And then she said: 'But life's not that bad.' I noted that she seemed quite happy in spite of all the health problems she had and she responded: 'Oh yes, oh I lost my husband 15 years ago, it was a bit of a struggle, a lot [of people] say you forget but you never forget, I know [it gets] a bit easier, a bit easier but in the end you never forget.'

Violet has bad leg ulcers, the worst I have ever seen, and I have seen plenty, having worked in a vascular ward. She says she has had them for more than 20 years. She can't move her legs herself, but needs someone to lift each of her legs if she needs to move at all. Despite her many health problems Violet has a wonderfully positive outlook on life. She said: 'You've got to accept what God gives you, haven't you?' She went on to explain:

> There's nothing else you can do, you can't say to Him I don't want my legs to be like this or that, but it's just that they are, you know. See I can move myself up here but I can't move the bottom part…my mother always said you take what God gives you till He stops giving, and you've got to do the best you can with it, well I use my hands, that's all I can do is use my hands.

Violet's attitude could be described as one of transcendence. Her physical problems were real, causing both immobility and pain, yet she seemed able to move through these to rise above the awfulness of her physical disabilities. Violet still experienced joy in her life. More than that, she had the ability to reach out to all who cared for her, so that by the time the staff member had completed their work with her and left the room, they felt uplifted.

Incontinence: a culture shift

A tremendous change is required in attitudes towards the weak and vulnerable people in need of care. Incontinence is just one of these issues. There is sometimes an attitude of blame associated with those who are incontinent. Some of the informants in this study spoke about what it feels like to have incontinence. Violet is incontinent. She said: 'Oh it's one of the worst things I think of anything that could happen to you, you know. I said to them "How could I get incontinent?" She said "It's the muscles of the bladder's collapsed…" well they've got those great big napkin things here and they put those on you and they pull them right up into the groin and they help, they absorb and that, but it's degrading, it really is degrading.' She acknowledged that the staff were as helpful as they could be with assisting her with this problem.

On another occasion I had been called to see a resident in another nursing home because the staff believed she was in spiritual distress. The source of this distress I discovered was a deep shame of being incontinent. I wondered how much this was a factor for Violet too. What can be done to help these people with such problems? Obviously the attitudes of staff are of first importance. It is hard for staff, who have never experienced incontinence, to understand what it is like. It is so important that staff do not take the attitude that the resident could do something to prevent being incontinent, so that blame must not be caste on the resident, the problem should be discussed openly and with great sensitivity. Ways of managing it should be discussed between the resident and staff in a trusting environment.

Being old and blind

Rebecca's only regret is her loss of sight. It is interesting that, although this is her only regret, due to her religious beliefs (she is a Christian Scientist) she did not feel it was possible to do anything about her sight. Rebecca became blind suddenly in 1985; she says she doesn't find it hard not being able to see: 'because I can feel, I can use the tactile sense'. I asked her why she had lost her sight: her response: 'I have no idea.' She said that she usually doesn't consult doctors, so she simply found she couldn't see and accepted that. She did remark that it was a bit frightening at first. Rebecca said one of her worries was not being able to find the toilet.

Max had a stroke about nine years ago. He lost his sight a few months ago.

> Well I had my left eye taken out at 75 and that had a problem and I was at the eye specialist a few months ago and I asked him what happened. I know something happened there, and he said, 'well your heart stopped beating'. I knew there was some problem. And that's all he told me.

He lost the sight of his other eye more recently. Max needs to have drops put in his eyes and complained that some of the nurses hurt him as they put the drops in. He also said that he can tell them how to do it, but he thinks 'they hate to be told by a patient'.

Sonya became blind seven and a half years ago, she is 90 years old. She likes to listen to as many tapes (from the Blind Society) as she can get. Sonya also loves to listen to music: 'Yes I love to hear music that I could dance to…' She said that brings back a lot of memories for her, but she doesn't like the tapes brought into the nursing home: 'but I don't like them brought in here because they make me too miserable, yes they make me melancholy'.

Living with diabetes in later life

A number of older people who have diabetes have lived with it for some years. Having an understanding of the person's perception of their illness and the way they have managed it will be important for continuing care and optimum well-being of the resident. This may include dealing with any misconceptions of their condition, and assisting them to maintain or reach their optimum weight, and to take part in sufficient exercise, as well as management of any medications and complications of diabetes. National Diabetes Associations have clear guidelines and resources available for people living with diabetes and their families. The Australian Diabetes Association website is at: www.diabetesaustralia.com.au/home/index.htm.

Fears

Fears held by frail elderly people in residential aged care in this study are less than those held by community dwelling elderly people (MacKinlay 2001a), however, fears do still exist. One source of fear is related to the very vulnerability of these fourth age people. Their vulnerability and needs may leave them open to exploitation and even abuse by those who care for them.

Violet, like most of the others I interviewed in the nursing homes, said she does not have any fears. I asked her: 'Quite a number of older people who are living in their own home have a number of fears. They are frightened about what might happen to them later. Do you think that's something that changes when you get into a nursing home?' Violet replied: 'Oh yes, definitely. But I think you've got to go into a decent nursing home, I'd say this is one of the best you could be in and 'cause I don't know any other, but they tell me there's a lot worse than this, you know.' A number of those who no longer held fears about their future said that now, in residential aged care, they felt safe, secure and cared for, and they knew that someone would come if they needed them.

A woman with dementia calling out in the night distressed Violet and it seems that some of the commonly held attitudes towards people with dementia were evident in her next sentences:

Oh Daisy [the other resident] is as cranky as anything with the staff, it's a shame, because the staff do so much for her. And she's so lazy she won't even bend over like that to pick up her meal, she wants them to feed her. Well they won't do that because it makes them an invalid altogether, you know, they say 'No you can't have that, you must feed yourself.' And then she'll drop it on the floor, you know terribly naughty and things like that, I wish I could get up and you know talk to them, let them know, that they're not the only ones here, she thinks she was the only one here. And I like getting attention and all that and I think oh dear, oh dear, don't let me get like that, you know, then I'm complaining oh.

Violet seemed very conscious of her own needs for care, and at the same time, the need to be a 'good' resident. Although Violet had said she had no fears, as she spoke it seemed there was something of a fear here of how she might be treated if she should become like the other resident she spoke of. These attitudes come out of a culture of ageism that is seen both in society and among some staff in nursing homes. There is an urgent need to address these attitudes and increase the quality of life for all residents of aged care facilities, including those who have dementia. The 'new culture' of dementia care that is espoused by Kitwood (1997) and Goldsmith (1996) is needed in all places that provide aged care.

Pain

Pain management in aged care facilities needs to be given high priority. The pain of arthritis, including back pain, and leg ulcers in particular, as well as other chronic conditions, is the cause of decreased quality of life among residents. Nurses working in aged care need to have a high awareness of pain among their residents, and the various manifestations of pain in elderly people. Effective pain assessment is an essential aspect of aged care, particularly in instances where residents cannot articulate their experience of pain. Pain may include the pain of suffering as well as physical pain. One factor to be noted is that acute pain of, say, myocardial infarction or mesenteric infarction, may be absent or atypical in older adults (Harkins 2002). While little has been studied of acute pain in older adults, in comparison with paediatric pain, there are no known differences in pain experienced by older adults undergoing various procedures.

One type of pain that deserves particular attention in older people is recurrent and persistent pain. Persistent pain has been defined variously, but perhaps best as 'pain that outlasts the normal healing period following tissue damage by about a month' (Harkins 2002, p.11). It is noted that people with Alzheimer's disease have difficulty in communicating specific pain symptoms. Often pain in older adults has been underestimated and under-treated. Elaine spoke of the pain from her arthritis and leg ulcer:

Once I got the bones broken in one leg and putting all the weight on the other one, it has broken out a bit again, so I've still got one ulcer on one leg, but the whole leg gets very sore, even in the muscles and everything you touch, is all, yeah.

She explained how hard it was for her to learn to take something for the pain on a regular basis, not waiting for the pain to get too bad before she took her medication, she said that had made it much more manageable.

Max, who had a stroke, said that at times: 'I'm full of pain, I'm untouchable.' He said that all he was offered was Panadol, and that didn't work. I asked if he had requested something else for pain, his response: 'Well see the way this place is run they got to talk to the head person here, you've got to give about a month's notice.' This was difficult from my perspective as a nurse and researcher. The resident was telling me something that I was not happy about, but I saw ethical issues with my coming into the home and interviewing people and then seeming to check up on care standards. I encouraged him to ask for pain relief, as he needed it and later discussed issues of pain management with the staff.

Katie spoke of her pain and the way that it interferes with her daily activities:

> It gets really monotonous you laying hour after hour and no one to talk to, sometimes I go downstairs to whatever's on, but up to date I haven't been able to go very often because I've been in too much pain. But now the pain seems to be disappearing which is much better but you can't sit and listen to anything if you're in pain all the time – it's impossible.

Suffering and pain

It is not simply a matter of providing adequate analgesia for pain to be relieved. There are times when pain is not only physical, but also emotional, existential and spiritual. Kestenbaum (2001) writing of healing and Jewish concepts of pain makes an important distinction in the understanding of pain and suffering. He writes: 'Suffering is a response to pain; it results from the emotional and spiritual meaning that the pain has in one's life. Medicine treats pain; caregiving responds to suffering' (p.5). He notes importantly that the point at which a situation become unbearable is not usually due to increase in pain, but rather has to do with the level of suffering. He notes estrangement as a core component of this suffering; in some circumstances this may even be estrangement from the self. He writes of the experience of an elderly woman feeling the loss of her role as a mother when she has to be cared for by her family, saying she finds it 'unbearably painful to be suddenly forced into a reversal of roles' (p.6).

Care of people who are suffering means to walk the journey of suffering with them, to be present with them, and authentic in caring. In other words, providing real spiritual care where a closeness or intimacy, albeit at a professional level, is developed between the person who is suffering and the carer.

This is often a difficult role for a health professional who has been socialized into a 'doing' role that emphasizes action rather than 'being with'. This involves not a sense of competence, but a sense of awareness of one's own inability to 'fix' anything, beyond being with the person and connecting with that person at their point of need.

Sleeping difficulties

Sleep seems to be a problem for numbers of residents in aged care, and many are prescribed sedation for sleeping. Just how much do sleep patterns change over the lifespan, and what problems do older adults in residential care encounter with sleep? Recent research was reviewed to answer these questions.

Floyd *et al.* (2000) studied how people actually get to sleep and they note that although primary studies suggest that ability to initiate sleep declines as people age, their review of the literature has not identified the age(s) at which adults experience the greatest change in their ability to initiate sleep. Decline in ability to actually fall asleep may not occur at a steady rate over the adult lifespan. They suggest that further research is needed to pinpoint thresholds of change and possible gender differences in thresholds.

A study (Ohayon *et al.* 2001) comparing sleep between younger and older people found inactivity, dissatisfaction with social life and the presence of organic diseases and mental disorders the best predictors of insomnia; age alone being insignificant. Importantly, it found being active and satisfied with social life are protective factors against insomnia at any age. These findings are relevant for routines in residential aged care.

There are some factors within the environment of aged care residences that may make it more difficult for residents to sleep, and noise is one of them. Violet spoke about the woman over the hall from her room who called out repeatedly in the night: 'Help me', as so many people with dementia seem to do. It would seem that it is a cry of an existential nature, and people who are specially trained in dementia care are more likely to be able to effectively support these people in their distress.

Transcendence and the spiritual care role

The process of moving from doing to being, of self-transcending, is part of the spiritual tasks and process of ageing. In a Christian context, transcending self means dying to self; not simply to be emptied of self, but taking it to the next step, to be engaged in an active growing into Christ. With the continuing decline of the physical body, the opportunities for growth of the spiritual dimension abound. Clements (1990) wrote of this, explaining that as the person moving through mid-life finds their roles stripped from them, and if they have no spiritual core, they may be found naked at the core. If we take our generic spirituality as a starting point, we may then ask, what kind of spiritual life do I want? Each of us has the capacity for spiritual development, what will we choose, and is spiritual growth a priority in our lives? So the questions emerge, what kind of spiritual portfolio do we have? Are we aware of the spiritual needs of those we care for?

The spiritual and pastoral role in transcendence

The spiritual and pastoral care role is to affirm each individual as a person of great value, and loved by God. Honouring the personhood of each individual includes blessing them by offering the possibility of sharing sacred space, that is, a place of intimacy. Spiritual care and pastoral roles mean being present with the person and listening to their story, using spiritual reminiscence, appropriate liturgies and making sacraments available to the person according to need. The spiritual and pastoral role includes, where appropriate, the opportunity for confession of past matters that are on the conscience, and the need for forgiveness and reconciliation. Spiritual and pastoral care aims for wholeness and spiritual growth.

Humour and transcendence

Humour may be a way into transcendence (MacKinlay 2004), and has been noticed to be a strategy used by a number of participants in both the study of frail ageing people and the current study of people with dementia. In small groups in a study of finding meaning in dementia (MacKinlay *et al.* 2002–2005), people engaged in conversations around memory loss, and laughed about it, however, it is noted that memory loss was identified as part of growing older, but not dementia. Behind the jokes may lie a fear of memory loss and its possible implications. It is possible that humour was being used to distance oneself from the feared situation, and may act to lessen its impact. We have found in our studies a stigma attached to the word 'dementia' (MacKinlay, Trevitt and Hobart 2002).

One of the spiritual tasks of the process of ageing is transcendence and humour may be a way into transcendence. It is only when one can move beyond the self, as in self-forgetting, proposed by Frankl (1985), that transcendence is possible. Thus humour may assist in self-forgetting (Figure 11.1). The process of self-forgetting allows the individual to see ultimate meaning, even in and through loss and disability. Study participants would quite spontaneously use humour to lighten or transcend a situation. However, authentic humour cannot be forced and it seems that authentic humour is actually a sign of self-transcendence. It is only when one is able to 'self-forget' that one is able to engage in humour.

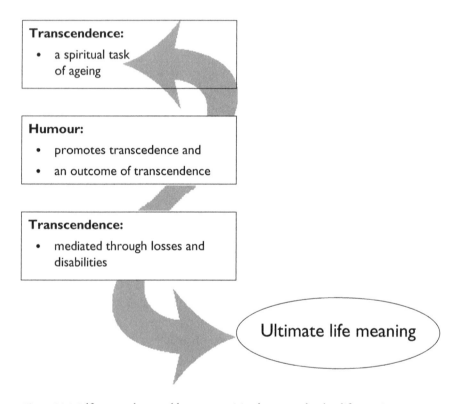

Figure 11.1 Self-transcendence and humour: a spiritual process related to life-meaning

Stroke

Stroke presents many challenges for those who are affected by it and their families. Deficits in communication, mobility, and activities of daily living are just some of the issues that reduce quality of life for these people. Depression is often associated with stroke. Kauhanen *et al.* (1999), in a study of depression post-stroke, found that more than half of the patients suffered from depression, and the frequency of major depression seemed to increase during the first year after the stroke. In addition to dysphasia, post-stroke depression is correlated with other cognitive deficits.

From a psychological or spiritual point of view, stroke presents enormous questions of meaning and quality of life post-stroke. The individual has suddenly lost abilities and their world has, in a sense, imploded around them. There may be an initial sense, both for the person who had the stroke and their family, that life will never be the same again. Being able to draw on effective past coping styles and the ability to transcend difficulties and losses, may contribute to greater recovery, provided that the degree of cerebral damage is consistent with recovery.

Life often continues to be hard for people who have experienced a stroke. Sufficient rehabilitation is not always possible, and then placement in an aged care facility may be required, as the burden on family to care for them at home becomes too great. However, one study in a review of stroke care (McKevitt *et al.* 2004) found that early discharge to home-based rehabilitation had a positive impact on rehabilitation, 'encouraging patients to practice activities on their own and devise their own solutions to problems' (p.1502), thus making the treatment more relevant to the people who had experienced the stroke. One problem found in this review of stroke studies was less than optimum communication between health care providers and patients. It is noted that shared goals on treatment between therapists and patients would aid in raising outcomes for those with stroke.

Hafsteinsdottir and Grydonck (1997) in their review of literature on 'being a stroke patient' reported that health care providers measured recovery in terms of task performance, improved mobility and independent self-care, whereas stroke *patients* measured their recovery in terms of a return to previously valued activities (p.583). This is an important distinction in perception, and certainly agreed goals of recovery are essential to well-being and maximum recovery levels for those who experience stroke. In aged care facilities, there is often at least the potential for improvement in well-being of these people, post-stroke. Certainly, their quality of life can often be improved with effective care that involves the facility staff working in cooperation with the person who has had the stroke and their family.

Physical care is important as these people often have difficulty with even simple activities of daily living. For the severely disabled person, mobility may be very restricted and pressure area care and physiotherapy will be needed, along with adequate nourishment, hygiene and prevention of infections. However, this physical care, even though extremely important, is not all that is needed by the person with a stroke. Equally important is that the person in the poorly functioning body, perhaps even feeling trapped within the disabled body, is not neglected. It is often said that care providers look at what the person with stroke can do (or perhaps even, what they can't do), while the person with the stroke looks at what life is like (Hafsteinsdottir and Grydonck 1997). Emotional and spiritual care are essential components of wholistic care for these people. Without this dimension of care these people may fail to thrive, and give up hope. Effective support may enable these people to find meaning in their disabilities and loss, and thus to transcend these difficulties.

Agnes has diabetes and she had a stroke about 10 years ago. She was initially unconscious for three weeks and had a right-sided paralysis. After long rehabilitation, she did learn to walk again. Agnes acknowledged that 'it was a bit hard'. While she was recovering she received strong support from one daughter, who would come and assist her with showers and feeding. A long period of rehabilitation followed, but she still wasn't well enough to go home. Agnes spoke of her fight to get well again:

> Oh yes, I don't believe in sitting down and doing nothing [laughs], mainly because out at [the aged care facility] there was a man living there…he had an accident at work and lost a leg and he could walk around and dance and do everything, and he sort of said you never sit down and do nothing. Because there was another poor old chap out there that wouldn't do a thing but moan about his one leg [laughs], and this fellow sort of inspired me, you know [laughs].

Although Agnes has not been able to live independently and struggles with diabetes and disabilities from her stroke, she still finds meaning in life. She seemed to find a lot to laugh about, even as we talked; she was in fact transcending her losses and disabilities. She has found a number of activities in the nursing home that she could take part in; she enjoys craft work, and having her daughter visit. Agnes has a sense of resilience in her outlook on life. This sense of resilience is a vital and perhaps elusive component in the mix that makes for well-being of any individual. Ramsey and Bleisner (2000) have written of the importance of faith in promoting resilience in the lives of older women in a cross cultural study of older American and German women.

Again, the suddenness of stroke makes it hard to adjust. Max was a busy building construction manager before he had a massive stroke. Subsequently Max found it very hard to come to terms with his disabilities. Max is confined to bed, and can only see shadows of people when they move. To complicate things still further, his wife died less than a year ago. Max seemed to have few resources for working with his disabilities. With his lack of mobility and sight loss, and grief as well, he seemed very isolated. He was in a single room and did not like being out in the community area of the nursing home, he seemed to feel even more vulnerable there. The result was that he had little contact with staff, except when they came into his room to give direct care to him. His family was busy, and although his daughter came to take his washing home, he felt guilty about her having that extra work to do. Max was depressed, a not uncommon occurrence with residents in aged care, and more so with those who have had strokes. According to Kauhanen *et al.* (1999), 42 per cent of patients in their study were diagnosed with depression 12 months after their stroke (they were not followed up further than that). Max's recent grief, lack of mobility and sight, would have made depression even more likely. Depression and ageing are discussed in Chapter 7.

Experiencing dysphasia

Both the residents discussed above could communicate reasonably well, however, difficulty with communication can be a major problem for people with stroke. Vreugdenhil (2004) has written a valuable article on communication and non-speech-based pastoral care. Dysphasia presents considerable difficulties for those who experience it and makes wholistic care challenging. Too often staff respond to residents who have dysphasia as being unable to understand and this is far from being true. It is vital that staff always err on the side of assuming that residents can understand, and that communication is the problem. So that, for instance, all care is resident-focused, and effective communication skills are used by staff, even in simple procedures such as showering, feeding and dressing. Adequate explanations should always be provided to residents before any procedure is begun, so that the resident may cooperate to the best of their ability, and is not confused by what the staff member is doing. Allowing a resident time to process what is happening is important too; hurrying residents with their care may end by being more time consuming than would have been the case had the carer simply taken the procedure at a suitable pace for the resident in the first place.

Difficulties in communication present barriers even for family members and carers in aged care facilities. In a busy environment, there is too little time for the carers to wait for the person with the stroke to find the words they need to express their needs and there is little incentive to let the person try to feed themselves if they need a lot of assistance; it is quicker to feed them. It is also quicker for the staff to shower and dress them, even though they may be able to do a lot for themselves, if given the time and appropriate assistance. Thus these people may lose the skills they could have retained, leading to helplessness, hopelessness and further depression.

Supporting people who have had a stroke

As Hafsteinsdottir and Grydonck (1997) note, recovery after stroke cannot be measured by functional abilities alone. It is necessary to also look at psychological, social and spiritual aspects of life, along with the activities of daily living. One man, who recently had a stroke, and was able to return home, said to me, 'It's a hard road back.' There is a real tendency for people's friends to forget them, and they become isolated, even when they are able to return home. Being admitted to long-term aged care raises even more challenges for the already disabled person. Loss of mobility and loss of speech are two of the most difficult disabilities for these people to transcend.

In the new environment of an aged care facility, the person needs to become familiar with the system, which includes knowing how to obtain the services they need. Often orientation into the home does not include introduction to other residents.

Connecting with people when communicating effectively is a problem

- Sight and hearing loss make it harder for these people to become familiar with their new environments. Assessment for such disabilities at admission and provision of appropriate aids in a timely manner, will make the settling in period much easier.

- Careful orientation to the new place of residence will be very helpful for the person experiencing an aged care facility for the first time.

- Adequate access to staff such as physiotherapists and occupational therapists and/or diversional therapists is needed.

- Attention to their specific cultural and spiritual requirements and consideration of these is needed.

- Facilitating opportunities to meet and make new friends will help with settling in.

- Staff being available and spending sufficient time with residents to listen to their needs will be very helpful.

Conclusion

This chapter has addressed common physical health problems that may have effects on psychosocial and spiritual well-being in later life and consequently, on quality of life. It has examined the relationships between physical decrements and the development of self-transcendence. Living in the fourth age is often complicated by multiple chronic conditions and associated physical ill-health, for example, the effects of incontinence, sensory deficits, dysphasia, issues of pain, suffering, sleep problems and mobility difficulties. The factors involved in the development of self-transcendence were discussed, including humour and transcendence and ways of connecting with people experiencing physical health issues.

Summary

- *This chapter considers the move from human doing to human being and transcendence and the task of body transcendence versus body preoccupation to be able to self-forget and move beyond the inevitable physical decrements of ageing.*

- *Issues of incontinence, pain and suffering and the sudden onset of stroke produce challenges for older people and may threaten their identity and sense of integrity.*

- *Pain is sometimes hard to assess in older people, and some pain at least is existential or spiritual pain and needs recognition and appropriate intervention.*

- *Dysphasia may complicate effective communications with people who have had a stroke.*

- *The process of body-transcendence may be facilitated through physical disabilities, or it may be blocked in the face of disabilities.*

- *Spiritual and pastoral care involves journeying with these people, and supporting needs for forgiveness and reconciliation where appropriate.*

Further reading

Jamieson, D. (2004) *Walking with Forgotten People: Some Aspects of Pastoral Care with Older People.* Canberra: Centre for Ageing and Pastoral Studies.

CHAPTER 12

Relationship and Intimacy Needs among Nursing Home Residents

This chapter focuses on the need for relationship and intimacy in later life. For many older people their deepest human relationships are almost synonymous with meaning (MacKinlay 2001a).We have found this to be so for both cognitively intact older people, and for those who have dementia. For some older people relationship means a deepening intimacy with their God, and a life centred on God may become a reality for some frail older people.

The need for intimacy in later life

Intimacy is connecting at a deep level with another human: the human need for intimacy is at its deepest an expression of the spiritual dimension. Intimacy can be expressed at sexual and non-sexual levels. For most human beings, the need is for human relationship and many also search for relationship with God, in whatever form that may take for the individual. Often intimacy is seen in sexual connotations, in a more narrow sense. However, Carroll and Dyckman (1986, p.123) describe intimacy as 'the ability to let myself be known by another and to be comfortable in that revelation'. They go on to say: 'At the deepest core of my being I need to be known and loved as I am.' They acknowledge this need as a reciprocal one. Intimacy is a deep and safe place to be, to simply 'be' with another, without the masks, the facades, the inhibitions; it is connecting and touching deeply with another human being.

In the Christian understanding of spiritual growth, Tillich (1963) has described the process of sanctification, or the process of moving toward spiritual maturity, that he says conquers loneliness by providing both for solitude and communion in interdependence. He notes that a decisive symptom of spiritual maturity is the power to sustain solitude. 'Sanctification conquers introversion by turning the personal centre…toward the dimension of its depth and its height. Relatedness needs the vertical dimension in order to actualise itself in the horizontal dimension' (p.234). Here Tillich is acknowledging what he sees as a human need, both for human relatedness and God relatedness. Further, Tillich writes that 'relatedness implies the awareness of the other one and the freedom to relate to him by overcoming self-seclusion within oneself and within the other one' (p.233). Tillich notes that there are many barriers to effective relatedness. In his terms, relatedness is a two way process, involving both parties in the relating. Thus, when frail elderly people or people with dementia need care, there are implications in relatedness both for them and their carers, yet the need for relatedness does not diminish.

The spiritual task to find intimacy with God and/or with others

In the model of spiritual tasks of ageing (MacKinlay 1998; 2001a; 2001c), one of the tasks of older people who have lost important relationships is to establish new intimacy with others and/or God. This task, identified with the independent living group of older people, was reinforced by the stories of these elderly residents of aged care facilities. For many humans, primary life-meaning is found through relationship (Figure 12.1). Maintaining social contacts becomes more difficult as frailty increases, and those in the fourth age who live alone may have few resources for developing new friendships and lack opportunities for intimacy. Social isolation may lead to depression and increasing need for care. Often the need is for new intimacy, as the many losses that the elderly person has experienced prior to entry to residential aged care may tend to accumulate, perhaps becoming overwhelming. These losses include loss of home but, most essentially, loss of relationship and intimacy of loved ones. As well, these people are dealing with multiple chronic conditions that make the transition to aged care very difficult to say the least.

The task for the elderly person entering aged care is to establish new relationships. This can be a daunting task, as one resident said 'this is a big place for one person like me'. Who may be the potential new friends and emotional support for this person? For those fortunate enough to have family close by, these relationships can be supported and continued. For those who have a community of faith near by, they may continue to be involved in the life of that community outside the aged care facility.

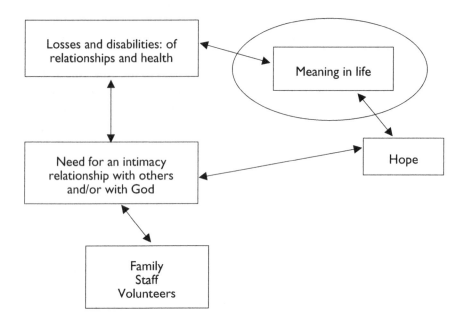

Figure 12.1 Spiritual tasks of ageing: the need for intimacy in residential aged care

Quality of relationship: elderly person and carer

The quality of relationship that staff develop with the residents is just as important as the ways residents communicate and relate with staff. It must be said, however, that often in residential aged care, the advantage in communication lies with the staff, as many residents experience either compromised cognitive function or sensory disabilities that may make communication and relationships with others more difficult than would normally be the case. Add to that the burden of grief and loss that many residents carry. Thus particular responsibility lies with staff to ensure that their communication skills and attitudes towards residents are open, encouraging and supportive. Relationships between staff and residents may become, for some residents, the only source of intimacy in their lives as any family members may live at a distance from the aged care facility. It is crucial that staff providing aged care know about the needs of the elderly people in their care, and do not rely on hearsay and myths to guide their actions, however well-meaning.

Intimacy and frail older people

Needs for intimacy may not be the first priorities for care within residential aged care, yet the need for intimacy is crucial to human well-being. For these frail residents of nursing homes, the need for intimate relationship is too easily forgotten when the focus is placed on meeting their physical care needs. The need for intimacy does not decline with either age or frailty. In one sense, recognizing a person in their fullness of personhood, in the context of relationship and social being, with an attitude of respect and trust, as described by Kitwood (1997) is an important part of this concept of intimacy. While Kitwood was writing specifically about personhood in people with dementia, this concept is equally important for all people.

In our latest study of quality of life for people with dementia (MacKinlay *et al.* 2002–2005), we have found that relationship is almost synonymous with meaning for people with dementia. To deprive them of family at a time of real vulnerability is a form of deprivation and punishment. Too often I have heard it said to relatives of people with dementia who are newly admitted to care, 'don't come to visit for about a week, as that will give them time to settle in'. That could not be further from what the new resident needs. It may be that they will 'settle' into the aged care facility; deprived of any familiar persons, they may become quieter, and 'easier to manage' because they are becoming depressed. Their primary need at this time is to have some connection with a person who is familiar to them, even if they cannot remember the name of that person. Knowing goes far deeper than this. Christine Boden, living with dementia (1998), said of her children, 'even if I can't remember their names, I still *know* who they are'. Knowing in this way has a deeper meaning; it is an awareness of deep connections with another person.

Eighty per cent of participants were widowed. This was a higher proportion than in the independent living group. Lack of a carer is one reason for admission to a nursing home, although with the introduction of Community Aged Care Packages (CACP) this has meant more people living alone can stay in their own homes and have services brought to them there. As in the earlier study that mapped the spiritual dimension of independent living older people (MacKinlay 2001a) (see Figure 1.2), one of the major themes arising from the data was the need for relationship. However, because of the frequency of bereavement in later life, often a lifetime partner of more than forty years has been lost; the person has lost perhaps the most important relationship of their lives. Therefore, at a time when the individual may also be facing physical disability and learning to live with chronic conditions, the need for intimacy may be both desired and at the same time difficult to achieve. One of the spiritual tasks of the model was to find intimacy with God and/or others in later life. Finding new intimacy in the midst of increasing frailty may be a challenging task (de Vries 2001).

Married and living in a nursing home: acknowledging sexuality in ageing

Fifteen per cent of the participants in this study were married and one was divorced. For a number of reasons the married residents did not have their spouse residing in the same institution. Thus the human need for intimacy could not easily be fulfilled. The need for relationship in these frail older nursing home residents presents particular problems. Sexuality is a very private concern and this cohort of older people did not easily discuss matters of sexuality openly; however, that does not mean that they are by any means 'asexual'. Numbers of residents spoke of their loneliness and missing their partners; however, none in this study specifically mentioned sexuality. In a subsequent study that focused on finding meaning among elderly residents who had dementia (MacKinlay *et al.* 2002–2005), sexuality certainly was spontaneously talked about. While the willingness of those with dementia to speak of sexual needs may be related to having fewer inhibitions in the process of increasing dementia, reasons for the differences can only be assumed.

Margaret is one of the few whose husband is still alive and she says her husband is a very good support to her, however she has needed to come into residential care, and they are now separated.

Bob spoke of his relationships with friends:

> I've been so fortunate, so fortunate in having a lovely number of friends, of all religions and all the same, why blame the religions, why blame the beliefs and when my friends confide in me and help me and it's just meant a lot to me. And if I didn't have this I wouldn't have any of the other that I was telling you.

Bob's wife is still alive but she lives in Sydney, so he doesn't see her much, now he's in the nursing home. And he said: 'I've been fortunate enough to have a wonderful wife whose still loves me, we've had a few ups and downs, nothing bad, you know. As a matter of fact I've got to tell you that my main support would come from my wife.' Both Margaret and Bob seemed resigned to the fact that they were not able to have their spouse living with them. Of his friends Bob shared: 'whereas I might sound a bit tearful, the tears come not from any grief, but from I'd like you to know this, it's important, not from any grief. A deep happiness that's always kept me, that the people I've known have been so wonderful.'

Roach (2004) found that despite growing recognition of the importance of sexual expression for nursing home residents, sexual activity remained a neglected component of nursing home care. Her study of staff in residential aged care in Australia and Sweden showed that both staff perceptions and responses to resident sexual behaviour were influenced by staff members' comfort with issues of sexuality. She identified a need for staff and management of aged care facilities to work towards developing a culture within the homes of openness to the topic of sexuality and establishing the rights of residents for sexual expression.

Roach described the central phenomenon of the study that she termed the 'guarding discomfort' paradigm, meaning 'individuals and organizations guarding against behaviours that caused them to be uncomfortable' (p.377). Roach provides an example of this paradigm from one of the staff interviews where staff members had decided that 'a married couple were "allowed" to share a room because their relationship was deemed to be "normal" and therefore asexual'. She noted that the way staff responded to resident expressions of sexuality depended on attitudes that were influenced by the staff member's own comfort levels with sexuality, which in turn were influenced by their religious views and cultural backgrounds. Thus staff (and management) could oppose or facilitate expression of sexuality within the nursing home. She noted in her study that:

> This basic human right is intimately related to other fundamental human rights such as freedom of choice, and a measure of control over one's own life. In situations where residents are given choice and some level of autonomy, there is an increase in self-esteem and improved sense of fulfillment in life. (p.378)

Myths of what is normal sexual behaviour in elderly people abound. The view that older people are not interested in sexual activity may be even more emphasized in residential aged care should a medical view of ageing exist. In this case, the elderly people are likely to be assumed to be ill, and in this model of care, expressions of sexuality are not seen as appropriate, and staff can make the decision as to whether a relationship is 'normal' or not. In this case, and others like it, freedom for sexual activity does not exist, even within marriage, between partners.

In entering residential aged care, elderly people who are still married face a fracturing of a marriage relationship that may have lasted for 40–50 years or even more. The loss of intimacy that has developed over the years can be a devastating experience for these people. Being together is part of living for them. An elderly couple I met with recently knew each other so well that they answered for each other in conversation; others in long but conflicted relationships still have need of each other.

Ways of supporting residents in freedom of expression of sexuality

The first need is to develop 'an environment supportive of the sexuality rights of residents by encouraging freedom and choice in daily activities' (Roach 2004, p.378). Recommendations for action based on Roach's study have been made for maintaining sexuality rights, noting that these actions need to be proactive. These actions are important in the change of culture to one that supports and affirms frail and elderly residents within aged care facilities and include:

- providing therapeutic tactile stimulation
- providing a socially stimulating environment, facilitating access to others both within the residence and in the wider community
- promoting freedom for expression of sexuality, including education and counselling of others where required
- facilitating shared and common interests between residents
- encouraging resident input into management processes
- investigating the causes of any inappropriate sexual behaviour
- acknowledging residents' rights.

(Roach 2004, p.379)

Roach has looked only at aged care staff in her study, but her findings equally apply to all who are associated with residential aged care. Treating older people with respect is basic to recognizing their sexuality. Non-sexual touch that is appropriately used is beneficial. Further, touch can be used therapeutically with older people and 'Giving touch has the power to shed new light on health care professionals' experiences of caring for older patients suffering from dementia and/or pain, giving them the power to be a valuable person and professional' (Edvardsson, Sandman and Rasmussen 2003, p.208).

Relationships and adapting to living in an aged care facility

Of the residents in the study, Bert was particularly fearful of the future regarding his relationship with his wife and he said: 'I'm concerned about, selfishly so, if my wife gets to the stage where she can't drive the car still or something like that. Our communication, or our ability to communicate in an institution like this…' He went on to talk about the difficulties of getting a smaller house or unit, and the costs involved, having come to the conclusion that his admission to an aged care facility was the only possibility for him and his wife. Bert said that he went home often for visits on weekends, but he was dependent on having his wife come and pick him up to take him home.

Bert has Parkinson's disease and he felt now that emotional and spiritual supports he might otherwise have had from his friends were unavailable. He expressed his feeling of stigma of being in a nursing home, combined with his condition:

> Well not your friends, you find they don't know how to handle it, so they avoid coming to see you. But I have obviously explained to my family now and they understand it. 'Don't expect to bring my friends to see me over here, it's a bit like a zoo or something you come and you stop for a while. They don't seem to know what to say, you know they can't say well you'll be getting out next week or something and they don't know what to do.' … I never thought of being there permanently. When it spells itself out to you, your own individual self, you find it's pretty, it's scary, [that] you're in this institution.

It had taken three visits prior to this one for Bert to be ready to talk with me. It seemed that he mostly just sat, not engaging in much social interaction at all, in fact it could be said that Bert was socially isolated within the nursing home environment. Initially, as I sat with him, he would only comment briefly on things like the food in the residence. It was at this third visit that the conversation emerged into a time of sacred space. It seemed for me that he was letting me into his deepest feelings about what his experience of the nursing home was like. In this meeting there was a sense of there being no one present but the two of us; it was a time of deep connecting. I asked him: 'Well, what was the scariest thing for you about it?' Bert replied: 'The most scary thing is how much longer it will go on for.' He went on to say: 'One of my sons says "I don't know what's wrong with the place, there's your meals, your washing's done, everything is done for you."' He paused, 'but that's not normal'. There was a sense of frustration in his voice as he said this.

There were considerable losses for him although, on one level, the nursing home was providing for all his basic activities of daily living. At another and important level, he was missing his wife and the former relationships with his friends. He had come to some compromise here, and that was to go home for a visit and have his friends see him there. It seems that what Bert was expressing here was a sense of stigma in being in a nursing home and, of course, most of his time was now spent away from home and family.

Reminiscing, Bert told a story of his grandmother and the struggles she had living in very primitive conditions in the early days on a farm. She was evidently a special influence in his life. Bert also lent me the notes he had written on his life story. I felt honoured to be given this to take away and read. The story was full of meaning and tales of the early days of his family and farm life. There was a real joy in these stories and Bert smiled as he spoke of those times.

The importance of children and grandchildren

For these mostly widowed older people, other relationships emerged with more importance, for instance, children, grandchildren and friends. It must be said though, that for many of these people, most of their friends have died, or they have moved to aged care facilities distant from where their family and/or friends live. For some who were admitted to nursing homes geographically remote from family and friends, staff of the nursing home may be the only source of intimate relationship. Sonya had most of her family living in other states, so it was difficult for them to visit; a daughter and granddaughter kept in regular contact by phone. Residents who have family and friends close by often seem to find more reasons for living, although this was not invariably so.

Geographical distance of family members presents particular difficulties in regard to the lack of family support and the need for intimate relationships for these elderly people. If these frail older people are to have any kind of emotional and spiritual support from anyone, it will probably need to come from neighbours, if living at home, or from staff and volunteers in aged care facilities. This in turn raises questions of how appropriate relationships with staff are developed. The need for intimacy for frail and vulnerable residents need to be acknowledged, as this is a basic human need. Failure to thrive may be a possible outcome for older people who are starved of loving relationships and care. Because these people are often vulnerable and could be at risk of exploitation, ethical dimensions of appropriate relationships between residents and staff must be held as important principles of care.

Staff of the aged care facility may be the only people with whom residents may make regular contact. This makes the staff the obvious people with whom to establish new relationships. However, it is possible that in endeavouring to meet the needs of frail elderly people, blurring of boundaries of professional caring may occur. It is important to consider ramifications where close bonds are established between staff and residents that may then be broken when staff members move to work in other areas, or rostering practices that may include regular changes of residents cared for.

Dora is one person from the study who has good spiritual and emotional support from her adult children. Elaine also finds her main support from her children and grandchildren as well as from her friends. She treasures memories of getting married and bringing her first child home. She spoke of happy times of hard work when they were young. Rebecca finds her emotional and spiritual support comes from her two children. Her church (Christian Science) also provides her with spiritual support. Concern for children is still present in frail older people. The only fear Agnes has is for her daughter who has Crohn's disease, which is the cause of a lot of ill health.

Regrets and guilt

There was a variety of responses from residents in this study as they looked back on their lives. Elaine noted that she had no regrets or sense of guilt. On the other hand Dora says that: 'Oh I think we've all got guilt in our lives, I can't put my finger on it, whatever it is, but there's guilt there all the time.' Dora says that for her the only way of dealing with guilt is through prayer. Violet has one regret, that she has a long-standing rift with her son, lasting more than 20 years. This is complicated by non-acceptance of her by her daughter-in-law. Violet feels regret and guilt about this and she longs to be reconciled with her son, but does not see how that could happen. Issues of regret and sometimes guilt can be addressed by staff who are willing to listen, who are non-judgmental and give the resident time to reflect on past issues that are still of concern to them. Spiritual reminiscence may facilitate healing of past grief, regrets and guilt. It may be that a referral to pastoral care or counselling, with the resident's consent, may be beneficial.

Violet wishes for reconciliation with her son. She worries about their family, does not get on with her daughter-in-law, and thinks she is cruel to her children. And yet she says: 'My children were the best things in my life, my son-in-law and daughter-in-law, your family, there's nothing on earth like your family, working with the Lord, against them or whatever, they're still your flesh and blood, aren't they?' Violet's biggest regrets in life are over her broken relationship with her son and his family; she does, however, admit some responsibility for that as she says: 'Well I suppose I'm guilty of...because no one can have a row with themselves, it takes two to make an argument, doesn't it?' Violet's emotional support comes from family and she looks at the photos on the wall of her late husband and her mother and father for support. This importance of photos of deceased loved ones was also noted in the research of independent living elderly people (MacKinlay 1998). This has also been understood by many carers in nursing homes who have encouraged the use of photos for residents, including the making of collages with photos. Violet said: 'Oh yes, I get a terrible lot of help I think, from those two photos up there. Well of course, my mother too, but mother's been gone so many, many years, …you never forget your mother.' Violet's father died when she was 18 months old. It is now understood that following loss through death (de Vries 2001), the relationship with the one who died does not terminate, but in the process of grief a new form of relationship develops for the one still alive. Photos of loved ones who have died form an important connection for many of the elderly residents. Violet has been widowed for many years; she can't remember how long ago her husband died of a massive heart attack.

Loneliness and isolation

Issues of isolation seemed to occur too frequently within residential aged care. Although these frail older people often said they felt safe and cared for in the aged care facility, there was also a great deal of loneliness and isolation. It must be said that simply taking part in the daily activities of the nursing home or hostel does not fulfil the needs for intimacy of many of these older residents. Heidi was one who said she felt lonely in the nursing home. Heidi was confused as to time, but otherwise able to converse adequately.

Katie, in particular, longed for someone she could be friends with, to help her unfold her spiritual journey, to search for the meaning of life events. She felt lonely even as a resident of a large nursing home. Activities were not sufficient to provide her with the depth of relationship she longed for. Katie said:

> I keep wishing I'm getting better, the wishes I think might be coming true but very slowly. I'm on a lonely scale as a matter of fact, because my daughter had to have an operation for her heart and I can't see her and I don't ever see her daughter, she's only got the one, and I've got nobody in Canberra that I know. They just gave me 24 hours notice to come here and they have done a lot for me since I've been here, I'm much better.

Katie said: 'I get down sometimes you know, I do really get down.' I asked her to tell me about that, and she responded: 'Because you've got no one to talk to, something will come…and you think oh, I wish so and so was here we could have a talk about that but see there's nobody… I've just got to think things out for myself.' Katie's loneliness came out in this part of the interview:

> Yes someone that you know was, oh, I just don't know it's hard to explain really. But it's a lonely life for one person to come into a big place like this, there's 136

of us I think here and I didn't know one person when I came in. But I've made friends with one and she's a lovely person, she's really lovely.

But still, Katie wonders:

Well I just wonder what the end's going to be like you know. If I'm going to get any worse or get any better or get any help, and I think well what's the use of worrying it doesn't help you any, because there's no one to tell you, yes, I'll help you, you know. You've got to make all new friends again and you don't see them often enough, you know. They have everything going here, I mean every morning and afternoon there's always something on you can go to but it's not the same as having a personal friend that you can talk things over.

Loneliness and intimacy with God

Katie said she felt very lonely in the nursing home. However, she did find comfort in her prayer, and she described her prayer life:

Well, I often pray to Him and particularly at night and I ask for help, and I tell Him I know that I'll get it when I pray through His Son. I do thank God for all He has done for me in the time that I've been with Him. Sometimes it seems hard that you should be left on your own, then I think well there's a reason for it, because I think He has a reason for us all. I do really! It mightn't suit us always.

There was a sense in which, although Katie was lonely in the nursing home, she was finding intimacy and closeness with her God.

It is not sufficient to provide for the physical needs of residents, nor even the psychological needs, nor to provide activities. Too frequently in aged care facilities the activity officers or diversional therapists have large numbers of people who can only be provided for within the funding constraints of the facility by using large group activities. These activities are often set in a context of making the residents feel happy, providing some entertainment, and passing the time in the nursing home. Activities need careful planning with consideration of the resident's needs as a primary goal. High proportions of residents have some hearing loss and perhaps sight impairment as well, coupled with physical problems that make it hard to sit and concentrate for long, particularly if the activity is not of interest to them. Further, those with dementia also find it hard to participate in large group activities. It is hard, sometimes, not to be reminded of the older style mental institutions where large groups of people would be got up and dressed and sat around the walls of the room all day. It is of concern that where such mental hospitals have been closed decades ago, aged care institutions might be providing similar care, at least in some situations.

Residents, no matter what their age, still need intimacy with others. Not only have these people lost many or all of the significant relationships of their lives, by the time they need residential care, but they are especially vulnerable. The very disabilities that were the reason for their admission make it more difficult for them to get to know other residents and to make new friendships within the nursing home environment, as in the cases of Bert and Katie.

Max had a stroke and he has few visitors and he was further isolated through his loss of sight, just in the last few months. He named the nursing home chaplain as possibly the main source of emotional and spiritual support. Max worries about his adult children; there does not seem to be any particular problem but he says: 'I'm a bit of a worrier.' It was some way into the interview that I asked about his wife, and he said she had died about five months before. He said that she had been in hospital a number of times over the last years. Later when I asked him about his grief for his wife he did not respond to that, but talked of when his father had died.

Sharing accommodation with another person

Sonya finds it hard sharing a room with someone. She talked about the difficulties of this: 'Well with this sharing a room you've got to be very compatible, you know, now for instance, like this little woman now she, she has her wireless on and I can't hear my talking book.' There are other problems too: 'Because there again of course, there's a conflict and then I have to say I must have air and she gets too cold, so you're bound to do this hard.' I asked if she had tried to talk with her roommate about these things and she replied: 'No I don't, because she's recovering from a stroke, see it's a very ticklish situation isn't it? The whole thing is that you shouldn't have to share a room because they're not big enough... The [rooms are] only built for one bed.' Sonya went on: 'Once you start complaining then they think about moving you to somewhere. Well then it's a very hard thing to have to be able to be what's the word with another person, ...compatible.'

These are some of the difficulties that living in residential aged care can bring. It must be hard for older people who have been used to being independent and having their own homes most of their lives to suddenly have to live so close to strangers, with little privacy and space. More aged care facilities now have single ensuite rooms, and although these provide for the needs to have one's own space and some privacy, people living in them may feel isolated, wanting someone to talk to, yet prevented by mobility problems of getting to communal areas to talk with others.

Moving residence in later life

Sonya's one big regret is that she moved from Darwin, where she had lived for 25 years, to the South Coast in another state to live in a 'granny flat' with one of her children. Not long after she had moved there her daughter needed the flat for her own daughter who had come home to live with twin babies. So Sonya was asked to move out. It was too late for her to go back to Darwin as she had lost her accommodation there. She was assessed and admitted to a nursing home. She said, she could still be at home, if she had some place to be, she just needed help with showering, she can walk with a frame. Sonya said she ended up in a nursing home in Canberra because she couldn't get into one nearer her family who live several hours away.

> I shouldn't have left Darwin, I was there for 25 years, now I had a Housing Commission unit, two bedroom and I could have got the same attention, like what exists with home care, meals on wheels... So I didn't have any other alternative only to come here [from the granny flat]. But I'm sorry, I had home care there and meals on wheels but I think they were really scared that they would have me on their hands and somebody would have to come down and look after me, but that's life! I could still shower, and I can still dress myself; I do it here and undress and I can wash myself. I can do that, the shower's no problem.

Sonya was brought up as a ward of the state; she lived in foster homes as a child. Now in the home she looks forward to seeing visitors, although she has few contacts living close enough to visit. She is one person who would benefit greatly from a visiting programme of volunteers.

These older people have lost so many relationships, but still have a need to be able to share and to form new relationships with others. This is illustrated by Veronica who says her emotional support is from her family, and that she can talk about the deep things of her life with the craft person in the aged care facility.

Use of activities and strategies to support relationship within the aged care environment

Activity for activity's sake, or to provide a means of passing the time, has little place in aged care. Too often in aged care activities are viewed as entertainment, and while there is room for entertainment that is compatible with residents' wishes, entertainment is not the only activity to be available within residential care. Some years ago I was conducting a survey with some residents of an aged care hostel and at the end of the survey, I thanked the small group of residents profusely for their time and readiness to complete the survey. I was surprised when they responded, 'No, thank *you!*' When I asked why they said that, they responded that it was rare to have anything to think about! They had actually enjoyed filling in a survey. Activities need to be meaningful for the residents, and residents should have an opportunity to be involved in both the selection and process of activities, wherever possible.

Activities that allow residents to meet and get to really know other residents are valuable; too often activities do not give residents time or space to get to know others in the aged care facility. Small groups that enable residents to engage and share with each other and not just with the group leader are important. Activities such as quizzes and bingo certainly bring people together in one room, but contribute little to developing relationships between residents.

One study that provides useful understanding of group activity for residents was conducted by Hodges, Keeley and Grier (2001) using hermeneutic pheno-menology and masterworks of art as a centre point for dialogue. They studied perceptions about chronic illness among three groups: registered nurses, nursing students and elderly people living with chronic illness. Content analysis of focus group interviews revealed themes of social isolation, inevitable role change, and inertia–movement. Of the three groups, only the elderly group of participants acknowledged hope and a steadfast refusal to give up. Themes of social isolation and role change are consistent with other studies of the elderly. The researchers suggest using masterworks of art as a way to generate energy exchange between elderly people and care-givers, providing a plausible catalyst for meaningful interventions that transcend age and practice settings.

The use of touch with elderly residents

The use of touch with residents in aged care has gained attention in recent years. Like infants deprived of loving touch, frail older people too need loving touch. Without it they will fail to thrive (see Chapter 10). In a study set in Sweden, Edvardsson, Sandman and Rasmussen (2003) studied the meanings within giving touch in nursing care of older patients, using a phenomenological–hermeneutic approach influenced by the philosophy of Ricoeur. 'Touch is central to nursing and health care workers frequently touch their patients, consciously or unconsciously in their interactions with them' (p.602). Most literature has studied touch from a patient perspective, thus inquiry about professionals' experiences are rare. Edvardsson *et al.* found that giving touch in the care of older patients is a transforming experience, 'where one suddenly perceives oneself as both a valuable person and professional who no longer powerlessly confronts patients' haunted and disrupted bodies, but who, by means of touch, has gained power to ease this suffering' (p.602).

They found that the effective use of touch could transform staff attitudes towards patients: 'Instead of seeing a severely demanding patient suffering from dementia and/or pain, one is able to see the person behind the disease as a human being, like oneself.' They noted the importance of the quality of relationship created between care-giver and patient, having characteristics of being calm, friendly and humane when giving touch. They argue that a relationship built in this way may transcend the moment of touch and influence one's way of caring.

Time seems to be a constant pressure for staff working in aged care. Work practices need to be carefully examined to see that maximum time is given where it counts most. Establishing trusting and caring relationships with residents must surely come high on the list of what is important in aged care. Workers in aged care need first class communication skills so that they may connect quickly and effectively with those in their care. The nursing assistant, the pastoral carer or the activity officer may become the person with whom the new resident can develop new intimacy. This is privileged work, and requires a high level of communication skills, the ability to be other-centred and to strive for and maintain highly ethical standards of care.

It may be that valuable and creative use of volunteers can be made. These are the people who may have time to sit with a frail elderly person, or a person with dementia and listen. The volunteer may become the new confidante. Again, this is a privileged role, and confidentiality of the resident must be guarded. Volunteers need adequate and appropriate in-service training and guidelines in their roles, including effective communication skills and establishing ethically appropriate relationships. Out of the establishment of new close and caring relationships, developed between volunteers and residents, may spring hope. Hope is essential for the flourishing of human beings.

Relationship in later life and being frail and elderly

A number of these informants resided in a nursing home distant from family and friends, indeed, the patterns of geographical dispersal of families common in Australia mean that often family is scattered across several states. The need for intimacy was clearly expressed in this study. Loss of long-term relationship left these people in need of the development of new relationships and new intimacies; not an easy task, considering both the frailty of these people and their limited access to people with whom they may develop new relationships.

The task becomes even more important and urgent at a time when these people do not have the skills and energy to establish new relationships. It seems that current western societies present problems for the establishment of effective intimacies for older people that would not have been present either before the current increase in longevity or before greater mobility within society occurred. First, older people are currently living longer with multiple chronic health conditions that may compromise well-being and the ability to interact socially. Second, in the fourth age of life, the ability to drive is likely to be restricted or lost, thus restricting the mobility of these people and limiting their opportunities for social engagement. Thus the establishment of new intimacies to replace those lost may be difficult. Third, many people live at long distances from their families, making them dependent on friends or volunteers for relationships. The impact of demographic trends will continue to grow as more blended families grow older.

Aged care providers need to seriously consider how new intimacies may be established for older residents. This may come in the form of examining health professional relationships with residents and the more effective use of volunteers with adequate training in human communication skills. For frail elderly people to find new intimacies is central to having hope and to finding meaning in life.

Conclusion

Among this group of nursing home residents loss of relationship was common. To deal effectively with this important task of ageing may have budget implications for aged care, both for the increasing numbers of older people living alone in the community, and also for those who reside in nursing homes. Yet the cost of caring for older people who feel nourished through inclusive and effective relationships may in the long term be lower than treating the effects of isolation, loneliness and depression in aged care. Research is needed to examine the effects of changed cultures and establishment of effective relationships on the well-being of residents within aged care.

Summary

- *Research shows that the need for close relationship does not diminish in later life.*

- *Among a group of nursing home residents loss of relationship was common, with 80 per cent of the sample being widowed. Not one of those who had a spouse alive shared accommodation with their spouse.*

- *Loss of significant long-term relationship left elderly people in need of the development of new relationships and new intimacies in an aged care facility.*

- *The task of establishing new relationships becomes even more important and urgent at a time when these people do not have the skills and energy to establish new relationships.*

- *Staff have important roles in supporting and affirming frail older people, sometimes even being the only significant friends these older people have.*

CHAPTER 13

Grief, Death, Dying and Spirituality in an Aged Care Facility

Death and dying in later life

Current western societies are ageing societies that continue to deny that death is part of life. Guroian (1996, p.29) writes of this denial of death, suggesting that as we have removed death from 'the moral sphere of the home', with a consequential move of the scene of death to the technological environment of hospitals, we have also become accomplices in our own spiritual suicide. Guroian notes that one consequence of this is a growing insensitivity to those who are terminally ill. In one way medical technology has removed us from the need to face death on a personal level, and death most commonly occurs in clinical and institutional surroundings. Often we assure ourselves that this move will provide the best treatment for our loved one. Yet, as Guroian states:

> A society that routinely commits its elderly and chronically and terminally ill members to institutional care away from loved ones is a society in jeopardy of losing its soul and becoming truly monstrous. There is, in fact, nothing more monstrous or deadly than shutting our fellow human beings off from love. (p.33)

These are strong words, and they present a challenge to the very way that frail elderly and terminally ill people are routinely cared for. While this move during the twentieth century to have more deaths occur in hospitals was in some part influenced by social changes and advances in medical technology:

> It remains the case that our elaborate technologies often separate people from those whose love they need most of all when they are dying. And it is not only

those who are dying who are deprived by this mechanization of medicine and institutionalization of death. Consciously or unconsciously, we all begin to anticipate in fear the same isolation and abandonment when our turn comes. (p.29)

While this may not be so much the case for older adults dying in aged care facilities, it is certainly by now part of the ethos surrounding death in our society. Those who work in aged care have been enculturated into this way of regarding death and at least some, maybe a high proportion, of aged care staff, will find it distressing coming face to face with death. Death has become medicalized and removed from the mainstream of life. Many people do not experience death in anyone close to them until late in life, and then often death occurs in a hospital, not at home.

Thus death is still very much seen as a failure in at least some parts of the acute health care systems of western societies. At times I find it challenging to assist some nursing students to come to terms with their own attitudes towards people who are dying. Some of them have never come near to death, and they cannot imagine what it can be like to be near to people who are dying. Some, not unnaturally, project their fears onto residents and patients they care for.

One of the most profound clinical nursing experiences I have had with students has been to walk the journey with them and a dying patient or resident, and where possible, the resident's family. There is a particular case that I have in mind, where I was with a small group of nursing students in a district hospital and an elderly woman was dying. The journey involved the students and me working together to provide wholistic care, including management of distress and pain, provision of fluids as required, the care of mouth, keeping the person comfortable and my modelling presence with the dying person. Importantly this clinical experience of caring for a dying person also involved journeying with the students and their personal experiences of grief. It was a time of closure and coming to the end for the person who was dying and their family, and also a time of learning and almost a sense of awe, in the presence of the drama of life that was being played out in our presence. We spent a long time reflecting and debriefing on the journey that we had shared, a time of privilege for all involved. It is not easy to walk that journey into death in a busy hospital setting, but sometimes the busyness of a hospital is not so much related to the need of care to patients, but the business of being a hospital. I am suggesting that hospitals are not good places to die: the context is wrong, hospitals are about preserving life, often at all costs, not about honouring life and letting it go.

Dying and fear of dying

Dying alone is a fear for many older people and the journey into death is feared by many. Yet all the participants in this study had personal experience of grief through the deaths of at least someone close to them. Now they were facing their own dying. Forty-five per cent of participants in the residential group study expressed fears related to the process of dying and/or losing control of their situation. However, this is lower than the 100 per cent of independent living older people who expressed fears of future vulnerability. The final career, that is the journey into death, is unknown still today; each of us has to make that journey, unless we meet with sudden death. Death reminds us of our fallibility in a society where:

> Death has become a symbol of our precarious societal condition. It reminds us that we are fallible and fragile within a society built upon 'expendableness,' throwaway resources built by dispensable workers. Coupled with the idea that death is proof of our ontic contingency, death takes on a power that makes it 'socially unacceptable'. (Jones 2001, p.103)

Jones says we seek to compartmentalize death, and in a way our nursing homes do that well. Older people who are dying are removed from the wider society to the safety of an aged care facility. Nursing homes are sometimes referred to as 'God's Waiting Room', and yet dying and death are not often spoken of in nursing homes. Often the societal attitudes of death denial carry over in attitudes of the staff of aged care facilities. The staff are, after all, members of society and reflect the attitudes of society towards dying and death. In an aged care facility, death is common and needs acknowledgement – it is hard to deal effectively with something that is not named. Often, both in the aged care environment and in the wider society, the word 'death' is not used but rather people talk about someone 'passing on' or 'passed away' or some similar term.

Two perceptions of grief in aged care: staff and residents

There are two perceptions of grief that are experienced in aged care facilities. First, the residents (and many of their families) who already know grief personally, and second, the staff, many of whom have not known personal grief. Thus a wide gulf of experience that includes membership of different cultural groups as well as different generations may separate staff from the multiple experiences of death among the residents. The younger people often employed in aged care may have little experience of grief, and some may have experienced grief, but not dealt with it effectively due to societal attitudes of denial of death.

Talking of dying and death

If we consider dying as the last career in a long life that has probably held a number of careers, this has important implications for people approaching the end of life. Just as other taboo topics like sex and cancer have come into the open in recent decades, it is now time for death to be openly acknowledged, spoken about and prepared for. A central component of the process of dying is the spiritual dimension. In an earlier study of staff awareness of spirituality in aged care (MacKinlay 2001e) I asked registered nurses to use a questionnaire on spiritual well-being (Highfield 1989) with residents they cared for at their place of employment. This questionnaire raised issues around death in a sensitive way, and the staff were surprised that some of the residents expressed a wish to speak of dying and death. It is noted that prior to this survey a number of the registered nurses were reluctant to raise issues of death and dying with the residents. Comments from these nurses after the surveys included 'it was like opening the floodgates'. These elderly residents did wish to speak of these issues; on the other hand, some other residents did not wish to speak of their grief.

Among the older people in this study, only 2 out of the 20 frail elderly people interviewed did not wish to speak about dying, and when I asked them, they did not object to being asked. Margaret had a son who had died. She did not go into details, it was sufficient for her simply to name to me the nature of her loss. Sonya too said she had experienced a lot of grief, but she didn't want to talk about it because it stressed her too much. It is noted that it is important to be sensitive to whether the resident does wish to discuss issues of dying and death; however, if the topic is not raised, residents may feel uncomfortable about raising it themselves, even if they do wish to speak of it. Giving permission for residents to speak of personal and difficult issues is an important aspect of care.

At a hostel for older people, I began a first meeting with a woman who has dementia, asking her where she found meaning in life. She began with these words: 'I've had a good life, I love this world and all creation, and I can feel God's presence so much more lately, [she paused] I think it won't be long before I die.' Her response to my question on life-meaning suggests that questions surrounding the topic of death are on the minds of at least some elderly residents. Unless staff working with elderly people are comfortable discussing these issues and can affirm the possibility of raising such sensitive issues with those they care for, then the questions may go unasked and, of course, unexplored.

Concern not to ask intrusive and/or personal questions and not to ask residents about their religious or spiritual beliefs may have such a high priority that residents are never asked. Yet, equally personal questions relating to physical status, such as bowel movements are quite regularly asked and not always only within earshot of the person being questioned. Somehow questions of spirituality are too frequently relegated to the background. People who are resident in aged care facilities may be only too well aware that this is likely to be their last place of residence before they die, yet, often in nursing homes, programmes and activities seem designed to prevent dying or death being mentioned. Thus elderly residents feel alone in God's waiting room.

Religious and spiritual beliefs in bereavement

So, are religious and/or spiritual beliefs important in the process of bereavement? Walsh *et al.* (2002) conducted a prospective study (the participants were recruited before they were bereaved) of how religious beliefs affected subsequent bereavement. This study was conducted in the UK in a secular palliative care unit that had no religious affiliation. In their sample, a total of 21 out of 129 people (16%) reported no religious or spiritual belief; 53 (41% of all participants) reported spiritual beliefs of low intensity and 55 (43%) reported strongly held beliefs. Marital status and ethnic origin were significantly related to spiritual belief, people with partners had stronger beliefs, and almost everyone in the low belief group was white. Ninety-five participants (74%) completed all follow up assessments. The study found those with strongly held spiritual beliefs recovered from their bereavement in a linear fashion, whereas those with low strength of belief showed little change by nine months but recovered rapidly thereafter. Participants with no spiritual beliefs showed a temporary gain at nine months but their symptoms of grief had intensified again by the final assessment.

The effect of belief remained significant when they entered the demographic variables of sex and age into the model. Adding social isolation and emotional closeness of the study participant to the deceased reduced the effect of strength of belief. Closeness to the dying patient predicted higher grief scores at all follow ups. It is noted that finding intimacy is one of the main spiritual tasks in ageing (MacKinlay 2001a), thus the effects of closeness and isolation found in this study are consistent with these spiritual tasks.

Walsh *et al.* (2002, p.1554) note:

> spiritual beliefs may provide an existential framework in which grief is resolved more readily. Most spiritual beliefs, whether or not associated with religious practice, contain tenets about the course of human life and existence beyond it. Strong beliefs may be a proxy for better adjustment and less psychological

distress. But our analysis suggests that strength of belief affected the course of bereavement, independently of psychological status.

It is important to note that Walsh *et al.* see beliefs as separate from psychological status; too often, in grief work and counselling, psychological needs are addressed at the expense of spiritual needs. Further, Walsh *et al.* concluded that the absence of spiritual belief is a risk factor for delayed or complicated grief, although replication of the study would strengthen their findings. Most palliative care units try to involve family members and friends who are important and close to the person dying. However, attention to spiritual matters may be a component in this work that is often overlooked or avoided by secular services. Walsh *et al.* are careful not to say that an intervention concerning spiritual matters is appropriate for people with no professed beliefs. Rather, their findings might help to identify people who are having difficulty in readjusting to life after their loss (p.1554). In an aged care facility providing a range of services, pastoral care and perhaps other types of grief counselling may be needed for people with no religious belief. Referral to community-based care, for those whose bereavement may be likely to be complicated, should be considered. However, it is noted that in numbers of aged care facilities pastoral care teams work ecumenically and will provide care that is not religion-based for those without professed beliefs.

Spiritual tasks of ageing and grief, dying and death

The spiritual tasks of ageing (MacKinlay 2001a) provide a framework for the final journey towards death. One of the important spiritual tasks is to make sense of the life we have lived, to find meaning and purpose in our lives as we come to the end. In applying the model of spiritual tasks, ultimate meaning lies at the centre, and the means of finding ultimate meaning lies in the spiritual tasks of transcending loss, disabilities, the loss of energy and dealing with pain; in coming to final life-meanings; finding hope in the midst of frailty and/or suffering. A final task that is important to the person facing death is finding intimacy with God and/or others. Having someone to walk that journey into death is a blessing for the person dying, and a privilege for the person travelling that final journey with them. This may only happen when dying can be shared and openly spoken about, with a hope of overcoming much of the stigma and sense of failure that death is treated with in the present society, which expects that even death can be 'cured'. Applying the spiritual tasks of ageing model may help guide the broad areas for conversation with the resident.

Experiences of grief among aged care residents

Grief had deeply and often touched the lives of the older nursing home residents in this study. Andrew's wife had died about a month before the interview. He spoke of his grief around the theme of their home. I asked him: 'What gives you energy for keeping on going in life now?' He replied:

> I would have told you without hesitation if you, [had asked] a few weeks ago I was keen on getting my wife well again not knowing that she'd never get better... Anyway, my wife dying it was to be, and the sadness of the house sitting there doing nothing seems to be a waste. I doubt if we'll ever go back there.

A little while later he said: 'my wife and I [decided] some months ago that we are too old for gardening anymore'. When I asked him directly about his grief later in the interview he changed the subject. Yet he returned to talk about his wife frequently during the interview. He said that he felt more deeply about God after his wife's funeral. Andrew was still struggling with the reality of his wife's death and its meaning for him.

As de Vries (2001) has written, the grieving process does not include closure of the relationship with a loved one, but a reprocessing of this relationship, to hold it as a part of life, even though that person is no longer there. For many older people the loss of a spouse through death is devastating, as it terminates an intimate relationship of perhaps 50 or more years. It seems natural that in grief, the bereaved person will be so aware of the absence of their loved one, while at the same time part of the work of grief is to find a new way of relating to this lost person and incorporating them into the continuing fabric of living.

Grief comes from a variety of losses

Like many other older people Agnes stated she is not afraid to die. In summing up her life Agnes said: 'I've had a good life and did things I wanted to do. Maybe it might have been better with grandchildren but I can't help that.' Not having grandchildren was a regret for Agnes and the loss of something she had hoped for, but she had grown to accept it. Agnes also has grief for the death of her husband and loss of two babies who died soon after birth. Those losses are now part of Agnes' identity.

It is now believed that grief is not only a response to what once was, that is – former relationships – but is also evidence of what persists. What persists is an enduring but changed relationship with the deceased person. Part of the grieving process is the struggle to establish a place in the griever's life for that changed relationship (de Vries 2001). In keeping with this perspective of grief Rebecca remembers her husband, who died some years before, she thought it was 1975. She said that his loss was still hard for her.

Older adults have experienced many losses through their lives. The main grief Angus had experienced was over the death of his wife 15 years ago; a sister died many years ago. Dora said about grief: 'Oh it's a big part, you never, never ever lose track of your husband.' He died about 16 years ago.

Grace's husband died about seven weeks before the interview. She said she has 'a little cry in my bedroom at night'. She talked about the funeral, saying she is coping 'OK'. And then she said: 'I'm lucky to be alive.' I asked Grace what she looks forward to now and she replied: 'To see [husband] in Heaven.' It is still important for Grace to be able to talk of her grief. And it may be that staff are the only people with whom she can talk. If they are too busy – there is no one.

Joyce has experienced much grief; her mother had left her and her father when she was less than 10 years of age. Her father cared for her, but he died in his 50s. Her husband also died before he was 45. She apparently coped very well with bringing up a young family by herself. Then her son committed suicide a couple of years ago. She talked of her grief and pain surrounding these losses. Despite the pain, she had a deep sense of acceptance and joy in life. At the same time, early in the interview Joyce remarked that she didn't think about emotional and spiritual supports. The death of an adult child through suicide, as Joyce had experienced, is likely to be very difficult to grieve. At the time I talked with Joyce, she said she has no fears as she faces the future:

> Well I don't have any, I'm not frightened of dying, I've got no fears about that, the only fear I've got is that living too long and becoming totally useless like this... I mean, firstly I can wipe my own bottom. Now I can do that and I can feed myself, so those two things if I can hang onto. I think I always have my mind on something...it would gradually get worse, you know, then of course, it affects you, it does affect your heart, the muscle, the muscle where...you know, it's not likely to kill me overnight. So I'll make the most of it while I'm here, you know [laughs]. My grandchildren are so loving and caring you know, so...

Joyce said she had trouble in talking of God and she has questioned why she had lost so many important relationships. Even so, Joyce continues to attend church services, and it would seem she obtains some comfort from them:

> I find it hard to really think that He [God] helped me because I mean, you know of the things that happened in my life and I think is there a God there? You

know I mean, I still go to church here most Thursdays I mean I'm not an atheist, sometimes I think if there is still a God there He wouldn't let those things happen to people.

Joyce has raised a question that is common in human experience. While this is not a theological book, this question deserves reflection and is a question that will be heard and asked by those who work in aged care. In the Christian experience, first we acknowledge that we live in a world where death had been defeated through the cross and resurrection. Thus for Christians, death does not mean annihilation. However, we still live in an imperfect world where suffering and pain do occur. God walks with us in our pain and suffering. A world in which a god controls all would deny human freedom, creativity and dignity.

The stories of farmers

Bert too had experienced his share of grief and he described the death of his son at 43 years of age, about three years before. This is a particularly hard grief for a parent. He said:

We had six sons; we had a boy who was accidentally shot about three years ago… He was out shooting and he came back to the car that was on the highway, and I haven't got any, any evidence of what happened, he was getting through the fence and it was a loaded rifle, so that's where they found him, he was halfway through the fence… So we ended up with one son less.

Farmers and their families often seem closer to the rhythm of life and death in creation than city folk. The death of Bert's son was a tragedy, and while this had touched Bert deeply, his life goes on. This experience of loss is somehow woven into the fabric of Bert's life. Another source of grief for Bert was selling his farm, about 13 years before the interview, to move into a city to retire. The farm had been part of their lives for more than a generation, and it formed one aspect of his identity; this was a big loss that was also associated with his ability to provide for his family as well as a sense of meaning in his life. Perhaps the life experience of rural living keeps people more grounded through the many experiences that form a rich tapestry of life, with grief and new life interspersed. In these circumstances much grief work has been accomplished by the time the person is in the later stages of a long life.

Katie had lived on a dairy farm with her family and she spoke of that part of her life and her husband's death:

I forget how many cows we used to milk, I never used to, but he used to, and his helper, but it was a good life, we had our own little garden there and our veggie garden as well in our…it was…we were happy, although we didn't see people very often but we were happy within ourselves, we didn't need other people to make us happy, no. But I missed him when he went though because no one, you'd turn around to say something and there's no one there. It would be about 10 or 12 years now and it takes a while to get used to being on your own because you tend to turn around to say something and there's nobody there. But he was a wonderful man! Oh yes, very sick when he went so…

Two of her four children had died in recent years, a son in a car accident and a daughter from cancer. And now another daughter had just had major cardiac surgery. Katie struggled to find meaning in these losses, and she remarked several times that it would really help her if she had someone with whom she could talk about her family.

Katie spoke of the fears she had experienced when her husband died:

Oh yes, I'm not so bad now but I did then afterwards, on my own because it's the most dreadful feeling to know that you're in a house on your own, there's nobody there that you can call out to if you get sick or if you just feel a bit lonely, you don't…it's a terrible feeling. And the fact of being together for so long…

I responded: 'And now that you're in the nursing home do you still have the same sort of fears?' Katie replied:

No I don't worry about those sorts of things now because I think well it's pointless. I'm going to be here for the rest of my life however long or short it's going to be, I don't know, so I've just got to make the most of what I've got here. Perhaps as time goes on I might make more friends, you know.

Katie was acutely aware that she would end her life in this aged care facility. She seemed to be wanting to work through her life and its meaning and would have valued a listening friend or staff member. Her sense of loneliness was obvious.

Experiences of grief and faith over the lifespan

Bob spoke of his grief, particularly of his mother who died when he was 11 or 12 years of age. He experienced that as a 'terrible trauma':

Because of the trauma you not prepared for you know, war and that you might be prepared that something is going to happen but in peace time…it's had an effect on me. But it made me change, not from the grief; [it] came mainly from the feeling that there was someone around. That made the world, gave the world much more meaning than everyone would normally seem to have.

Bob said that after his mother died it brought him into a closer realization of the presence of God. His father also died while he was still a child.

> It did. But being a young lad I hadn't thought about that before very much, you know, at that age. Except that I also had the same thing only in a different way, it happened with my son, who was only six when he died.

Bob reflected on how his loss of his parents had affected him as a child:

> But they were the most wonderful people and I could never be influenced from the point of view that I had a feeling they were such wonderful people, about them, my parents I couldn't afford to be, you know…I was awfully lonely, after all let's be honest, it's these things that affect you.

Bob spoke about the death of his mother and his faith development:

> No to tell you…when mum died as she did in a car accident and I was told…it seemed easier to work out, if I believed in God, and I mean there were all the worldly things at the start, a peculiar world, there's a life and death kind of thing that other people had for you. Didn't seem at all like a problem you know. Still doesn't seem a problem. Anyway enough said; how does it rebound on your behaviour, well it had a pretty big effect on my behaviour, but I haven't need to have anything curtailed with my behaviour, nobody's asked me to be anything but what I am, which is important. And I saw people so close to sickness, probably a bigger message in there, that one day I'll be able to work out for myself, and pass on to others. But I think there's a bigger message there to be found; that I could be useful, in telling people how in trouble, all I felt was to serve God, which was perhaps be helpful to them.

Bob spoke at length about his faith and the grief through his life and as he spoke there were tears in his eyes. This was important time for Bob to be able to process his grief. Again, the importance of someone having time to listen is emphasized; death is often an unspoken topic in aged care facilities.

These older people were still on their final career of life, reflecting on life-meanings, reframing and moving towards final life-meanings. There is still struggle, and tension in some parts of their lives. The processing will probably continue until their death.

Moving into a nursing home

Not all loss and grief in later life is associated with death, but the loss of independent residence is an important loss. It is both a real loss and at the same time, symbolic of other losses, for example, moving to a nursing home also signifies a loss of control over activities of daily living, a loss of the opportunities for intimacy and a general loss of freedom. Consequently, deciding to move from home to an aged care facility is one the hardest decisions that older people and their families face. Bert found it hard settling into the nursing home. He had been fully involved in making the decision to move, but the loss of the closeness of relationship with his wife, who still lived at home, was hard. Bert felt that the move had given him more security, but:

> I don't like the rest of it. As a matter of fact I don't aim ever to like it. I suppose depending on how long the future I've got. But there's not much purpose in being in one of those places, there's not a great purpose of being able, well it's a world all of it's own. You're not achieving, or at least, I don't feel I'm achieving anything.

Veronica's husband died six years ago; she says she still gets too upset to talk about his death. Recent studies have shown that older people express strong feelings for people who have died, and particularly so for parents and partners (Troll 2001). This seems to run contrary to Bowlby's (1980) description of the process of mourning, that resolves by detachment from the dead person. Veronica was still very much attached in her relationship with her husband. She also gets upset when other residents in the nursing home die. This is an important area for spiritual and pastoral care to be involved with grief work in the nursing home. Veronica remarked that just last week a woman she had known since she was admitted to this nursing home two years ago died, and she is really missing her. It is also a source of sadness for Veronica that she has to be in a nursing home. Again, this woman is dealing with multiple grief and loss.

Fear of death

Charlie was one of only two people from both these studies (MacKinlay 1998; 2001a) who said they feared death. Others in the studies drew a distinction of being fearful of the process of dying but not of being dead in later life. Most informants, however, feared a protracted and painful path to death.

Other concerns Charlie has relate to his former wife; they were divorced, apparently many years ago, and it appeared that Charlie had never really resolved the loss of that relationship. Charlie feels he has handled the grief badly. He became angry as I asked further questions there, so I did not pursue that line of questioning. Yet later in the interview, Charlie raised the question of death himself and he said: 'Everyone does no matter what they say, they fear death. I know I've tasted death.' I asked him if he would like to talk to someone about death and dying, he replied: 'Yes'. I asked who he might like to talk to, and he replied: 'My ex-wife.' But in fact, Charlie said he thought she would not want to talk with him.

Then I asked Charlie: 'Is there anyone else that you think might be able to help…who could perhaps listen to you about your fears?' His response: 'No,' he said, very perceptively, 'they all want to talk, no one wants to listen.' As the interview progressed I asked Charlie when he first became aware of God. He answered, that it was about the age of 14. I asked what this first awareness was through and he replied: 'fear of death'. He could not remember the circumstances. Charlie had spent seven years in the navy and seemed not to want to talk about his time there. Overall Charlie seemed isolated with few contacts in the nursing home, he could be described as a 'loner', and he appeared to block possibilities of help; it may take considerable skill and time to gain his trust.

Elaine, on the other hand, seemed to have learnt to overcome many of her losses and disabilities; she has in a sense transcended many of her problems. In this is a way of coping with life, through pain, and disability and grief. She spoke of her room mate at the home dying, just a week before I spoke with her, and she said: 'That put me back this last week, you know, I'm starting to get over that again now.' She reflected about the former room mate:

> Oh she was a good room mate you know, we got along so well together, and she was so crook the last few days. Every morning you'd wake up and you'd look over and it didn't matter whether it was 5 o'clock in the morning and she'd be sitting in the corner in her chair, she couldn't sleep, you know. And it was that way after she'd gone. Every time I woke up I could see her sitting in the chair. So I took her seat, I sit in that corner now and I can't see her, you know, it's sort of relief that [pause].
>
> That was hard the last night, the poor thing, she was trying to tell me something, but I couldn't catch it, and that sort of got me down, you know, what was she trying to tell me, and I couldn't hear it, you know. As I say I'm over that now and every day I'm getting better.

As I thought about her reflection, I kept wondering what it was that the dying woman had been trying to say, maybe she needed help in the last stages of her life. We cannot be sure what it might have been. And I wondered, if the nurses had been aware of this woman's needs, or if there had been pastoral care staff available, may they have picked up on some issue? It seems to me that what the dying woman wanted was most likely to be some emotional and spiritual support, perhaps a question answered, an assurance, even that she was not alone as she died. I can only make assumptions.

Dying alone: how do we bring love into the nursing home?

It has been said on many occasions that no one should have to die alone. It seems to me that at least some people in nursing homes do die alone. What can be done? Perhaps nurses who are tuned to the spiritual needs of older people might be able to give spiritual care, and be present to them in their need. Then my thoughts turn to Elaine, and her concerns; she couldn't make out what the dying woman wanted to say. I wonder if there was a fear there for Elaine too, will she have a need before she dies, and find no one to help? I remember an elderly woman who was living alone in another study (MacKinlay 1998) who said she was afraid of dying and not being found for a week, as had happened to her friend.

Is there a solution to the problem of being alone when dying? Is it education? Is it funding and increased staff levels? Is it increased awareness of spiritual needs? No one should have to die alone, unless they genuinely choose to do so. While it seems important not to regard aged care from a medical model, as this opens up possibilities for wholeness of life in the later years, it is also important within this wholistic model to affirm the process of dying as a natural part of living.

Elaine was the only person who spoke of euthanasia. When I asked her if there were any things she was worried about, she said she was worried about being unable to help herself as she became more frail and she went on:

> When you see others can't move in their beds, got to be fed and things like that, I wouldn't like come to that. I still say, I always did say when you come to that and you're old and know you're not going to get better, that law should come in that you can say put me to sleep.

I wanted to be sure how she understood euthanasia, so I asked: 'When you say that, you're sort of saying that you'd be wanting someone to actually give you an injection or something, and end it at that point?'

Elaine replied: 'Yes, 'cause I can't see any sense laying around.' Still exploring, I asked her: 'Rather than say if you were really very, very ill, that they just maybe wouldn't treat you or give you antibiotics, do you see a difference between the two things?' Elaine replied:

> Yes, I don't think that any use in giving us stuff just to keep you alive, when you know you can't get any better, and just laying there waiting for the last breath to go. I can't see, it's – it's a big strain on your family and it's no good to yourself. I always think that law should come in.

Love and compassion are needed to walk with these older people. It may be that an older person's wish for death may be because they see no hope in life. However, it may also be because they have walked their journey to the end, and know that God waits for them. In this case, they are truly ready to die. If we are able to recover the final career of life that leads into death, then some of the fear that surrounds death may be dissipated.

Ageing, disability and quality of life

A number of studies have shown a wide discrepancy between perceptions of quality of life of staff and people with disabilities. One very telling study (Bach, Campagnolo and Hoeman 1991, in Kilner, Miller and Pellegrino 1996) surveyed 82 ventilator assisted persons with Duchenne muscular dystrophy (DMD) and found that persons with DMD 'reported nearly the same rate of life satisfaction as the general population' (p.196). When surveying non-disabled emergency room (ER) providers and quadriplegic spinal cord injury survivors (Gerhardt *et al.* 1994, in Kilner, Miller and Pellegrino 1996) it was found that both groups rated themselves at 95 per cent as persons of worth. However, when the ER group were then asked to rate themselves as persons of worth, should they sustain injury leading to quadriplegia, these same staff rated themselves at only 55 per cent, a 40 per cent decline in worth. This same kind of perception is also common among nursing students, in fact one group of students questioned an assessment form that we were using with elderly people, saying that I should not ask residents if their life was worth living, as it could be assumed not to be worth living, and it was suggested this question was too personal to ask.

However, as can be seen from the studies cited above, perception of quality of life between health professionals and patients or residents may differ considerably. Differences in perception may occur because autonomy is consistently promoted as one of the highest values in western society; consequently, if a person can no longer retain their autonomy, their quality of life is assumed to decline. These staff perceptions of quality of life for severely disabled and/or older people will have enormous implications for the quality and range of options for care that will be available to these people.

The final career: dying well

In our desire to remove dying and death from within the family setting to institutions we have medicalized dying and death and have lost the knowledge of the way to die (Heinz 1994; MacKinlay 2001a). For residents in aged care, the journey on the final career of life may have begun before being admitted to aged care, or their admission may have raised their awareness of their impending mortality. (Of course, some people may be temporary residents in aged care, being there for respite care before returning home.) One of the important tasks in residential aged care is to make the final journey well. The final career consists of two parts, to hand on one's story to the next generation and to make the journey to death. Bonnie reflected on her stage in the journey:

> Yes, I mean I'm prepared to die, I'm not frightened of dying as you can imagine. But OK Lord, if I'm still to be here give me something to do, let there be some reason, and I've found as I go through, been through life latterly, that I must sow a few seeds somewhere, because different ones say now, you know you said so and so last week, I'm mean I'd forgotten that.

Perhaps what is needed is a midwife for dying; that is palliative care in residential aged care. The need overwhelmingly is for someone to walk the final journey with these elderly people. We have midwives trained to assist at our birth into this world; so we need to develop skills that will enable carers to walk the journey towards death with the elderly person who is in the process of dying. The term 'a good death' has come to mean, to those who advocate for euthanasia, a physician assisted death or assisted suicide.

A good death for an older person should mean a death with true dignity, where the dying person is able to come to final life-meanings and is able to be at peace with themselves and with God and to give up their soul, that is to die spiritually, when the time is right. Courage is needed to deny the use of futile treatments and heroic actions, and a sense of wisdom to know when the time is right. Dying with dignity means to have one's family and friends with you, or when they cannot be, then some person, that we may call the midwife for that final journey, should be with the dying person. Even in death there are different wishes, and some people do seem to want to spend the very last time alone, sometimes waiting until loved ones are out of the room before dying.

Dora spoke about her current situation: 'Well firstly it's my faith that keeps me going and secondly it's the help I'm getting here with physio and the help with the nurses and thirdly I wonder why God doesn't take me when I pray every night that He will.' This is a question many residents ask. The meaning lying behind the question may differ depending on the people who ask it, for example Dora, a Christian, sees that her life is over and she is waiting to die and go to be with the Lord. Others may ask the question out of a sense of despair and hopelessness. The role of palliative care and pastoral care is to bring ageing and palliative care together, palliative care is not only for those dying from cancer, and palliative care must be truly wholistic, including physical, psychological, social, cultural and spiritual care.

An important part of this journey, for most people, is to have someone to walk with the dying person on their journey, so that the person may make this final journey in the presence of loved ones, respected and cared for until the end of the journey.

Some older people do seem to come to a time of peace and the end of the struggle before they die, and this seems obvious to those about them, although those who observe might not know the source of the peace. Barbato (2002) writes of the importance of being with people who are dying, even when they have slipped into a coma, and can no longer seem to respond to those around them. While they are still alive, they may still be aware and processing life experiences, although it seems that the responses to others and to their environment becomes more selective. At this stage, often the person will respond only to events that are meaningful to them. For example, there are many accounts of elderly people who live until their child or sibling has travelled from a great distance to be with them before dying, perhaps waking from a coma to say their goodbyes.

Funeral rites and ceremonies

Specific religious needs of older people are dealt with in Chapter 9. Rituals and services for burial of the dead will be carried out according to the established rites of the different religious faiths and it is important to honour the particular faiths and traditions (Cohen *et al.* 2000). Memorial services are held in many nursing homes, some are held for particular people, while in other settings regular services give the families and staff the opportunity to openly acknowledge their grief for all the deaths that have occurred in the home over a period of time, perhaps every three months, perhaps annually. It is important to acknowledge and include residents in these services.

These are important marks in the process of grieving for family, friends and, within an aged care facility, both the other residents and the staff. In my earlier work in aged care (MacKinlay 2001a; 2001b) I found that death was not a topic that many residents or staff felt comfortable with. A task of the chaplain in aged care contexts is to help family, residents and staff to acknowledge the grief and to begin the process of grieving.

Horst (2000) in a study of the impact of death of a resident on relationships in a nursing home setting in Canada, found that those bereaved spoke of the empty space left by the resident who had died and the comfort they received through rituals offered both in the facility and wider community-based memorial services. At the same time staff and residents spoke of their distress at the sudden replacement of another resident in the room the person who had died had lived in. That space, it seemed, took on a sacred quality and ritual was needed to 'honour that space, to give thanks for it, and to affirm the lasting contribution that the one who had occupied it has made' (p.41) It was suggested that much of this occurs in the memorial services that are commonly held in nursing homes, but Horst was adding that this space, once occupied by the resident, should be the site of recognition for those who had most deeply shared and been touched by the life of this person. This ritual would aim to connect to the Holy and bring healing, and affirm the work of grieving for all members of this community. It would also, finally, prepare the way to welcoming the new resident to that sacred space.

Staff and grief and loss in aged care facilities

The previous grief experiences of staff may be raised as they again lose people they have cared for through death. Continuing education is valuable in assisting staff to acknowledge grief in their lives and to understand something about dying and grief. This is especially needed in the current death denying cultures that most of us live in. Rituals like those suggested by Horst may assist staff to healing in their own life journeys and enable them to walk with those they care for, family, staff and residents.

Conclusion

The fourth age of life is the time of the final life career, the time when the person may become more aware of their own mortality and begin preparing for dying and death. It seems that most people fear what the dying process might bring, though few older people seem to fear death itself. Much can be done to walk this journey into death with those who are dying.

Fortunately now, principles of palliative care are being practised in aged care. Older people might not always want to talk about dying, but dying and death are important topics at certain times.

There is work to be done as older people come to accept the meaning of their life journeys and to actively engage in the final career of life. There will be the need to process and revise provisional life-meanings that were set down in earlier life, perhaps to seek reconciliation with others, to celebrate life, and to say goodbye to family and friends. Pastoral care may be very important at these times. On the other hand, some older people will continue to deny death, and not wish to speak of it. These people also need sensitive pastoral and spiritual care: care that respects their need, either to talk, or not to talk, and to be listened to.

Summary

- *Many people in western societies do not experience death in anyone close to them until late in life, and then often death occurs in a hospital, not at home.*

- *Dying alone is a fear of many older people and the journey into death is feared by many.*

- *Grief in ageing affects older people, their families, friends, staff and other residents.*

- *Giving permission for residents to speak of personal and difficult issues, including dying, is an important aspect of care.*

- *Finding meaning in the last career of life is a spiritual journey into death.*

- *The means of finding ultimate meaning lie in the spiritual tasks of transcending loss, disabilities, the loss of energy and dealing with pain; in coming to final life-meanings; finding hope in the midst of frailty and/or suffering.*

- *A final task that is important to the person facing death is finding intimacy, with God and/or others.*

- *Walking this final journey in life with the one dying is a special position for those privileged to be a part of this journey.*

- *A task of the chaplain in aged care is to help family, residents and staff acknowledge the grief and to begin the process of grieving.*

- *Funerals and memorial services provide an important basis for grieving.*

- *Rituals before and after death are important markers of events; these should be sensitively developed with input from those who grieve.*

CHAPTER 14

Ethical Issues in the Fourth Age of Life

Throughout the book, ethical issues have been raised and addressed, to some extent implicitly. In this chapter, ethical aspects of care are addressed more explicitly. A number of important ethical issues arise in later life; the more obvious are end of life care and advance directives; assisted suicide and euthanasia; issues of autonomy, consent and competency; issues of quality of life and access to appropriate health care services. This chapter cannot cover the whole field of ethical issues in ageing, but attempts to highlight the issues. The list of further reading at the end of the chapter provides valuable resources.

How do we care for the frail, the weak and vulnerable people in our complex post-modern societies? What is the duty to care? What are the responsibilities and rights of older people to provide for their own care? What are the responsibilities and rights of those who provide the care?

There are many ethical issues in aged care. One of the most difficult currently surrounds questions of end of life care. With increasing means of extending life, an expectation may develop that life must be prolonged, no matter what the quality of life experienced by the individual. Underlying these struggles, to come to terms with questions and decisions, between what is possible and what is morally appropriate, lie some very basic questions that warrant exploration. First, what does it mean to be old and living in a western society in the early twenty-first century? What does it mean to be old and suffer? And what does it mean to grow old, and be isolated and rejected? These are deeply ethical questions that an ageing society must grapple with.

Being old and living in a western society in the early twenty-first century

Most western societies these days are both multicultural and multifaith. These changes from a mono-faith and mono-cultural society create new scenarios for setting values and moral perspectives. Most western societies also have embraced post-modernism with its set of relative values and humanism. Thus there are a number of ways that health providers might look at ethical issues of ageing, just as there will be different ways that elderly people may look at ethical issues affecting them.

A biomedical perspective on ethics will emphasize genetic breakthroughs and the use of sophisticated technological interventions to prevent and repair the physiological problems of ageing. Thus ethics approached from a bio-medical perspective may include the search for eternal youth, translated into an ageing view of how to delay/deny the ageing process. This ethical perspective will focus on the search for the greatest good for all. At the same time, it will focus on maintaining personal autonomy and the ethical principles of bene-ficence and non-maleficence. A psychosocial perspective on ethics in later life will emphasize ways of creating a society in which older adults can relate effectively, and live active and creative lives. That also includes a search for autonomy and human rights. A spiritual perspective on ethics will emphasize the need for community and for care of the weak and vulnerable, and growing to wholeness in later life. Thus the spiritual approach in later life is a search for meaning and integrity in life, and relationship with God and/or with others.

The value of the lives of older adults

On what basis do we argue for the value of life in later life? Perhaps, at a more basic level, on what do we base the value of human life at any age? There are a number of perspectives from which we can respond, perhaps to consider the years left to live, and therefore the potential to give to the community; perhaps the contribution of the person to others during their lifetime. The former view may give younger people potentially more value than older people, as it could be argued that the young ones have not yet had a chance to live and contribute, while older people have had their chance, their experiences and use of resources; therefore their lives are of less value. Do we value human *doings* or *beings*? The major faiths of the world hold views of the sacredness of life, and the value of life in the Abrahamic faiths lies in humans being created in the image of God.

Being old and suffering

It has been said that the way a nation treats its old, its weak and its vulnerable is the measure of that nation. An ethical perspective that values autonomy and the ability to produce goods and make a contribution to society is a perspective that will place low value on those who can no longer maintain independence and can no longer contribute to society. Thus people with dementia or other mental disabilities and frail and/or disabled older people will be seen as a burden on society rather than a repository of wisdom and experience to be shared with the coming generations and to be respected, loved and cared for, treasuring the contributions they have made to the community, even once they are no long capable of doing so. The view that affirms older people will only be available when societal values uphold the goodness and integrity of human beings because they are, because they exist, rather than for a value that can be costed and weighed as being worthy of care and love.

In the Abrahamic faiths, human life is valued as being from God, and it is not given to human beings to dispose of. This stance provides for an attitude of reverence for life and respect for others. This stance does not say though, that life must be prolonged at any cost; it is acknowledged that human life in this world has a beginning and an end. There are times when it becomes futile to try to extend life, for example a person being maintained on life support without any hope of recovery. An example of this would be an elderly person who is in the terminal stage of dementia, and the decision is made to institute palliative care, rather than use more aggressive means of treatment that would merely serve to prolong the dying period.

However, there are times when suffering is a part of the journey into ageing. A society has choices to support and care for those who are suffering, or to ignore them or deny those who suffer access to care. Debate in recent decades, particularly based on the work from the Hastings Center and Callahan (1996) has focused on resourcing appropriate aged care and the cost of doing so.

The bioethical perspective and alternatives

Modern thinking in bioethics has used ethical principles of autonomy, benefi-cence, non-maleficence, justice and veracity to frame ethical issues. However, these principles used in a biomedical frame alone have been shown to be less than adequate in the practice of care, not least aged care. Recent review of virtue ethics (Pellegrino and Thomasma 1993) has enlarged the scope of ethical decision making, taking important account of the character of the health professional as agent in ethical decisions. Virtue ethics is based on the view that persons characteristically act in certain ways, for certain reasons, in a variety of situations, and hold certain attitudes and emotions (Copp and Sobel 2004). Thus it is maintained that ethical principles are more adequate when virtue ethics are applied at the same time. Pellegrino and Thomasma (1993) and Campbell (2003) argue that ethical principles and virtue ethics are complementary to each other.

Over recent decades autonomy has become the major ethical principle on which professional health practice is based. However, an important complication for ethical consideration is compromised autonomy, which may occur during the ageing process. It is not possible for a frail elderly person or a person in later stages of dementia to be wholly autonomous. Indeed, if we are honest, we all mostly function as interdependent beings, most of the time. Not one of us is completely independent in every way. Thus we have inadequate guidance for practice should we base our caring on autonomy. We need another way to underpin ethical practice in aged care.

The recent changes in the areas of medical technology, ageing of societies, and the valuing of life in secular societies have produced their own sets of challenges for older adults and their care. A major challenge is the regard for elderly people as commodities to be treated, based on economic outcomes (Meador and Henson 2003). Against this it is argued that a human being is more than a body and medical condition to be treated; each person should be valued based on acknowledgement of their personhood. However, varying definitions of personhood render this a problematic term (Kitwood 1997; Post 2000). For instance, philosophers of recent times have relied heavily on rational criteria, on decision making capacity and, to some extent, having sentience, that is, the capacity to feel and experience sensations, for personhood to be conferred (Johnstone 1999, p.41). This would render certain types of people, for instance the mentally disabled and those with dementia, as lacking in personhood and therefore being less worthy of treatment, care and, indeed, life. Two important understandings are needed, first, what it means to care, and second, what it means to be a person.

Caring

Caring first assumes the presence of a relationship. Caring is a relationship of giving and receiving between persons; it cannot take place unless the attitudes of trust, generosity, integrity and respect for the person being cared for are present in the giver and normally (but not necessarily) a willingness to receive in the person being cared for. However, caring can also take place when the receiver of care is unable to respond to the giver of care, for example a care recipient who is unconscious or has late stage dementia. In these cases, the care-giver cares in the absence of a response from the care recipient; this demands a higher ethical commitment than if the care recipient was able to assent to the care. The way care is delivered to a recipient unable to respond will largely depend on the attitudes and beliefs of the care-giver in relation to the personhood of the care recipient. Thus it is necessary to consider what it means to be a person.

Personhood

In recent decades dementia has become a major focus for what it means to be human and, consequently, our understanding and valuing of human persons informs standards of duty of care for the weak and vulnerable of society (Cheston and Bender 1999; Kitwood 1997; Post 2000). In my first study (MacKinlay 2001a), and even recently in some situations in the wider community, I have heard the myth that people with dementia really do not know what is going on and cannot recognize people, thus justifying the provision of less than desirable care. This approach is also used in some instances to justify non-involvement of these people in care decisions (Goldsmith 1996). Post (2000) notes the problems that may confront care-givers from biomedical ethicists: 'the category of "need" is arrogantly displaced as the dominant source of moral obligation by the category of "personhood," often defined in terms of rational capacities for "moral agency." Non-persons count less, if at all'(p.79). Post sees this view of ethics for people with Alzheimer's disease denying them a place as human beings, and reducing their options in life. While a rationalist approach to defining personhood is one way of valuing persons, it is, fortunately, not the only way. According to Kitwood (1997, p.8) there is another way of viewing the human person; Kitwood says personhood is:

> A standing or status is bestowed upon one human being, by others, in the context of relationship and social being. It implies recognition, respect and trust. Both the according of personhood and the failure to do so, have consequences that are empirically testable.

Viewed this way, people are to be treated with respect and love; in fact there is an ethical imperative to do so, even if they are unable to respond to others. This creates a radical shift from the biomedical perspective that demands certain capabilities of the care recipient before they can be deemed worthy of having the status of personhood bestowed upon them and, then, deemed worthy of care.

The ethical perspective of virtue ethics

Having considered the perspective of caring, and then personhood of the one being cared for, it is now important to consider the relationship between the two. Virtue ethics is a way of considering the moral agent in ethical acts. Virtue ethics were adopted in the ancient medical ethical codes of the Greeks, Indians and Chinese, but were long neglected in western ethics (Pellegrino and Thomasma 1993). They argue that the 'moral essence of a health profession is the special relationship that sickness and the response to illness creates between healer and the patient' (Pellegrino and Thomasma 1993, p.xii).

Attitudes of staff to frail and vulnerable older people

An important aspect of care is closely associated with the attitudes of staff towards those they care for. Bird (2002) found that different staff held different attitudes toward and different perceptions of the same residents. Bird notes one instance of a resident who was often violent towards staff during showering, needing three people to shower her, but was showered by one staff member without incident at the weekends. It emerged through conversation with the resident's husband that she was 'an excessively shy person and almost socially phobic' (p.55). The staff involved in her care had very different perceptions of that resident. What was the difference – the same resident but different staff. The weekend staff member used basic dementia nursing skills of going slowly, constantly acknowledging the resident's fears and backing off, and continuing to provide calm reassurance when she became disturbed. Bird found in his study, that faced with exactly the same potential workplace stressors, staff had very different emotional reactions, suggesting that the difference must lie with the staff members. This raises issues of attitudes of staff towards those they care for. As Bird suggests, these people with dementia don't deliberately decide to be aggressive, or to deliberately annoy the staff. Too often staff working in residential aged care have insufficient training in specific areas of aged care, and especially in dementia care.

Pellegrino and Thomasma (1993) describe virtues for health professionals:

1. Fidelity to trust and promise (encompassing a recognition of the importance of trust to healing).

2. Compassion and caring (so that patients can be assisted in their healing in the fullest sense).

3. Prudence (encompassing the qualities of practical wisdom and the ability to deal effectively with complexity).

4.   Justice: 'justice has its deepest roots in love... Love testifies that the claims of others upon us are the claims of our brothers and sisters in a community of compassion and care'(p.94).

5.   Fortitude and courage (they suggest that fortitude is sustained courage, and courage is distinguished as moral courage).

6.   Integrity and intellectual honesty (to ensure competent practice).

7.   Effacement of self-interest (to help protect patients against being exploited).

These virtues are exercised by those who work as care providers in the process of everyday decision making. At a very basic level these ethical characteristics will be seen in simple acts, such as providing privacy for an elderly person assisted in showering, and taking time when assisting a person to eat. Always asking the care recipient how they would like care provided; always thinking of the residents, before thinking of the routine of the aged care residence.

Guidelines for ethical care of people who have dementia

Post (2000) reported the development of the Fairhill Guidelines on ethics and the care of people with Alzheimer's disease. These guidelines set important pointers for ethical practice, addressing relevant issues for people who have dementia and their families, and to some extent they can be applied to other late life ethical issues not related to dementia. The main guidelines are:

1.   Being truthful: issues in diagnostic disclosure.

2.   Preserving privileges: issues of driving.

3.   Respecting choice: issues of competency and autonomy.

4.   Valuing freedom: issues of behaviour control.

5.   The right to die: issues of death and dying.

6.   Quality of life: issues of the cultural perception of dementia.

(Post 2000, pp.44–65)

These guidelines will be used to discuss ethical issues, both related to people with dementia and other older people who do not have dementia.

Issues of truthfulness and openness

Being truthful in issues of diagnostic disclosure is always important, and no less so in dementia than other conditions. First, physicians should sensitively inform affected individuals and their families about the diagnosis of probable Alzheimer's disease. Disclosure comes with responsibility to direct the affected individual and family to available resources. However, while this has been the dominant western view of the use and importance of truthfulness, other faiths may differ; Clarfield *et al.* (2003) in a comparison of the approach to end of life issues in Judaism, Catholicism and Islam, provide examples of scenarios to illustrate ethical approaches to decision making. In the scenario, a question is raised by the children, about sharing with the husband the news of the bleak prognosis for his elderly wife who had suffered a massive stroke. The Jewish perspective is to protect the father from the news in respect for his health and to not disclose the truth, or at least delay telling. The Catholic approach to the same question is that the truth must be told, unless the husband states specifically that he does not want to be told. In the case of Islamic ethics, it would be difficult to justify withholding information from the husband, first because he is her surrogate decision maker and, second, truth must be upheld at almost any cost, except in the case of risk to one's life. Thus, while a secular western view is to first respect the wishes of the patient or resident and to then, with permission, tell their next of kin, when other cultures and faiths are considered, the ethical issue of disclosure may be different.

Supporting autonomy

Issues of autonomy centre around respect for choice and competency. These issues will include crucial decisions such as whether it is safe to remain living alone, when unable to remember to turn off the gas after cooking, and when possibility of the person burning themselves in the shower exists. People with dementia should retain the choice of making decisions with whatever competencies they retain; not to do so is denying their independence and dignity. Careful assessment and discussion with the person, and instituting safety measures to prevent accidents in the home, may allow the person the dignity of risk in remaining independent (with sufficient and appropriate services) at home.

With decreasing capacity for decision making, it is vital that people are supported in making the decisions that are important for them; this becomes a complex issue for people with dementia. The aim is to preserve privileges appropriately, in the best interests of the person with dementia, while also considering the safety of others. Driving becomes an issue of concern for many of these people. The Fairhill Guidelines present three points, first, a diagnosis of Alzheimer's disease is never sufficient reason for loss of driving licence. Second, the person with dementia, if competent, should be part of the decision making process regarding driving restrictions. And, finally, whether the physician or other health professionals should have a role in setting restrictions remains unclear, but the guidelines note that the decision is probably best left with the family and community. However, there may be a role for medical intervention in some cases.

The experience of moving from independent living to residential aged care

Allowing dignity of risk may also be an issue in making one of the hardest of all decisions of later life, the decision to leave the family home and move to live in an aged care facility. Some older people living alone may be at risk of injury, of frequent falls, and may not be safe in food preparation, and concerned carers may feel that residential care is to be preferred. The decision to move to residential care must be made carefully, with real involvement of the elderly person wherever possible. The elderly person must be allowed the dignity of risk as assessed in their living situation, if this is their desire. Community services should be tailored to deal with issues such as provision of meals if they are no longer able to cook safely. The Fairhill Guidelines note that it is important to plan for global incompetency of late stage dementia through the use of advance directives and durable power of attorney. This needs to include advance directives for health care.

Valuing freedom versus behaviour control

The Fairhill Guidelines note the best approach to problem behaviours relies on social and environmental modifications and creative activities to preserve independence and self-esteem. Further, physical and chemical restraints should not be substituted for social, environmental and activity modifications. Behaviour-controlling drugs should be used cautiously and only for specified purposes. In residential aged care, with residents who fall easily, it is preferable to use hip protectors and allow the person dignity of risk rather than to deprive them of their mobility and freedom. An individual profile of the person with dementia should be available to facility-based care-givers (nursing homes, assisted living or other care settings), highlighting an interactive and activity-based care plan known to be most effective for the individual (Post 2000, pp.53–55).

End of life issues

First is the need to acknowledge Alzheimer's as a terminal illness and, although death may not be imminent, treatment and care decisions are made on the basis of this belief. At some point in the progression of the disease, palliative care will be needed. The person who has Alzheimer's (if possible) and their family and carers should be included in discussions of what constitutes a good death for this person. The person with dementia may wish to have decisions regarding end of life treatment made by trusted family members who will act in their best interests, when they are no longer able to make their own decisions. In some cases there will not be any family, or the person may not trust family members with these decisions. A further complication is the increasing number of blended families in western societies; contact may have been lost with adult children when one of the parents marries again. This can prove to be isolating for an ageing and vulnerable person, as communications may have been lost or a breakdown in relationships may prevent notification of close relatives.

In end of life issues Post (2000) makes careful distinction between refusal of treatment, voluntary euthanasia and assisted suicide, noting the importance of knowing the person's wishes, which may be recorded in advance directives and known and respected by the family.

Provision of artificial nutrition and hydration to people who are dying

Provision of nutrition and hydration is more often an issue in dementia care than in any other condition in later life. First, it is important to be clear about whether the person is dying or not. Knowing the person well and being aware of their personal and family history and assessment for depression and overall health status will help to build up a picture of the person and their wishes at end of life. Sometimes artificial nutrition and hydration may be an important treatment. For example, a person who has head and neck cancer may not be able to take oral fluids, but is not in the process of dying and needs artificial nutrition and hydration to survive. If the person is not dying then certainly appropriate provision of nutrition and hydration is required, and this may sometimes be by artificial means.

However, in any case where the person is dying, it is appropriate to withhold nutrition and hydration. In a ruling that reflects current thinking from international medical, ethical and legal opinion, the Court decided that artificial nutrition and hydration provided through a percutaneous endoscopic gastrostomy tube (PEG) to a woman in a persistent vegetative state may be withdrawn (Ashby and Mendelson 2004). The woman was aged 69 years, and in the advanced stages of dementia; the tube was inserted at the request of her husband while she was still ambulant and still able to communicate with him. Once she reached a permanent vegetative state, her husband requested the removal of the tube, saying this was not what she would have wished. Staff in the home were uncertain what could legally be done and the Public Advocate assisted in the process. The judge ruled that 'any form of artificial nutrition and hydration is a medical procedure, not part of palliative care, and that it is a procedure to sustain life, not to manage the dying process' (Ashby and Mendelson 2004, p.442). Sometimes it has been harder to have a treatment discontinued than to begin it in the first place. This ruling clearly demonstrates the possibility of discontinuing treatment, recognized through legal processes. Ashby and Mendelson (2004) note that during the dying process there is a normal gradual reduction and eventual cessation of oral intake. While the person retains a sense of thirst and hunger, food and fluids must always be available, and adequate assistance with drinking must be given, but artificial means of providing these should not be used when oral intake ceases. Measures for comfort, such as mouth care and. of course, pain relief must be continued. There is no evidence that medically administered nutrition and hydration improves comfort or dignity during the dying process and, further, they make the argument that fluid infusion may lead to overload and reduce the dying person's comfort (Ashby and Mendelson 2004; Post 2000).

Quality of life issues

Quality of life is an important dimension of life. Without it, hope diminishes and life may cease to be worth living. But how is quality of life measured, and what does it consist of? The guideline set out by Post (2000) is written for people with Alzheimer's disease, however, issues of quality of life emerge in a range of instances in later life, including depression, extreme frailty, stroke and aphasia, and chronic health conditions that cause pain and suffering, such as arthritis.

A major difficulty of quality of life measures lies in the necessarily subjective nature of assessment, for example a person with dementia may not be able to effectively communicate about their quality of life. In the absence of clear articulation of what quality of life is, it may be easy to assume that because the person can no longer participate in life in the same way as previously, then life is not worth living. However, this is a very subjective judgment and particularly unhelpful for the person with dementia. Over the progress of the disease, people with dementia come to a point where they live mostly in the present, without memory of the past or a sense of the future. Yet, this life experience may not be bad (Bryden 2005), and a new sense of the appreciation of life in the present moment may come at this time. At late stage dementia, quality of life may be more obviously compromised and it becomes obvious when the person is in the process of dying. At this stage life extending treatments can no longer be justified, and it would be cruel to extend the dying process.

Informed consent

The right to informed consent must be guarded among vulnerable elderly people. Goldsmith (1996) found that people with dementia did have needs and opinions about their care, and it is in dementia that informed consent is most likely to be omitted from care. Too often people with dementia are showered, dressed and fed without explanation, and they are not asked or offered choices in their care. Paternalism is still practised in numbers of health care settings, particularly in acute care settings, where staff may not be well informed about the ageing process, and may make assumptions that older people won't understand information about procedures and new technologies. Thus procedures may not be well explained. Perceived slowness of mobility of an elderly person may result in the person being placed in a wheelchair instead of being encouraged to walk, because it takes too long to walk; dependency can thus be fostered within health care settings.

Rationing of health care services based on age

In his book *Setting Limits: Medical Goals in an Aging Society* (1987) Callahan opened the debate on the allocation of scarce health resources and how these may be restricted on the basis of age. There have long been limits in western societies to the amount of medical technology that can be afforded based on the numbers of people with needs for its use. An easy way to balance need would be to ration access to health care based on age; older people have lived their lives, the argument goes, therefore the resources should go to younger people. Few would argue the case for heart transplants for elderly people who are living with co-existing chronic conditions and already compromised body systems. Further, no one would at this point argue for fertility treatments to be offered to people in their sixties or older. However, there may be other valuable treatments used for older people that will greatly increase their quality of life. It would be unjust not to offer these where the treatments are available.

Callahan (1996, p.744) continues the argument that it is important to be aware of the possibilities of other measures being used to limit health care costs for elderly people, for example through advance directives, guidelines for futile treatment and decisions on the use of appropriate care, covert rationing based on age and physician-assisted suicide may be condoned.

The case for provision of aged care by religious organizations

In a number of western countries there has been a definite division between functions of the state and the church. For most of the twentieth century churches have provided aged care services, with varying levels of support from governments. With the rapid ageing of societies and changing structures and standards of care provision, the way that these services are provided has in some places become less clear.

Funding seems to be a constant tension within the aged care industry and there seem to be pressures to develop large aged care providers based, for the most part, on matters of efficient use of available funds. It may be argued that a continuance of use of a medical model for aged care may not present the optimum environment for resident well-being. It is argued further that as the baby boomers grow older and need services of aged care, they will not accept the current medical focus and institutional model. They will be looking for care that will enable them to continue to live independently, and to retain an autonomous lifestyle. Yet, realistically, these goals for living independently will have to be balanced against the need for complex health care.

A shift in emphasis of care and room for independence is needed. It is desirable that older people remain as independent as possible, retaining responsibility for their care to the extent they are able, while being able to buy into services they need to retain a good quality of life. Perhaps grouped housing, such as serviced apartments with access to health services and care, may be one model that can be used effectively.

So, should aged care that is provided by a church or religious group be any different from that provided by a secular provider? Both religious and secular providers need to meet any accreditation guidelines, that is, guidelines that are acceptable to the whole community. However, a church group that provides aged care, provides that care out of the ethos of their faith vision. Therefore, a religious backed aged care provider will adhere to the government guidelines and standards and in addition they will provide care according to the beliefs of their faith. In the major religions, care will be provided on a basis of love and care for others. In the Christian view, the duty of care is summed up in the words that Jesus spoke in Matthew 25:

> I was hungry and you gave me food, I was thirsty and you gave me something to drink, I was a stranger and you welcomed me, I was naked and you gave me clothing, I was sick and you took care of me, I was in prison and you visited me.

This vision has long provided a sense of purpose in social justice, and certainly this has been so in providing aged care. It is challenging these days to hold both the government standards and the faith ethos together in practice, but it can and must be done, if the churches are to continue to have a role in providing care.

However, Thobaben (1996) takes the view that the church in the west 'has essentially abdicated its responsibility and role in health care to the funding sources' (p.197). He accuses some 'Christian' institutions of identifying with secular 'healthcare providers or organizations in the marketplace more consistently than with the church' (p.199). He states that this situation need not continue, and rightly challenges the churches to minister to persons in need. To do this Thobaben advocates Christian organizations and practitioners adopt seven specific institutional intentions, adapted from US structures:

- Improve staff education in the sociology of healthcare and culture of disability.
- Improve staff moral education and development.
- Begin formal patient and family moral education.
- Begin educating accreditation bodies and those working in government aged care policy regarding the need for increased funding of rehabilitation and long-term care alternatives.
- Develop further facilities for transitional and open residential living, perhaps with the establishment of parish nursing programmes and associated with parishes.
- Develop in-home transitional and independent living support.
- Develop respite care.

Owning the vision and the mission statement

No one can provide care out of a vacuum. Each provider brings their own belief structure and vision to what they do. This will become the basis on which they provide care, based on their beliefs about human persons and the value of human life, and in particular, care of older and vulnerable people. Each aged care provider must carefully establish their mission statement, based of their beliefs about people in their particular setting, establishing a clear understanding of who they are as providers of care.

Conclusion

This chapter has outlined the more important ethical issues that arise in later life; including end of life care, advance directives, assisted suicide and euthanasia, issues of autonomy, consent and competency, issues of quality of life and access to appropriate health care services.

Most western societies these days are both multicultural and multifaith, and most have also embraced post-modernism with its set of relative values and humanism. In recent times ethics have been approached from a biomedical perspective and may include the search for eternal youth, translated into a view of ageing that seeks ways to delay/deny the ageing process. The ethical perspective that focuses on the search for the greatest good for all may deny access to care and quality of life for older people. Modern thinking in bioethics has used ethical principles of autonomy, beneficence, non-maleficence, justice and veracity to frame ethical issues. However, it is maintained that ethical principles are more adequate when virtue ethics are applied at the same time. Virtue ethics are a way of considering the moral agent in ethical acts and include characteristics of fidelity, compassion, prudence, justice, fortitude, integrity and self-effacement.

Summary

The main ethical issues in later life include:

- *end of life care*
- *advance directives*
- *assisted suicide and euthanasia*
- *issues of autonomy*
- *consent and competency*
- *issues of quality of life*
- *access to appropriate health care services.*

Bioethics has used ethical principles of:

- *autonomy*
- *beneficence*

- *non-maleficence*
- *justice*
- *veracity*

to frame ethical issues.

Virtue ethics is a way of considering the moral agent in ethical acts and includes characteristics of:

- *fidelity*
- *compassion*
- *prudence*
- *justice*
- *fortitude*
- *integrity*
- *self-effacement.*

Further reading

Jeffery, P. (2001) *Going Against the Stream: Ethical Aspects of Ageing and Care.* Gloucester: Gracewing/The Liturgical Press.

Johnstone, M.J. (1999) *Bioethics: A Nursing Perspective.* Marrickville: Harcourt Saunders.

Moody, H.R. (1992) *Ethics in an Aging Society.* Baltimore: John Hopkins University Press.

Post, S.G. (2000) *The Moral Challenge of Alzheimer Disease: Ethical Issues from Diagnosis to Dying.* Baltimore: John Hopkins University Press.

Thobaben, J.R. (1996) 'Long-term care.' In J.F. Kilner, A.B. Miller and E.D. Pellegrino (eds) *Dignity and Dying: A Christian Appraisal.* Grand Rapids, Michigan: William B. Eerdmans Publishing Company.

CHAPTER 15

The Model of Spiritual Growth and Care in the Fourth Age of Life

A framework for caring

The traditional model of ageing and aged care, developed in the twentieth century, is a medical model that assumes an illness perspective of ageing; this is the biomedical paradigm. In this book an alternative model has been proposed, a model that assumes a wellness approach to ageing. The model implies a wholistic and wellness perspective that recognizes ageing as a process involving biological, psychosocial and spiritual dimensions. Further, and importantly, ageing may be considered to be a social construction and a spiritual journey. Thus ageing as understood in this book is a complex interaction of biological, psychosocial and spiritual factors. The model used is a dynamic one that is open to change and to the challenges and opportunities of ageing.

This book is based on a model of spiritual tasks and the spiritual process of ageing; it is a developmental model for ageing in the twenty-first century. Each of the six themes of the model have been outlined in the appropriate chapters of this book. This final chapter reviews the parts of the model and attempts to bring it together in a wholistic model to guide both spiritual growth and spiritual care in the fourth age of life.

Ultimate meaning in life

The continuing search for meaning in the final stage of life is probably the most important task of life. It is in this final and fourth age of the life cycle that this task and process becomes more urgent for many people. A growing realization of their own mortality raises the importance of the task. Some older people, however, do not find this a natural task, and may continue to deny that they are growing older.

The focus of this book has been on that fourth and final part of the lifespan. Its subjects are those who are frail, and in need of a variety of services to meet activities of daily living and maximize well-being. These older people may still be living in the community, with services delivered to them, or they may be in residential aged care, because they are no longer able to be cared for adequately at home.

It is at this fourth stage of life that the model becomes really interactive. The search for ultimate life-meaning may be spurred on by the person having less energy to continue to take part in activities, and gerotranscendence theory (Tornstam 1999/2000) provides a model for understanding this aspect of ageing. In Tornstam's model, energy lack is associated with components of disengagement, thus recognizing that disengagement theory (Havighurst, Nergorten and Tobin 1968), largely disregarded during the 1970s and 1980s, does once again have currency in theories of ageing. If disengagement theory is now applied more appropriately to frail older people experiencing decreasing energy levels, it is likely their frailty is the key to their decreased involvement in social roles and activities. As a consequence of decreased energy levels, it could be as Moody (1995) suggests, that the latter part of the life cycle may become a natural monastery. This time of frailty could be a time where the person is forced back into themselves, to become even more introspective. The practice of mysticism, where solitude, meditation and contemplative prayer are practised, may be become the norm for some fourth age people. There was certainly an increase in private prayer reported by many of the frail people in the study of those living in residential care. Mysticism may be a means of exploring life-meaning, while it may also provide the means of growing into greater intimacy with God for Christians.

The search for meaning, then, does not occur in isolation within the ageing person, it is not as if the person wakes up one morning and thinks, 'I must begin my search for meaning.' It is rather that a combination of factors within the ageing process provides the stimulus or the key to begin to unlock the meaning and purpose of this person's life. Atchley's Continuity theory (2000) also provides a basis for understanding the process of growing older, against a background of continuing to hold similar values and attitudes throughout life, while adapting to changes as these occur. During the fourth age of life, the search for meaning takes on a new sense of urgency and importance.

Loss of significant relationships during later life is yet another factor that seems to push the older person to reevaluate their lives, against the sense of devastating losses that they might never really recover from. Further, loss of roles, either by mutual withdrawing or because those roles can no longer exist, for example being a parent to growing children, also become reasons to reflect on life and its meaning.

Thus the search for meaning is raised in a number of ways. Among the frail older people in residential care in this study, the search for meaning became more central. More of them were spending more time alone (not always through choice) and in reflection of their lives. During in-depth interviews and question-naires a higher proportion of these older people than of those who were living independently, found God at the centre of their lives. The question: 'What brings greatest meaning in your life now?' was more likely to bring an immediate response of 'God'. It seemed that these older people were on a spiritual journey that brought them, in the face of increasing frailty, into closeness with God. But this was not so for all, and some of the participants in the study did not find meaning in God. These older people were more likely to find greatest meaning through human relationship. While most of these older people did find meaning and purpose in life, and affirmed that life was still worth living, some of the participants experienced a sense of despair in their frailty. This is, as Erikson *et al.* (1986) described, the final stage of psychosocial development, the search for integrity versus despair.

In any kind of spiritual or pastoral care, it is important to find out what provides greatest or ultimate meaning for the particular person. This is a starting point for care, and involves assessment and effective listening to the older person.

Finding intimacy in later life: the importance of relationship for frail elderly people

One of the six themes that the model of spiritual tasks of ageing is based on (MacKinlay 2001a) is the search for intimacy. This search is one that recognizes both the need for human relationship, and for relationship with the tran-scendent, for example with God or a deity. In this study of frail elderly people, the need for relationship was almost synonymous with meaning. Many of these people, resident in aged care facilities, had lost the most significant relationships of their lives, and there was a deep sense of loss and a deep yearning for new and intimate relationships. Some were able to fulfill their needs for intimacy through contact with adult children, grandchildren and great-grandchildren, others had no family at all who could visit. For the latter group, staff and visitors, sometimes volunteers to the aged care residence, were their only human contacts.

Numbers of frail residents expressed a real sense of loneliness in their experience of being in an aged care facility. For those frail older people remaining in the community, there was often loneliness and social isolation. It is also important to note that these responses did not change for people in residential aged care who had dementia. For these people also, meaning was almost synonymous with relationship (MacKinlay *et al.* 2002–2005). It is too often assumed that people with dementia do not recognize others, even family members, and therefore that relationships are not important for them. This could not be further from the truth. The names may be forgotten, but knowing remains more than being able to address someone by name (Boden 2002). Connecting deeply with another person is critical to the well-being of those with dementia too.

Failure to thrive

Failure to thrive occurs where there is a lack of nourishment of the soul. The soul is nourished through human contact; that involves recognition of the value of the person, and the person feels and knows that they are affirmed and loved, (*agape*). As Kitwood (1997) has stated so well, it is the responsibility of the carer to affirm the personhood of the person who has dementia. The model of spiritual tasks of ageing recognizes the importance of intimacy for frail older people, noting that with the loss of previous crucial relationships, there is a need for developing new human relationships and new intimacies.

Developing new relationships in an aged care facility

Being admitted to an aged care facility is almost always a time of uncertainty and vulnerability. The person moving into the facility is facing numerous losses and a reduction in their ability to control and choose life activities. Often the move has involved both loss of important relationships and loss of material possessions. At such times in life, it is hard to find meaning. Recently I was talking with an elderly couple who had felt obliged to sell up their home and move 'into something more appropriate for their age'. Now they are very unhappy, they have had to get rid of most of their belongings and feel they have lost a way of life.

According to one study (Fleming 2001), about 50 per cent of older people admitted to aged care facilities are depressed. Simply being occupied does not necessarily bring a sense of meaning into the person's life. These people will probably be grieving multiple losses and may also be depressed. Often there is no chance for new residents to grieve and to have their depression recognized. Many of these problems will lessen and/or disappear when staff really care about the person – as Kitwood (1997) wrote it is we who affirm the dignity and personhood of the individual – we can also withhold that affirmation of the person.

Too often when a person is admitted to an aged care facility, the orientation to the facility does not include meeting with other residents. Such orientation could support the development of new friendships among frail and vulnerable older people. Activities do not often allow for developing new friendships, particularly if the groups are large and run by facilitators, leaving little possibility for interaction between residents. Limited mobility, hearing and sight deficits make meeting and making new friends even more difficult. Some of the residents of this study reported an important reason for attending church services in the aged care facility was to meet other residents. An important focus in the orientation of new residents must include welcoming them into the community of the aged care facility, and assisting them to get to know others, both residents and staff.

Self-transcendence

Self-transcendence or self-forgetting (Frankl 1986) is one of the six major themes of the model of spiritual tasks of ageing (MacKinlay 2001a). The occurrence of self-transcendence was discussed above in relation to stimulating the search for life-meaning. Transcendence is a means of moving from self-centredness to other-centredness and it forms an important component of the ageing process, both from a psychosocial and spiritual perspective. Those who remain self-centred will continue to focus on bodily complaints, such as pain and symptoms of constipation, sleeplessness and other problems of an ageing body. This is not to minimize the significance of these issues of bodily decrement, but to suggest that there is another way of being, in frailty. This involves a move to human *becoming*, or human being; that is a move from human *doing* to human *being*. Those who develop body transcendence are able to move beyond the constrictions of body preoccupation (Peck 1968) to find a place where they may still be able to enjoy life, to face life and find meaning, in the midst of frailty. This is one aspect of the struggle between moving towards integrity in later life compared with a decline into despair that Erikson *et al.* (1986) have described.

Loss of energy and the threat of loss of control may cause some people to retreat into themselves in fear and a denial of the implications of bodily loss and disabilities. Yet others, faced with marked disabilities and loss during the fourth age, will find meaning and hope, and come to a place of wisdom and joy (Erikson *et al.* 1986). To those who watch the development of self-transcendence in another person, this is a mystery, and it may be asked: 'How can this person be so joyful and at peace, as they experience chronic pain, losses of significant relationships, and disabilities?'

Moving from provisional to final meanings in life

This task in the model is also related to other tasks; there are obviously close interactions between self-transcendence and the search for final life-meanings. The diminished energy levels, the losses of relationships, the bodily losses and decrements leading to self-transcendence are linked with a renewed search for final meaning. Again the questions become more urgent, one question that may begin to surface is: 'How much time do I have?' And yet again, 'What has been the purpose of my life? What has been its meaning?' In a sense, at this time of life, people are beginning to live into their life-meanings; some who are using reminiscence may be finding that there are number of 'Ah ha' times – suddenly events from their past have taken on new meanings, and the whole of their story begins to come together.

For some people major issues of past trauma and family rifts, perhaps even abuse, come to the surface and there seems to be an urgent need for confession, forgiveness and reconciliation. For some of the current cohort of elderly people unresolved issues of experiences during war re-emerge and need attention and healing. Peter Coleman (1999) and others have done valuable work in this field, showing that reminiscence therapy and work may be effective in bringing peace and closure to such memories. Faith Gibson (2004) has been another pioneer in reminiscence work, especially with people who have dementia. Further researchers and authors in this field are Kenyon, Clark and de Vries (2001), and Webster and Haight (2002). Reminiscence, and specific spiritual reminiscence, with a focus on life-meaning, and religion, where relevant, shows much promise for psychosocial and spiritual growth in the future.

Assisting older people to find final meanings

Many people search for meaning – this is more so as people grow older, and begin to become more aware of their own approaching death. Other people seem content to accept life as it comes.

We can't 'give' meaning to any other person, each person has to find meaning for themselves, but it is possible to journey with them to find meaning. We may listen to their life story, be present with the person, so that we may be a sounding board for their reflections and questions. The diversional therapist or pastoral carer can facilitate the search for meaning by introducing activities that encourage reflection and reminiscence. Meaningful activities are often more effective in smaller groups than in large groups and, certainly, reminiscence, if it is to be at all useful, needs to be within a small group where the participants are taken seriously and have a chance to reflect on their lives. There is a tendency in some aged care facilities to use large group work that becomes more of an entertainment than an activity, and is of little value to the older people. For some people with dementia, no one has listened to them for a long time, and Malcolm Goldsmith's book *Hearing the Voice of People with Dementia* (1996) shows the importance of listening.

Response to life-meaning

While finding ultimate meaning in life lies at the core of the search for each person, this meaning is then the starting place for living. It is out of the perceived meaning of life that the person responds to meaning. Thus for each person there will be both similarities and differences. Assessment of spiritual needs is an essential first step to assisting these older people. Response to meaning in the study varied, according to what formed ultimate meaning for the person. For many of these elderly people, meaning was about relationship. Meaning is related to response to meaning and, indeed, the response affirms the meaning. The ability to have quality time with close family and friends will affirm the meaning of these relationships and the well-being of the older person. The opportunity to worship in a manner that is meaningful to the person will connect with their faith, and affirm this sense of ultimate meaning. The chance to engage in music or art or interact with the environment will affirm life-meaning for those for whom this is important; gardening is a joy to many older people. Those who become too frail to work in a garden may well still enjoy being taken for a walk in the garden. Principles of the Eden Alternative (Thomas 2002) are helpful in connecting frail older people with life.

For frail elderly people, responding becomes more difficult. Those with a history of attending church services often find they can no longer get to church easily, needing to depend on others for transport if they are still living in the community, and for assistance with being ready in time for the service if they are in residential care. Energy loss can affect the person's ability to stay the distance in a service of worship and even concentration may be difficult, with sensory losses and mobility problems. Often the intrinsic aspects of religion, that is, prayer, meditation or the reading of scripture become more important to these frail elderly people.

The nursing home environment

Older people newly admitted to residential care will need to make adjustments to the differences in their new environments. For a start they will probably have had to part with numbers of personal items, such as furniture, that won't fit into the usually smaller space of an aged care residence. They may be in a setting that allows pets but, on the other hand, they may have had to part with a long-term pet that has provided much comfort for a number of years.

The environment within aged care facilities can be supportive of the development of high standards of care and a sense of well-being in residents, as, for example, in the Eden Alternative project (Thomas 2002). However, in some instances, high standards of care are delivered in less than optimally planned aged care buildings. While the physical environment is influential on the well-being of both residents and staff, the human elements of aged care are the most important. Many aged care facilities in the early twenty-first century endeavour to provide a home-like atmosphere for residents. Providing an appealing environment that will support resident well-being is a complex undertaking as the needs of frail older adults are numerous; they would still be living at home if they were able to meet their needs independently. Care is required for physical, psychosocial, emotional and spiritual needs and a supportive environment may assist residents to respond to life and its meaning.

Finding hope in the fourth age of life

Hope is essential for human survival and human flourishing. We can't necessarily replace what the person has lost, we can't necessarily repair their disability, but we can connect with them – giving person-centred care that affirms and nourishes the soul. Finding hope in life can be challenging for these frail older people who have lost so many significant relationships, so many roles, and even their ability to have control over their lives. Yet hope is possible in the fourth age of life. The ability to find hope lies in the interaction within the model of finding ultimate life-meaning; without meaning in life, all is hopeless. Without the ability to respond effectively to meaning, hope will be diminished. Without intimacy of relationships, it is often hard to maintain hope. Self-transcendence is a critical factor in finding hope in the face of increasing disabilities and losses. The ability to review life and search for meaning may assist the person, however frail, to find meaning and hope. Thus hope is influenced by the other tasks of the model, finding ultimate meaning, responding to meaning, moving from provisional to final life-meanings, finding intimacies and transcending losses.

Spiritual strategies for care

Spiritual strategies for care may be based on the model of spiritual tasks and process of ageing (MacKinlay 2001a). Chaplains, pastoral carers, diversional therapists or activity officers may be regular providers of spiritual care. Other aged care professionals will have the opportunity to provide spiritual care at particular times.

Assessment of spiritual needs is important (see Chapter 3). The focus of questions will be on where people find meaning in their lives, asking what brings purpose and meaning to life, what interests do they have and what interests did they have earlier in life? Based on where they find meaning, how do they respond to that meaning? Perhaps it is through relationship, perhaps they have recently lost an important relationship (highlighting the spiritual tasks of transcending loss and disability, and finding new relationships and intimacy in later life).

Perhaps people find meaning through music, through art, through dancing, perhaps through reading or gardening. An exploration of life-meaning is important, and it cannot be assumed that everyone will want to respond to life in the same ways. Religion is an important means of connecting for some older people and use of liturgy often involves words, music, use of the senses, including sight, hearing, smell, taste and touch. Spiritual strategies, or the spiritual portfolio that the person already has may prove to be a source of strength as they settle into an aged care facility. Spiritual strategies include prayer, meditation, contemplative prayer, reading of scripture, attendance at worship, keeping of a personal journal. Small groups for Bible or other scripture reading or other religious purposes may be valuable.

Being able to respond to life-meaning is a way of fulfilment and connecting with life, and it is affirming for the individual that their life has a purpose. Finding final meanings is an important task of ageing, and reminiscence work, especially spiritual reminiscence, is valuable in assisting older people to make the meaning connections in their lives. The process is outlined in detail in Chapter 6. All these spiritual tasks are associated with finding hope in loss, disability and increasing frailty.

The contribution of aged care staff to well-being of residents

First, the contribution of staff has enormous potential to facilitate well-being or its reverse within an aged care facility. While the building design and environment are important to morale and well-being of residents, staff attitudes are even more important. Bird (2002) studied the behaviour of residents with dementia and their responses to different staff members who cared for them, and found that staff approaches and attitudes made a marked difference to the behaviour of residents with 'problem' behaviours. The onus is always on the staff to effectively communicate with residents, never the other way, as these elderly people may often have impaired communication abilities, and need sensitive support from the staff. Sometimes staff will engage in 'elder speak' using a higher tone of voice and speaking in a paternalistic voice. A number of people working in aged care have told me that it was easy to work with older people – just treat them like children! To work with this attitude is to deny the intervening years of life that these people have lived. If there is no difference between the knowledge and understanding of a child and an older person, then life has been wasted. Even for those who have dementia, there are differences; and the way they respond to life is still influenced by their life journey.

In a number of cases the staff who provide care may come from a much younger age group than those they care for. Thus a number of staff may hold different values and have different life experiences so that mutual understandings of events may not occur. Add to this the different cultures of both staff and residents, again this may make common understandings of culture and also of spiritual and religious practices difficult.

The role of staff in spiritual care

Spiritual care is a multidisciplinary endeavour. While pastoral carers and chaplains have a traditional role, other staff also have important input into spiritual care. One important and evolving role is that of the diversional therapists. While other aged care workers focus on physical care, be it provision of food, or nursing care – such as showering, dressing, and medications – diversional therapists have the privilege of being able to reach to the ultimate things of life – engaging with the residents – in life, and nourishing the spirit. Often, it seems in current aged care settings, nursing staff and personal carers do not have time to give to spiritual care, although some nurses will argue that by prioritizing and carefully planning care, spiritual care can be provided.

The clergy role in pastoral care

The specific role of chaplains is in gathering and ministering to the community of faith, and includes the administration of ritual and sacrament. Pastoral counselling and spiritual direction include dealing with grief and guilt, which may be a critical block to spiritual development. Confession and pronouncement of God's forgiveness, according to the tradition of the person being ministered to, may have healing qualities. Reconciliation, where it is possible, is part of the process of forgiveness, which allows the person to move to new spiritual growth and healing. In some cases, however, the other person(s) involved may no longer be living, and face to face reconciliation is not possible.

The nursing role in spiritual care

The spiritual tasks of ageing identified in this study would seem to be tasks that can be adopted into the nursing role; to assist older people in their vulnerability; in the transcendence of disabilities and loss; to search for final meanings; to find hope, and even to assist older people finding intimacy with God and/or others. Nurses can provide care by assessing, *being with*, listening and connecting deeply with the elderly person. Nurses do need to have skills in effective listening and, just as important, to be in touch with their own spirituality. Nurses need to be spiritually healthy and self-aware before they can be effective in providing spiritual care.

Pastoral care: who needs it?

Ninety-two per cent of participants in one study (MacKinlay 2001a) said they had a faith regardless of having any religious affiliation. This presents implications for spiritual and pastoral care. If we then assume that all people have a spiritual or faith dimension, assessment of spiritual needs must be deemed a necessary component of care, regardless of religious affiliation. Thus pastoral care becomes a way of being and journeying with all older people, not just those who identify with a religious tradition. This assumes that pastoral carers will live their roles out of their own acknowledged traditions, with an openness to the spiritual needs of those they care for. Thus, regardless of their own spiritual background, the pastoral carers will seek to meet the older people at the point of need of the older person.

The place of pastoral care and older people

One of the greatest gifts we can bring to our ministries is the gift of presence, of being there and being fully available to the person at that very moment. You may have shared what I call sacred space with those you care for, a time of feeling that the two of you were united in your spirits, a sense of deepest understanding and being with. There is in this a real sense of stepping on sacred ground and this experience is indeed a blessing for both the giver and the receiver. Pastoral care should be intentional and an authentic component of the team approach to spiritual care, working with registered nurses, assistants in nursing, diversional therapists and any others who engage in wholistic care of older people. The functions of pastoral care are to:

- assess individual needs
- work within the institutional framework
- advocate for the frail and vulnerable
- provide wholistic care for the aged person, for their family, and for staff.

Frail older people often give us far more than we can give to them. From a Christian context, it could be said that in some ways we are Christ to them and they in turn become Christ for us. It is a privilege to walk beside these frail and vulnerable people, to be, in some way, a blessing to them and, in turn, to be blessed by them.

If we acknowledge that pastoral carers are about meeting the spiritual needs of older people, then we also acknowledge the broad base of their caring roles. These may be carried out wherever older people are, in community as members of a parish, in the local community, in residential aged care. The role includes both supporting spiritual growth and development in the fourth age of life and spiritual care. It is also recognized that each cohort of elderly people will have their particular life journey, with its common experiences and values, and their individual and personal journeys, that constitute their spiritual and faith journeys too. The next cohort of ageing people coming to the point of needing care will be the baby boomers; a cohort that has made changes in each part of the life journey up to this point. It can only be assumed that these older people will experience later life in new ways; however, because humans are spiritual beings, and because the latter part of the life journey is a spiritual journey, baby boomers too will have spiritual needs. How they will want to meet these needs has yet to unfold.

Education in ministry in an ageing society

The demographics of society alone would set a high priority on including research-based content of aged care as a core component of all pastoral ministry programmes. As demonstrated in my studies, the spiritual dimension of ageing is a real component of the whole picture of ageing, and would thus be an important component of such courses. If staff are to provide effective wholistic care that includes spiritual care, then education needs to be provided.

Gerontology as a speciality subject should be available as a graduate studies course, both by graduate diploma or by masters degree. These courses should be readily available for all those who work in aged care, in parishes, in chaplaincy and other pastoral carer roles, and should be available both on campus and by distance learning.

The role varies for different types of professional preparation; ranging from therapy in life review for social workers and pastoral counsellors (as well as chaplains, and clinical nurse specialists in gerontology), to the non-professional but important functions of being with, listening to and being involved in individual and/or group work with older people. This non-professional role can effectively be done by pastoral visitors, who have attended short courses specifically designed for their needs.

For some providers of spiritual care, such as chaplains and pastoral carers, courses at post-graduate level may be required. For nurses, diversional therapists and other aged care workers, spiritual care is increasingly being included in basic education for practice. Continuing education programmes in aged care facilities should include work on spiritual care. There is no clear agreement for levels of education for practice in pastoral care. Various courses exist, some have a general pastoral care content, but few courses with a specific content on ageing are available. Yet there is a real content that is specific to ageing and pastoral care, that is needed for those working with elderly people. For high standards of spiritual care, staff need appropriate courses readily available to them. In addition to the discipline specific content, clinical pastoral education is a valuable background to anyone working pastorally.

One of the most important learning activities for people who work with frail and elderly people is to learn to listen to those they care for. It is too easy for people who have sensory or cognitive disabilities to be isolated because staff don't take the time to listen to them, and appear in a hurry to move on to the next person or task. It may be wrongly assumed that because a person has difficulty communicating that they cannot communicate or that they will not understand what others say.

Continuing education will provide workshops on grief and loss and on sexuality in later life. Other continuing education will focus on the process of ageing, palliative care and spiritual reminiscence. Often numbers of staff who work with elderly people have had little contact with people who are dying, or they may be living with their own unresolved grief. Grief is part of the nursing home culture, and all staff need to be able to understand their own grief before they can effectively work with people in their care who are grieving. Workshops on sexuality in later life are important for two reasons, first to dismiss the myths that older people are asexual, and second, to assist staff to provide appropriate care and sensitivity towards the sexuality of others and, especially, frail older people and those who have dementia.

Pastoral care: a team approach

Models of care: a model based on the aged care facility

This model uses the resources of the aged care organization to provide infrastructures for service provision. Often these organizations already have the required structures in place, and this avoids duplication of services. Where services are to be provided from outside the organization, knowledge of the organization assists in smoothly operating services. Chaplains may be employed by the aged care organization. Where this model of care is in place, linkages between community, parish and aged care facility are enhanced. Having a specialist aged care chaplain employed in the facility makes it easier to engage the chaplain as an integral part of the care team. In this case, pastoral care becomes readily recognized as a part of wholistic aged care, rather than an add on, optional component of care.

Models of care: a model of parish-based care provision

Aged care may be provided by clergy, or pastoral workers, or parish nurses, working in team with a local parish. Care is provided to community-based elderly people, or to residents in aged care. Numbers of these models work on an informal basis from the parish. As needs for pastoral support for older people rise, a more structured approach to care may be needed. Care providers will need education in both pastoral care skills and in working with elderly people.

Potential obstacles to implementing change

In the late 1990s when I completed my doctorate, I suggested that there were a number of obstacles to implementing change to move to wholistic care for older adults. I now wish to revisit these and make an assessment of changes that have occurred since then.

The first was the *need to recognize the universal nature of human spirituality*. At that time I wrote that the technological basis of the post-modern society tends to devalue the place of concepts that are difficult to quantify. Spirituality can be considered as an example of an area that does not easily fit the scientific model, or the medical model of health. I argued, based on my doctoral studies, that the spiritual dimension can clearly be seen to be a component of human being, and could reasonably be said to be a universal component, noting that those who did not have any religious affiliation acknowledged that there was a spiritual aspect of life. The ways in which the spiritual was worked out by different informants varied a great deal, nevertheless, it was recognized and acknowledged to be important. Now, a great deal more research is available to back these claims. In fact the time seems ripe to introduce spiritual care into health and aged care.

The second potential obstacle was: *Ageism prevents people being open to the possibilities of continued spiritual development in ageing.* I wrote then that an

> attitude of openness to possibilities in ageing is necessary before any changes towards the spiritual tasks of ageing can be addressed. This attitudinal change is required right across society; within the community, where opportunities are provided for learning and activities for older adults; in policy and planning to take account of the wholistic approach to care for older people, and not least in new attitudes of openness towards the wonderful resources of these older adults that await exploration. (MacKinlay 2001a, p.254)

Although it is evident from the amount of publishing in this field that much research is now being undertaken to dispel myths of ageing, there remain pockets of ageism, where myths still persist. The same is true of church communities and the need to recognize the opportunities that exist in being church in new ways in an ageing society. I wrote then that

> not only do the present and coming cohorts of older people need health care services, including spiritual care, but these older people are resources in themselves, thus, the great diversity of older people ought to be recognized, allowing for care and ministry by older people, with older people, to older people. (MacKinlay 2001a, p.254)

I believe that this has not changed. More than research is needed to make a difference in practice, attitudes need to change, and this can only occur as people see the need for change themselves; that is, when they are touched by others who can make the message come alive, or when they themselves grow older and become frail. But then it is perhaps too late. Will it be too late for the baby boomers too, when they learn about growing older?

The third potential obstacle to change was *the reluctance to push a particular belief system in a multicultural society.* I suggested then that tolerance of others' beliefs is valued, but that such a stance may be 'detrimental to the whole society, because we may fail to acknowledge our own belief systems. The result can be to develop a culture that has a spiritual vacuum' (MacKinlay 2001a, p.254). The number of articles published on multifaith perspectives of health and of spirituality now seem to acknowledge the multicultural and multifaith nature of most western societies. The literature points to the need to study, respect, and affirm the spiritual practices of the major faiths in an ageing multifaith society. However, we must continue to guard against a generic spirituality that fails to recognize the spiritual and particular needs of older people.

The final potential obstacle to change I identified in the 1990s was the idea that *the spiritual dimension is not really part of health care.* This is changing rapidly and it would be fair to say that most nursing textbooks now have at least some reference to spirituality and some have chapters on spiritual care. Spirituality in nursing is taught in most schools of nursing, although content probably varies a great deal. More medical and health conferences are being held where spirituality is being addressed as one of the themes, or in the title of the conference, for example a national conference on health and spirituality held in July 2005 in Australia. The third international conference on ageing and spirituality was held in Adelaide in 2004. It seems now that spirituality is openly acknowledged as a part of health and well-being. Now it remains to continue the research and to develop evidence-based practice in the multidisciplinary field of care involved with ageing and aged care.

Conclusion

Spiritual care and pastoral care are not optional extras, but need to be built into the main mission statement and to be actioned right through to resident and community-based care. A task now is engaging laity from the parish perspective, both as consumers and participants in growing spiritually in later life. It is necessary now to implement a model of service delivery that more intentionally uses the gifts of retired people. It is important to offer them training that may lead to involving more older people in positions where they are involved and accountable for service delivery. Offering well older people the opportunity to be involved in activities that are meaningful and useful too will greatly benefit them. This will be good for the older people who wish to be part of the provision of care, and it will also assist the professional care-givers by backing their professional service both in the community and in residential care. At the Centre for Ageing and Pastoral Studies in Canberra we are developing packages for pastoral care and spiritual growth for parish use with older adults in a variety of areas, the first of these was piloted during 2003 in a rural parish and is now in its second edition.

I also see important links between residential care and the faith community so that specialist aged care chaplaincy works alongside the parish clergy and community, and I think it is also important to give some context to models of service delivery, and that includes dealing with myths of ageing and opening up attitudes to new ways of seeing older people.

Summary

- *Ageing is understood here as a complex interaction of biological, psychosocial and spiritual factors.*

- *This book is based on a model of spiritual tasks and the spiritual process of ageing; it is a developmental model for ageing in the twenty-first century.*

- *This final chapter reviews the parts of the model and attempts to bring it together in a wholistic model to guide both spiritual growth and care in the fourth age of life.*

- *Each of the six themes of the model have been outlined in the appropriate chapters of this book.*

- *The role of staff in spiritual care is addressed noting the effects of staff attitudes on resident behaviours.*

- *Pastoral care includes: assessing individual needs; working within the institutional framework; advocacy for the frail and vulnerable; wholistic care for the aged person, for families and staff.*

- *Education in spiritual care is an important basis for appropriate care.*

Assessment of the Spiritual Needs of Older Adults: Level 1
Based on spiritual tasks of ageing (MacKinlay 2001a)

To be used at admission. May be self-administered, or with family or staff.

Name:_____

Address:_____

What makes your life worth living?

Are there things that are hard for you now?

What is hardest for you now?

How do you cope with difficult things in your life?

1   Religion/denomination (*optional*):_____

2   Are there any religious or spiritual practices that give you support, e.g. attending services of worship, prayer, meditation, reading scripture or other religious materials?

3   Are you a member of a church, congregation or faith community?

      ❑ Yes   ❑ No

4   Is there someone within that community that you would want contacted, for example your minister?

      ❑ Yes   ❑ No

      If yes, please provide contact details for that person.

Assessment of the Spiritual Needs of Older Adults: Level 2
Based on spiritual tasks of ageing (MacKinlay 2001a)

To be used in interview with resident/patient.

Name: _____

Address: _____

Religion/denomination (*optional*): _____

Are you a member of a church, congregation or faith community?

❑Yes   ❑No

Is there someone within that community that you would want contacted, for example your minister?

❑Yes   ❑No

If yes, please provide contact details for that person.

1   Ultimate meaning in life

1.1   Where do you find/what brings greatest meaning in your life?

1.2   What do you think God is like?

2   Response to ultimate meaning

2.1   Is religion important to you? If yes, in what way is it important?

2.2   Is your spiritual life important to you? If yes, in what way is it important?

2.3   Do you go to church? If no, did you use to go to church?

2.4   Which ways of engaging with life's meaning do you use and/or would you like to use? (*tick relevant boxes*)

❑ Worship   ❑ Music
❑ Prayer   ❑ Art
❑ Reading of scripture   ❑ Environment
❑ Meditation   ❑ Other

Comments:

2.5 Do you engage with meaning through religious traditions? Which of the following would you like to engage in? (*tick relevant boxes*)

❑ Attending church services

❑ Having the chaplain call

❑ Having your own minister/pastoral visitors visit

❑ Joining a small group for Bible reading/study/other religious studies

❑ Meditation

❑ Other

Would you like assistance with any of these?

2.6 Do you engage in life's meaning through any of the following? (*tick relevant boxes*)

❑ Music   ❑ Environment

❑ Art   ❑ Other

Comments:

3   Transcendence of loss and disabilities

3.1 What losses have you experienced in the past two to five years, e.g. spouse, other relatives, friends, work, home?

3.2 Do you have enough energy to do all you want to do?

3.3   Have you had any major illnesses and/or surgery?

3.4   What chronic illnesses do you live with?

3.5   What has helped you to cope in difficult circumstances in the past?

3.6   Has your faith been a help in coping? If yes, how?

4   Moving from provisional to ultimate meanings

Spiritual reminiscence may be used as a vehicle to explore issues and find relationship between ultimate meaning and growth.

4.1   What have been the hardest things in your life?

4.2   What is hardest in your life now?

4.3   What life experiences do you remember with joy?

4.4 What life experiences do you remember with sadness?

5 Finding intimacy with God and/or others

5.1 Do you share meaningful relationships with others? If yes, who, e.g. spouse, friend/s, relative/s?

5.2 Do you share your struggles and joys with God?

5.3 Social and spiritual intimacy/isolation. Do you feel lonely? (*tick one box*)

   ❑ Never   ❑ Mostly
   ❑ Sometimes   ❑ All the time

   Comments:

6 Finding hope

6.1 Do you have any fears?

6.2 What gives you hope in life?

Group Topics for Spiritual Reminiscence

These questions are based on the MacKinlay (2001a) spiritual tasks of ageing model.

Questions for participants to explore their life journey

A series of six themes of broad questions can be used to facilitate the process of spiritual reminiscence over six weekly group sessions. The questions below are suggested outlines of questions for each weekly session.

Week 1 Life-meaning

1. What gives greatest meaning to your life now? Follow up with questions like:

    • What is most important in your life?

    • What keeps you going?

    • Is life worth living?

    • If life is worth living, why is it worth living?

2. Looking back over your life:

    • What do you remember with joy?

    • What do you remember with sadness?

Week 2 Relationships – isolation

    • What are/have been the best things about relationships in your life?

Use this as a starting point for exploring relationships with the group. Think of a number of questions, such as who visits you? Who do you miss? Who have you been especially close to?

- Do you have many friends here? How many friends do you have?
- Do you ever feel lonely? When? Follow up on things that might be associated with time of day, place, etc.
- Do you like to be alone?

Week 3 Hopes, fears and worries

- What things do you worry about?
- Do you have any fears? What about?
- Do you feel you can talk to anyone about things that trouble you?
- What gives you hope now?

Week 4 Growing older and transcendence

- What's it like growing older, e.g. do you have health problems? Do you have memory problems? If so, how does that affect what you want to do?
- What are the hardest things in your life now?
- Do you like living here? What's it like living here? Was it hard to settle in?

and other questions of a similar kind.

Week 5 Spiritual and religious beliefs

- Do you have an image of God or some sense of a deity or otherness?
- If so, can you tell me about this image? Do you feel near to God?
- What are your earliest memories of church, mosque, temple or other worship? Did you used to go to Sunday school, church?

Week 6 Spiritual and religious practices

- Do you take part in any religious/spiritual activities now, e.g. attending church services, Bible or other religious readings, prayer, meditation?
- How important are these to you?
- How can we help you to find meaning now?

References

Achenbaum, W.A. (1995) 'Age-based Jewish and Christian rituals.' In M.A. Kimble, S.H. McFadden, J.W. Ellor and J.J. Seeber (eds) (1995) *Aging, Spirituality, and Religion: A Handbook*. Minneapolis: Augsburg Fortress Press.

Australian Capital Territory (ACT) Legislative Assembly Standing Committee on Health and Community Care (2001) *Elder Abuse in the ACT*, Report Number 11. Canberra: ACT Legislative Assembly.

Alexopoulos, G.S., Katz, I.R., Bruce, M.L. and Heo, M. (2005) 'Remission in depressed geriatric primary care patients: A report from the PROSPECT study.' *American Journal of Psychiatry 162*, 4, 718–725.

American Psychiatric Association (1994) *Diagnostic and Statistical Manual of Mental Disorders*. 4th edn (DSM-IV). Washington: American Psychiatric Association.

Ariyo, A.A. and Haan, M. (2000) 'Depressive symptoms and risks of coronary heart disease and mortality in elderly Americans.' *Journal of the American Heart Association 102*, 15, 1773–1779.

Arthur, D. and Lai, C. (2003). 'Depression.' In R. Hudson (ed.) *Dementia Nursing: A Guide to Practice*. Melbourne: Ausmed Publications.

Ashby, M.A. and Mendelson, D. (2004) 'Gardner re BWV: Victorian Supreme Court makes landmark Australia ruling on tube feeding.' *Medical Journal of Australia 181*, 8, 442–450.

Astley, J. and Francis, L.J. (1992) *Christian Perspectives on Faith Development*. Grand Rapids: William B. Federmans Publishing Company.

Atchley, R.C. (2000) 'Spirituality.' In T.R. Cole, R. Kastenbaum and R.E. Ray (eds) *Handbook of the Humanities and Aging*, 2nd edn. New York: Springer.

Australian Institute of Health and Welfare (2003) *Residential Aged Care in Australia 2001–02: A Statistical Overview*. AIHW cat. no. AGE 29. Canberra: AIHW.

Australian Institute of Health and Welfare (2004) *The Impact of Dementia on the Health and Aged Care System*. AIHW cat. no. AGE 37. Canberra: AIHW.

Bach, J.R., Campagnolo, D.I. and Hoeman, S. (1991) 'Life satisfaction of individuals with Duchenne muscular dystrophy using long-term mechanical ventilatory support.' *American Journal of Physical Medicine and Rehabilitation, 70*, 3, 129–35.

Baker, D.C. (2000) 'The investigation of pastoral care interventions as a treatment for depression among continuing care retirement community residents.' *Journal of Religious Gerontology 12*, 1, 62–85.

Baltes, P.B. and Baltes, M.M. (eds) (1990) *Successful Aging: Perspectives from the Behavioral Sciences*. New York: Cambridge University Press.

Barbato, M. (2002) *Caring for the Dying*. Sydney: McGraw Hill Book Company.

Bellah, R.N. (1969) 'Transcendence in contemporary piety.' In H.W. Richardson and D.R. Culter (eds) *Transcendence*. Boston, MA: Beacon Press.

Bellah, R.N., Madsen, R., Sullivan, W.M., Swidler, A. and Tipton, S.M. (1985) *Habits of the Heart: Individualism and Commitment to American Life*. Berkeley: University of California Press.

Bergman-Evans, B. (2004) 'Beyond the basics: effects of the Eden Alternative Model on quality of life issues.' *Journal of Gerontological Nursing 30*, 6, 27–34.

Bird, M. (2002) 'Dementia and suffering in nursing homes.' *Journal of Religious Gerontology 13*, 3/4, 49–68.

Birren, J.E. and Cochran, K.N. (2001) *Telling the Stories of Life through Guided Autobiography Groups*. Baltimore: The John Hopkins University Press.

Blanchard-Fields, F. and Norris, L. (1995) 'The development of wisdom.' In M.A. Kimble, S.H. McFadden, J.W. Ellor and J.J. Seeber (eds) *Aging, Spirituality, and Religion: A Handbook*. Minneapolis: Augsburg Fortress Press.

Boden, C. (1998) *Who Will I Be When I Die?* Pymble: Harper Collins Religious.

Boff, L. (1985) *Church: Charism and Power.* London: SCM Press Ltd.

Bowen, S. and Hudson, R. (2003) 'Creative care.' In R. Hudson (ed.) *Dementia Nursing: A Guide to Practice.* Melbourne: Ausmed Publications.

Bowlby, J. (1980) *Attachment and Loss.* New York: Basic Books, Inc.

Brenner, A. (2001) 'Prayer and presence.' In D.A. Friedman (ed.) *Jewish Pastoral Care: A Practical Handbook.* Woodstock, Vermont: Jewish Lights Publishing.

Bryden, C. (2005) *Dancing with Dementia: My Story of Living Positively with Dementia.* London: Jessica Kingsley Publishers.

Buckwalter, K.C. (1999) 'Depression and suicide.' In M. Stanley and P. Beare (eds) *Gerontological Nursing.* Philadelphia: Davis.

Butler, R. (1995) 'Foreword.' In B.K. Haight and J.D. Webster (eds) *The Art and Science of Reminiscence: Theory, Research, Methods, and Application.* Washington, DC: Taylor & Francis.

Callahan, D. (1987) *Setting Limits: Medical Goals in an Aging Society.* New York: Simon and Schuster.

Callahan, D. (1996) 'Controlling the costs of health care for the elderly: Fair means and foul.' *New England Journal of Medicine 335,* 10, 744–746.

Campbell, A.V. (2003) 'The virtues (and vices) of the four principles.' *Journal of Medical Ethics 29,* 5, 292–300.

Capps, D. (1990) *Reframing: A New Method in Pastoral Care.* Minneapolis, MI: Fortress Press.

Carroll, L.P. and Dyckman, K.M. (1986) *Chaos or Creation: Spirituality in Mid-life.* New York: Paulist Press.

Carson, V.B. (1989) *Spiritual Dimensions of Nursing Practice.* Philadelphia: W.B. Saunders Co.

Carson, V.B. and Green, H. (1992) 'Spiritual well-being: A predictor of hardiness in patients with acquired immunodeficiency syndrome.' *Journal of Professional Nursing 8,* 4, 209–220.

Chandler, M.J. and Holliday, S. (1990) 'Wisdom in a postapocalyptic age.' In R.J. Sternberg (ed.) *Wisdom: Its Nature, Origins, and Development.* New York: Cambridge University Press.

Cheston, R. and Bender, M. (1999) *Understanding Dementia: The Man with the Worried Eyes.* London: Jessica Kingsley Publishers.

Clarfield, A.M., Gordon, M., Markwell, H. and Alibhai, S. (2003) 'Ethical issues in end-of-life geriatric care: The approach of three monotheistic religions-Judiasm, Catholicism, and Islam.' *Journal of the American Geriatrics Society 51,* 8, 1149–1154.

Clements, W.M. (1990) 'Spiritual development in the fourth quarter of life.' In J.J. Seeber (ed.) *Spiritual Maturity in the Later Years.* New York: The Haworth Pastoral Press.

Close, R.E. (2000) 'Logotherapy and adult major depression: Psychotheological dimensions in diagnosing the disorder.' *Journal of Religious Gerontology 11,* 3/4, 119–40.

Cohen, C.B., Heller, J.C., Jennings, B., Morgan, E.F.M., Scott, D.A., Sedgwick, T.F. and Smith, D.H. (eds) (2000) *Faithful Living Faithful Dying.* Harrisburg, PA: Morehouse Publishing.

Cohen-Mansfield, J., Marx, M.S and Rosenthal, A.S. (1989) 'A description of agitation in the nursing home.' *American Journal of Geriatric Psychiatry 44,* M77–M84.

Cole, T.R., Kastenbaum, R. and Ray, R.E. (eds) (2000) *Handbook of the Humanities and Aging.* New York: Springer Publishing Company.

Coleman, M.T., Looney, S., O'Brien, J., Ziegler, C., Pastorino, C.A. and Turner, C. (2002) 'The Eden Alternative: Findings after 1 year of implementation.' *Journals of Gerontology: Series A: Biological Sciences and Medical Sciences 57A,* 7, M422–M427.

Coleman, P.G. (1986) *Ageing and Reminiscence Processes: Social and Clinical Implications.* Chichester: John Wiley and Sons.

Coleman, P.G. (1994) 'Reminiscence within the study of ageing: The social significance of story.' In J. Bornat (ed.) *Reminiscence Reviewed.* Buckingham: Open University Press.

Coleman, P.G. (1999) 'Creating a life story: The task of reconciliation.' *Gerontologist 39,* 2, 133–139.

Copp, D. and Sobel, D. (2004) 'Morality and virtue: An assessment of some recent work in virtue ethics.' *Ethics 114,* 3, 514–555.

Crisp, J. (2003) 'Communication.' In R. Hudson (ed.) *Dementia Nursing: A Guide to Practice.* Melbourne: Ausmed Publications.

Crisp, J. and Taylor, C. (eds) (2004) *Potter & Perry's Fundamentals of Nursing*. Australian adaptation. Marrickville: Mosby Publishers, Harcourt Australia.

Crystal, H. (2004) *Dementia with Lewy Bodies*. eMedicine. www.emedicine.com/neuro/topic 91.html, accessed 18 April 2005.

Csikszentmihalyi, M. and Rathunde, K. (1990) 'Psychology of wisdom: Evolutionary interpretation.' In R.J. Sternberg (ed.) *Wisdom: Its Nature, Origins, and Development*. New York: Cambridge University Press.

Cumming, E. and Henry, W.H. (1961) *Growing Old: The Process of Disengagement*. New York: Basic Books, Inc.

Cutrona, C.E. and Russell, D.W. (1987) 'The Provisions of social relationships and adaptation to stress.' In W.H. Jones and D. Perlam (eds) *Advances in Personal Relationships*. Greenwich, CT: JAI Press.

Davies, E., Male, M., Reimer, V., Turner, V. and Wylie, K. (2004) 'Pain assessment and cognitive impairment: Part 1.' *Nursing Standard 19*, 12, 39–42.

Davies, H. (1999) 'Delirium and dementia.' In J. Stone, J., Wyman and S. Salisbury, (eds) *Clinical Gerontological Nursing*. Philadelphia: W.B. Saunders.

de Vries, B. (2001) 'Grief: Intimacy's reflection.' *Generations*, Summer, 75–80.

Dempsey-Lyle, S. and Hoffman, L. (1991) *The Aging Game*. New Jersey: Slack Inc.

Denny, F.M. (1994) *An Introduction to Islam*. New York: Maxwell Publishing Company.

Draper, P. and McSherry, W. (2002) 'A critical view of spirituality and spiritual assessment.' *Journal of Advanced Nursing 39*, 1, 1–2.

Driscoll-Lamberg, A. (2001) 'Integrating spirituality in counselling with older adults.' In D.O. Moberg (ed.) *Aging and Spirituality: Spiritual Dimensions of Aging Theory, Research, Practice, and Policy*. New York: Haworth Press.

Edvardsson, J.D., Sandman, P.-O. and Rasmussen, B.H. (2003) 'Meanings of giving touch in the care of older patients: Becoming a valuable person and professional.' *Journal of Clinical Nursing 12*, 4, 601–609.

Ekval, G., Arvonen, J. and Waldenstrom-Lindblad, L. (1983) *Creative Organisational Climate, Construction and Validation of a Measuring Instrument*. Stockholm: Fa-Institute.

Ellison, C.W. (1983) 'Spiritual well-being: Conceptualization and measurement.' *Journal of Psychology and Theology 11*, 4, 330–338.

Emick-Herring, B. (2001) 'Impaired communication.' In M. Mass, M. Buckwalter, K. Hardy, M. Tripp-Reimer, T. Titler and J. Specht (eds) *Nursing Care of Older Adults: Diagnoses, Outcomes & Interventions*. Philadelphia, PA: Mosby.

Erikson, E.H., Erikson, J.M. and Kivnick, H.Q. (1986) *Vital Involvement in Old Age*. New York: W.W. Norton and Co.

Fiala, W.E., Bjorck, J.P. and Gorsuch, R. (2002) 'The religious support scale: Construction, validation and cross-validation.' *American Journal of Community Psychology 30*, 6, 761–287.

Fleming, R. (2001) *Challenge Depression*. Canberra: Commonwealth Department of Health and Ageing.

Floyd, J.A., Janisse, J.J., Medler, S.M. and Ager, J.W. (2000) 'Nonlinear components of age-related change in sleep initiation.' *Nursing Research 49*, 5, 290–4.

Folstein, M.F., Folstein, S.E. and McHugh, P.R. (1975) '"Mini-Mental State": A practical method for grading cognitive state of patients for the clinician.' *Journal of Psychiatric Research 12*, 189–196.

Fountain, J. (2003) 'The relatives' perspective.' In R. Hudson (ed.) *Dementia Nursing: A Guide to Practice*. Melbourne: Ausmed Publications.

Fowler, J.W. (1981) *Stages of Faith: The Psychology of Human Development and the Quest for Meaning*. San Francisco: Harper.

Fowler, J.W. (1986) 'Dialogue towards a future.' In C. Dykstra and S. Parks (eds) *Faith Development and Fowler*. Birmingham, Alabama: Religious Education Press.

Frankl, V.E. (1984) *Man's Search for Meaning*. New York: Washington Square Press.

Frankl, V.E. (1997) *Man's Search for Ultimate Meaning*. Reading, Massachusetts: Perseus Books.

Friedman, D.A. (2001) *Jewish Pastoral Care: A Practical Handbook from Traditional and Contemporary Sources*. Woodstock, Vermont: Jewish Lights Publishing.

Friedman, D.A. (2003) 'An anchor amidst anomie: Ritual and aging.' In M.A. Kimble and S.H. McFadden (eds) *Aging, Spirituality and Religion: A Handbook, Volume 2.* Minneapolis: Fortress Press.

Fulmer, T. (2005) 'Elder abuse and neglect assessment.' *Medsurg Nursing 14,* 1, 78.

Gatz, M. and Fiske, A. (2003) 'Aging women and depression.' *Professional Psychology: Research and Practice 34,* 1, 3–9.

Gauger, J., Kane, R., Kane, R. and Newcomer, R. (2005) 'The longitudinal effects of early behaviour problems in the dementia care-giving career.' *Psychology and Aging 2,* 1, 100–116.

George, L.K. (1999) 'Religious/spiritual history.' In Fetzer Institute (ed.) *Multidimensional Measurement of Religiousness/Spirituality for Use in Health Research.* Kalamazoo, MI: John E. Institute, 19–24.

Gerhardt, K.A. and Corbet, B. (1995) 'Uniformed consent: Biased decision making following spinal cord injury.' HEC Forum 7, 2–3 (March–May) 10–121.

Gibson, F. (1998) *Reminiscence and Recall: A Guide to Good Practice.* London: Age Concern Books.

Gibson, F. (2004) *The Past in the Present: Using Reminiscence in Health and Social Care.* Baltimore: Health Professions Press.

Glaser, B.G. and Strauss, A.L. (1967) *The Discovery of Grounded Theory: Strategies for Qualitative Research.* Chicago: Aldine Atherton.

Glaser, B.G. and Strauss, A.L. (1999) *The Discovery of Grounded Theory: Strategies for Qualitative Research.* New York: Aldine De Gruyte.

Goldsmith, M. (1996) *Hearing the Voice of People with Dementia: Opportunities and Obstacles.* London: Jessica Kingsley Publishers.

Goldsmith, M. (2001) 'When words are no longer necessary: A gift of ritual.' In E. MacKinlay, J. Ellor and S. Pickard (eds) *Aging, Spirituality and Pastoral Care.* New York: The Haworth Pastoral Press.

Goldsmith, M. (2004) *In a Strange Land... People with Dementia and the Local Church.* Southwell, Nottinghamshire: 4M Publications.

Gray-Vickrey, P. (2004) 'Combating elder abuse.' *Nursing 34,* 10, 47–55.

Greeley, A.M. (1969) *Religion in the Year 2000.* New York: Sheed and Ward.

Greeley, A.M. (1973) *The Persistence of Religion.* London: SCM Press Ltd.

Greeley, A.M. (1982) *Religion: A Secular Theory.* New York: The Free Press.

Guroian, V. (1996) *Life's Living towards Dying.* Grand Rapids, Michigan: William B. Eerdmans Publishing Company.

Hafsteinsdottir, T.B. and Grydonck, M. (1997) 'Being a stroke patient: A review of the literature.' *Journal of Advanced Nursing 26,* 3, 580–588.

Haight, B.K. and Webster, J.D. (eds) (1995) *The Art and Science of Reminiscence: Theory, Research, Methods, and Applications.* Washington, DC: Taylor and Francis.

Hair, J.F. Jr., Anderson, R.E., Tatham, R.L. and Black, W.C. (1995) *Multivariate Data Analysis with Readings.* Englewood Cliffs, New Jersey: Prentice Hall International Inc.

Hardin, E. and Khan-Hudson A. (2005) 'Elder abuse – "society's dilemma".' *Journal of the National Medical Association 97,* 1, 91–95.

Harkins, S. (2002) 'What is unique about the older person's pain experience?' In D.K. Weiner, K. Kerr and T.E. Rudy (eds) *Persistent Pain in Older Adults.* New York: Springer Publishing.

Hassan, R. (1995) *Suicide Explained: The Australian Experience.* Melbourne: Melbourne University Press.

Hauerwas, S., Stoneking, C.B., Meador, K.G. and Cloutier, D. (eds) (2003) *Growing Old in Christ.* Grand Rapids, Michigan: William B. Eerdmans Publishing Company.

Havighurst, R.J., Neugarten, B.L. and Tobin, S.S. (1968) 'Disengagement and patterns of aging.' In B.L. Neugarten (ed.) *Middle Age and Aging: A Reader in Social Psychology.* Chicago: The University of Chicago Press.

Hays, J.C., Meador, K.G., Branch, P.S. and George, L.K. (2001) 'The spiritual history scale in four dimensions (SHS-4): Validity and reliability.' *Gerontologist 41,* 2, 239–249.

Heard, K. and Watson, T.S. (1999) 'Reducing wandering by persons with dementia using differential reinforcement.' *Journal of Applied Behavior Analysis 32,* 3, 381–384.

Heinz, D. (1994) 'Finishing the story: Aging, spirituality and the work of culture.' *Journal of Religious Gerontology 9,* 1, 3–19.

Henderson, A. and Jorm, A. (1998) *Dementia in Australia*. Aged and Community Care Service Development and Evaluation Report No. 35. Camberra: AGPS.

Hide, K. (2001) *Gifted Origins to Graced Fulfillment, The Soteriology of Julian of Norwich*. Collegeville, MN: The Liturgical Press.

Highfield, M.F. (1989) 'The spiritual health of oncology patients: A comparison of nurse and patient perceptions.' Unpublished dissertation, Denton: Texas Woman's University.

Hildebrand, J.K., Joos, S.K. and Lee, M.A. (1997) 'Use of the diagnosis "failure to thrive" in older veterans.' *Journal of the American Geriatrics Society 45*, 9, 1113–1117.

Hill, P.C. and Pargament, K.I. (2003) 'Advances in the conceptualization and measurement of religion and spirituality: Implications for physical and mental health research.' *American Psychologist 58*, 1, 64–74.

Hodge, D. (1972) 'A validated intrinsic religious motivation scale.' *Journal for the Scientific Study of Religion 11*, 369–376.

Hodge, D.R. (2002) 'Working with Muslim youths: Understanding the values and beliefs of Islamic discourse.' *Children and Schools 24*, 1, 6–21.

Hodge, D.R. (2004) 'Working with Hindu clients in a spiritually sensitive manner.' *Social Work 49*, 1, 27–38.

Hodges, H.F., Keeley, A.C. and Grier, E.C. (2001) 'Masterworks of art and chronic illness experiences in the elderly.' *Journal of Advanced Nursing 36*, 3, 389–398.

Horst, G.R. (2000) 'The impact of the death of a resident on relationships in a nursing home setting.' Unpublished project in partial fulfilment of requirements for a doctor of ministry program. St Paul Minnesota: Luther Seminary.

Hudson, R. (ed.) (2003) *Dementia Nursing: A Guide to Practice*. Melbourne: Ausmed Publications.

Husain, S.A. (1998) 'Religion and mental health from the Muslim perspective.' In H.G. Koenig (ed.) *Handbook of Religion and Mental Health*. San Diego: Academic Press.

Idler, E. (1999) 'Organizational religiousness.' In Fetzer Institute (ed.) *Multidimensional Measurement of Religiousness/Spirituality for Use in Health Research*. Kalamazoo, MI: John E. Institute, 75–80.

Isenberg, S. (2000) 'Aging in Judaism: "Crown of Glory" and "Days of Sorrow".' In T.R Cole, R. Kasterbaum and R.E. Ray (eds) *Handbook of the Humanities and Aging*. New York: Springer Publishing Company.

Jackson, G. and MacDonald, C. (2004) 'Aggression.' In R. Hudson (ed.) *Dementia Nursing: A Guide to Practice*. Melbourne: Ausmed Publications.

Jamieson, D. (2004) *Walking with Forgotten People: Some Aspects of Pastoral Care with Older People*. Canberra: Centre for Ageing and Pastoral Studies.

Jamieson, D. (2005) *Exploring and Affirming my Life*. Canberra: Centre for Ageing and Pastoral Studies.

Jewell, A. (ed.) (2004) *Ageing, Spirituality and Well-being*. London: Jessica Kingsley Publishers.

Johnstone, M.J. (1999) *Bioethics: A Nursing Perspective*. Marrickville: Harcourt Saunders.

Jones, W.P. (2001) 'In wait of my life: Aging and desert spirituality.' *Journal of Religious Gerontology 12*, 2, 99–108.

Juthani, N.V. (1998) 'Understanding and treating Hindu patients.' In H.G. Koenig (ed.) *Handbook of Religion and Mental Health*. San Diego: Academic Press.

Kane, R.L. and Kane, R.A. (eds) (2000) *Assessing Older Persons: Measures, Meaning, and Practical Applications*. New York: Oxford University Press.

Kanitsaki, O. (2002) 'Mental health, culture and spirituality: Implications for the effective psychotherapeutic care of Australia's ageing migrant population.' In E. MacKinlay (ed.) *Mental Health and Spirituality in Later Life*. New York: Haworth Pastoral Press.

Kauhanen, M., Korpelainen, J.T., Hiltunen, P., Brusin, E., Mononen, H., Maatta, R., Nieminen, P., Sotaniemi, K.A. and Myllyla, V.V. (1999) 'Post-stroke depression correlates with cognitive impairment and neurological deficits.' *Stroke 30*, 9, 1875–80.

Kenyon, G.M. (2003) 'Telling and listening to stories: Creating a wisdom environment for older people.' *Generations 27*, 3, 30–33.

Kenyon, G.M., Clark, P. and de Vries, B. (2001) (eds) *Narrative Gerontology: Theory, Research, and Practice*. New York: Springer.

Kestenbaum, I. (2001) 'The gift of healing relationship: a theology of jewish pastoral care.' In D.A. Friedman (ed.) *Jewish Pastoral Care: A Practical Handbook from Traditional and Contemporary Sources.* Woodstock, Vermont: Jewish Lights Publishing.

Killick, J. (1997) *You are Words: Dementia Poems.* London: Journal of Dementia Care.

Killick, J. and Allan, K. (2001) *Communication and the Care of People with Dementia.* Buckingham: Open University Press.

Kilner, J.F., Miller, A.B. and Pellegrino, E.D. (eds) (1996) *Dignity and Dying: A Christian Appraisal.* Grand Rapids, Michigan: William B. Eerdmans Publishing Company.

Kimble, M.A. and McFadden, S.H. (eds) (2003) *Aging, Spirituality and Religion: A Handbook, Volume 2.* Minneapolis: Fortress Press.

Kimble, M.A., McFadden, S.H., Ellor, J.W. and Seeber, J.J. (eds) (1995) *Aging, Spirituality, and Religion: A Handbook.* Minneapolis: Augsburg Fortress Press.

Kirby, S.E., Coleman, P.G. and Daley, D. (2004) 'Spirituality and well-being in frail and nonfrail older adults.' *Journals of Gerontology 59B,* 3, 123–129.

Kirkwood, T.B.L. (1999) *Time of Our Lives.* London: Weidenfeld and Nicolson.

Kirkwood, T.B.L. (2000) 'Evolution of aging: How genetic factors affect the end of life.' *Generations 24,* 1, 12–24.

Kirshner, H. (2005) 'Frontal and temporal lobe dementia.' Available at www.eMedicine.com, accessed 15 May 2005.

Kitwood, T. (1997) *Dementia Reconsidered.* Buckingham: Open University Press.

Koenig, H.G. (1994) *Aging and God: Spiritual Pathways to Mental Health in Midlife and Later Years.* New York: The Haworth Pastoral Press.

Koenig, H.G. (1995) 'Religion and health in later life.' In M.A. Kimble, S.H. McFadden, J.W. Ellor and J.J. Seeber (eds) *Aging, Spirituality and Religion: A Handbook.* Minneapolis, MI: Augsburg Fortress Press.

Koenig, H.G. (ed.) (1998) *Handbook of Religion and Mental Health.* San Diego: Academic Press.

Koenig, H.G. and Lawson, D.M. (2004) *Faith in the Future: Healthcare, Aging, and the Role of Religion.* Philadelphia: Templeton Foundation Press.

Koenig, H.G., Cohen, H.J., Blazer, D.G., Pieper, G., Meador, K.G., Shelp, F., Goli, V. and DiPasquale, R. (1992) 'Religious coping and depression in elderly hospitalized medically ill men.' *American Journal of Psychiatry 149,* 1693–1700.

Koenig, H.G., George, L.K., Meador, K.G., Blazer, D.G. and Ford, S.M. (1994) 'Religious practices and alcoholism in a Southern adult population.' *Hospital and Community Psychiatry 45,* 225–231.

Koenig, H.G., Hays, J.C., George, L.K., Blazer, D.G., Larson, D.B. and Landerman, L.R. (1997) 'Modeling the cross-sectional relationships between religion, physical health, social support, and depressive symptoms.' *American Journal of Geriatric Psychiatry 5,* 131–144.

Koenig, H.G., McCullough, M.E. and Larson, D.B. (2001) *Handbook of Religion and Health.* New York: Oxford University Press.

Kubler-Ross, E. (1970) *On Death and Dying.* New York: Collier Books/Macmillan Publishing Co.

Kuhl, D.R. and Westwood, M. (2001) 'A narrative approach to integration and healing among the terminally ill.' In G.M. Kenyon, P. Clark and B. de Vries (eds) *Narrative Gerontology: Theory, Research, and Practice.* New York: Springer.

Kunz, J.A. (2002) 'Integrating reminiscence and life review techniques with brief, cognitive behavioral therapy.' In J.D. Webster and B.K. Haight (eds) *Critical Advances in Reminiscence Work: From Theory to Application.* New York: Springer Publishing Co., 275–288.

Lachs, M.S. and Pillemer, K. (2004) 'Elder abuse.' *Lancet 364,* 9441, 1263–1273.

Lai, C. and Arthur, D. (2004) 'Wandering.' In R. Hudson (ed.) (2003) *Dementia Nursing: A Guide to Practice.* Melbourne: Ausmed Publications.

Lang, S.S. (2005) 'Elder abuse cited as urgent problem.' *Human Ecology 32,* 3, 23.

Leenaars, A.A. (2003) 'Can a theory of suicide predict all "suicides" in the elderly?' *Crisis: Journal of Crisis Intervention and Suicide 24,* 1, 7–16.

Levin, J. (1999) 'Private religious practices.' In Fetzer Publication (ed.) *Multidimensional Measurement of Religiousness/Spirituality for Use in Health Research.* Kalamazoo, MI: John E. Institute, 39–42.

Levin, J. (2003) '"Bumping the top": Is mysticism the future of religious gerontology?' In M.A. Kimble and S.H. McFadden (eds) *Aging, Spirituality and Religion: A Handbook, Volume 2*. Minneapolis: Fortress Press.

MacKinlay, E.B. (1998) 'The spiritual dimension of ageing: Meaning in life, response to meaning and well being in ageing.' Unpublished doctoral thesis. Melbourne: La Trobe University.

MacKinlay, E.B. (2001a) *The Spiritual Dimension of Ageing*. London: Jessica Kingsley Publishers.

MacKinlay, E.B. (2001b) 'Health, healing and wholeness in frail elderly people.' *Journal of Religious Gerontology 13*, 2, 25–34.

MacKinlay, E.B. (2001c) 'Ageing, social and spiritual isolation.' *Journal of Religious Gerontology 12*, 3/4, 89–99.

MacKinlay, E.B. (2001d) 'The spiritual dimension of caring: Applying a model for spiritual tasks of ageing.' *Journal of Religious Gerontology 12*, 3/4, 151–166.

MacKinlay, E.B. (2001e) 'Understanding the ageing process: A developmental perspective of the psychosocial and spiritual dimensions.' *Journal of Religious Gerontology 12*, 3/4, 111–122.

MacKinlay, E.B. (2002) 'Mental health and spirituality in later life: Pastoral approaches.' *Journal of Religious Gerontology 13*, 3/4, 129–147.

MacKinlay, E.B (2003) 'Late-life depression – the role of the pastoral care giver in long term care.' In M.A. Kimble and S.H. McFadden (eds) *Aging, Spirituality, and Religion: A Handbook, Volume 2*. Minneapolis: Fortress Press.

MacKinlay, E.B. (ed.) (2004) *Spirituality of Later Life: On Humour and Despair*. New York: Haworth Pastoral Press.

MacKinlay, E.B., Trevitt, C. and Coady, M. (2002–2005) 'Finding meaning in the experience of dementia: The place of spiritual reminiscence work.' Australian Research Council. Linkage Grant.

MacKinlay, E.B., Trevitt, C. and Hobart, S. (2002) 'The search for meaning: Quality of life for the person with dementia.' Unpublished project report: University of Canberra Collaborative Grant 2001.

Marshall, M. and Hutchinson, S. (2001) 'A critique of research on the use of activities with person's with Alzheimer's disease: A systematic literature review.' *Journal of Advanced Nursing 35*, 4, 488–496.

Maslow, A.H. (1970) *Motivation and Personality*. New York: Harper and Row.

McFadden, S.H., Brennan, M. and Patrick, J.H. (eds) (2003) *New Directions in the Study of Late Life Religiousness and Spirituality*. New York: Haworth Pastoral Press.

McKevitt, C. Redfern, J., Mold, F. and Wolfe, C. (2004) 'Qualitative studies of stroke: A systematic review.' *Stroke 35*, 1499–1505.

McNamara, L.J. (2002) 'Theological perspectives on ageing and mental health.' *Journal of Religious Gerontology 13*, 3/4, 1–16.

McSherry, W. (2000) *Making Sense of Spirituality in Nursing Practice*. London: Churchill Livingstone.

McSherry, W. (2002) 'Dilemmas of spiritual assessment: Considerations for nursing practice.' *Journal of Advanced Nursing 38*, 5, 479–488.

Meador, K.G. and Henson, S.C. (2003) 'Growing old in a therapeutic culture.' In S. Hauerwas, C.B. Stoneking, K.G. Meador and D. Cloutier (eds) (2003) *Growing Old in Christ*. Grand Rapids, Michigan: William B. Eerdmans Publishing Company.

Meeks-Sjostrom, D. (2004) 'A comparison of three measures of elder abuse.' *Journal of Nursing Scholarship 36*, 3, 247–250.

Miller, C. (2004) *Nursing for Wellness in Older Adults*. Philadelphia: Wilkins and Williams.

Minardi, H.A. and Blanchard, M. (2004) 'Older people with depression: Pilot study.' *Journal of Advanced Nursing 46*, 1, 23–32.

Minichiello, V., Aroni, R., Timewell, E. and Alexander, L. (1995) *In-depth Interviewing: Principles, Techniques*. Sydney: Longman.

Moberg, D.O. (1990) 'Spiritual maturity and wholeness in the later years.' In J.J. Seeber (ed.) *Spiritual Maturity in the Later Years*. New York: Haworth Pastoral Press.

Moberg, D.O. (ed.) (2001) *Aging and Spirituality: Spiritual Dimensions of Aging Theory, Research, Practice and Policy*. New York: Haworth Pastoral Press.

Moody, H.R. (1995) 'Mysticism.' In M.A. Kimble, S.H. McFadden, J.W. Ellor and J.J. Seeber (eds) *Aging, Spirituality, and Religion: A Handbook*. Minneapolis: Augsburg Fortress Press.

Morgan, R.L. (1995) 'Guiding spiritual autobiography groups for third and fourth agers.' *Journal of Religious Gerontology 9*, 2, 1–14.

Morgan, R.L. (2003) 'Small group approaches to group spiritual autobiography writing.' In M.A. Kimble and S.H. McFadden (eds) (2003) *Aging, Spirituality and Religion: A Handbook, Volume 2*. Minneapolis: Fortress Press.

Morse, J.M. (ed.) (1992) *Qualitative Health Research*. Newbury Park: Sage Publications.

Morse, J.M. and Field, P.A. (1995) *Qualitative Research Methods for Health Professionals*. Thousand Oaks, California: Sage Publications.

Murphy, P.E., Ciarrocchi, J.W., Piedmont, R.L., Cheston, S., Peyrot, M. and Fitchett, G. (2000) 'The relation of religious belief and practices, depression, and hopelessness in persons with clinical depression.' *Journal of Consulting and Clinical Psychology 68*, 6, 1102–1106.

Musick, M.A., Blazer, D.G. and Hays, J.C. (2000) 'Religious activity, alcohol use, and depression in a sample of elderly Baptists.' *Research on Ageing 22*, 91–116.

Neugarten, B.L. (1968) 'Adult personality: Toward a psychology of the life cycle.' In B.L. Neugarten (ed.) *Middle Age and Aging: A Reader in Social Psychology*. Chicago: The University of Chicago Press.

Nursing Standard (2004) 'Trust trials spiritual care strategy.' *Nursing Standard 18*, 37, 5.

Norberg, K., Hellzen, O., Sandman, P. and Asplund, K. (2002) 'The relationship between organizational climate and the content of daily life for people with dementia living in a group dwelling.' *Journal of Clinical Nursing 11*, 2, 237–246.

Normann, H.K., Norberg, K. and Asplund, K. (2002) 'Confirmation and lucidity during conversations with a woman with severe dementia.' *Journal of Advanced Nursing 39*, 4, 370–376.

Ohayon, M.M., Zulley, J., Guilleminault, C., Smirne, S. and Priest, R.G. (2001) 'How age and daytime activities are related to insomnia in the general population: Consequences for older people.' *Journal of the American Geriatrics Society 49*, 4, 360–366.

Olson, D.M. and Kane, R.A. 'Spiritual assessment.' In R.L. Kane and R.A. Kane (eds) (2000) *Assessing Older Persons: Measures, Meaning, and Practical Applications*. New York: Oxford University Press.

Palapathwala, R. (in press) 'Ageing and death: A Buddhist-Christian conceptual framework for spirituality in later life.' *Journal of Religion, Spirituality and Ageing 18*.

Pargament, K.I. (1997) *The Psychology of Religion and Coping: Theory, Research, Practice*. New York: The Guilford Press.

Pargament, K.I. (1999) 'Meaning.' In Fetzer Institute (ed.) *Multidimensional Measurement of Religiousness/Spirituality for Use in Health Research*. Kalamazoo, MI: John E. Institute, 75–80.

Peck, R.C. (1968) 'Psychological developments in the second half of life.' In B.L. Neugarten (ed.) (1968) *Middle Age and Aging: A Reader in Social Psychology*. Chicago: The University of Chicago Press.

Pellegrino, E.D. and Thomasma, D.C. (1993) *The Virtues in Medical Practice*. New York: Oxford University Press.

Peterman, A., Fitchett, G., Brady, M.J., Hernandez, L. and Cella, D. (2002) 'Measuring spiritual well-being in people with cancer: The Functional Assessment of Chronic Illness Therapy-Spiritual Well-being Scale (FACIT-sp).' *Annals of Behavorial Medicine 24*, 1, 49–58.

Post, S.G. (2000) *The Moral Challenge of Alzheimer Disease: Ethical Issues from Diagnosis to Dying*. Baltimore: John Hopkins University Press.

Powers, B. (2003) 'The significance of losing things: For nursing home residents with dementia and their families.' *Journal of Gerontological Nursing 29*, 11.

Ramsey, J.L. and Bleisner, R. (2000) *Spiritual Resiliency in Older Women: Models of Strength for Challenges Through the Life Span*. Thousand Oaks, California: Sage Publications.

Randall, W.L. and Kenyon, G.M. (2001) *Ordinary Wisdom: Biographical Aging and the Journey of Life*. Westport: Praeger.

Raphael, B. (1990) *The Anatomy of Bereavement: A Handbook for the Caring Professions*. London: Routledge.

Raymond, J. (2002) 'Suicide in later life.' *Journal of Religious Gerontology 13*, 3/4, 117–128.

Richards Hall, G. and Gerdner, L. (1999) 'Managing problem behaviours.' In J. Stone, J. Wyman and S. Salisbury (eds) *Clinical Gerontological Nursing*. Philadelphia: W.B. Saunders.

Richards, K. and Beck, C. (2004) 'Progressively lowered stress threshold model: Understanding behavioural symptoms of dementia.' *Journal of the American Geriatrics Society 52*, 10, 1174–1175.

Roach, S.M. (2004) 'Sexual behaviour of nursing home residents: Staff perceptions and responses.' *Journal of Advanced Nursing 48*, 4, 371–379.

Rowland, F., Liu, Z. and Braun, P. (2002) 'The probability of using an aged care home over a lifetime (1999–00).' *Australasian Journal on Ageing 21*, 3, 117–121.

Scotton, B.W. (1998) 'Treating Buddhist patients.' In H.G. Koenig (ed.) *Handbook of Religion and Mental Health.* San Diego: Academic Press.

Seeber, J.J. (ed.) (1990) *Spiritual Maturity in Later Years.* New York: Haworth Pastoral Press.

Seeman, T.E., Dubin, L.F. and Seeman, M. (2003) 'Religiosity/spirituality and health: A critical review of the evidence for biological pathways.' *American Psychologist 58*, 1, 53–63.

Sloan, R.P., Bagiella, E., VandeCreek, L., Hover, M., Casalone, C., Hirsch, T.J., Hasan, Y., Kreger, R. and Poulos, P. (2000) 'Should physicians prescribe religious activities?' *New England Journal of Medicine 342*, 25, 1913–1916.

Sloan, R.P. and Bagiella, E. (2002) 'Claims about religious involvement and health outcomes.' *Annals of Behavioral Medicine 24*, 1, 14–21.

Snow, L., O'Malley, K., Cody, M., Kunik, M., Ashton, C. and Novy, D. (2004) 'A conceptual model of pain assessment for noncommunicative persons with dementia.' *Gerontologist 44*, 6, 807–817.

Snow, L., Rapp, M. and Kunik, M. (2005) 'Pain management in persons with dementia.' *Geriatrics 60*, 5, 22–26.

Snowden, D. (2001) *Ageing with Grace.* London: HarperCollins.

Snowdon, J. (1998) 'Management of late-life depression.' *Australasian Journal of Ageing 17*, 2, 57–62.

Soeken, K.L. and Carson, V.J. (1987) 'Responding to the spiritual needs of the chronically ill.' *Nursing Clinics of North America.* Sept. 22, 3, 603–11.

Stanley, M. and Gauntlet Beare, P. (1999) *Gerontological Nursing: A Health Promotion/Protection Approach.* Philadelphia: F.A. Davis.

Sternberg, R.J. (ed.) (1990) *Wisdom: Its Nature, Origins, and Development.* New York: Cambridge University Press.

Stoll, R.I. (1979) 'Guidelines for spiritual assessment.' *American Journal of Nursing*, September, 1574–1577.

Stone, J., Wyman, J. and Salisbury, S. (1999) *Clinical Gerontological Nursing.* Philadelphia: W.B. Saunders.

Stott, J. (1992) *The Contemporary Christian.* Leicester: Inter-Varsity Press.

Strang, S., Strang, P. and Ternestedt, B. (2002) 'Spiritual needs as defined by Swedish nursing staff.' *Journal of Clinical Nursing 11*, 1, 48–57.

Strauss, A. and Corbin, J. (1990) *Basics of Qualitative Research: Grounded Theory Procedures and Techniques.* Newbury Park: Sage Publications.

Strawbridge, W.J., Shema, S.J., Balfour, J.L., Higby, H.R. and Kaplan, G.A. (1998) 'Antecedents of frailty over three decades in an older cohort.' *The Journals of Gerontology 53B*, 1, S9–16.

Stroebe, M.S., Hanson, R.O., Stroebe, W. and Schut, H. (eds) (2001) *Handbook of Bereavement Research: Consequences, Coping and Care.* Washington: American Psychological Association.

Swinton, J. (2001) *Spirituality and Mental Health Care: Rediscovering a 'Forgotten' Dimension.* London: Jessica Kingsley Publishers.

Swinton, J. and Narayanasamy, A. (2002) 'Response to: A critical view of spirituality and spiritual assessment.' *Journal of Advanced Nursing 40*, 2, 158–160.

Tacey, D. (2003) *The Spirituality Revolution: The Emergence of Contemporary Spirituality.* Pymble, Australia: HarperCollins Publishers.

Tanyi, R.A. (2002) 'Towards clarification of the meaning of spirituality.' *Journal of Advanced Nursing 39*, 5, 500–509.

Tarakeshwar, N., Pargament, K. and Mahoney, A. (2003) 'Measures of Hindu pathways: Development and preliminary evidence of reliability.' *Cultural Diversity and Ethnic Minority Psychology 9*, 4, 316–332.

Teaster, P.B. and Roberto, K.A. (2004) 'Sexual abuse of older adults: APS cases and outcomes.' *Gerontologist 44*, 6, 788–796.

Thobaben, J.R. (1996) 'Long-term care.' In J.F. Kilner, A.B. Miller and E.D. Pellegrinio (eds) *Dignity and Dying: A Christian Appraisal.* Grand Rapids, Michigan: William B. Eerdmans Publishing Co.

Thomas, W. (2002) *The Eden Alternative.* Available at www.edenalt.com, accessed 24 March 2005.

Thorn, S. and Paterson, B. (1998) 'Shifting images of chronic illness.' *Image – The Journal of Nursing Scholarship 30*, 2, 173–178.

Thursby, G.R. (2000) 'Ageing in eastern religious traditions.' In T.R. Cole, R. Kastenbaum and R.E. Ray (eds) *Handbook of the Humanities and Aging*. New York: Springer Publishing Company, 155–180.

Tillich, P. (1963) *Systemic Theology Vol 3*. Chicago: The University of Chicago Press.

Tornstam, L. (1999/2000) 'Transcendence in later life.' *Generations 23*, 4, 10–14.

Touhy, T.A. (2001) 'Nurturing hope and spirituality in the nursing home.' *Holistic Nursing Practice 15*, 4, 45–56.

Tournier, P. (1972) *Learning to Grow Old*. London: SCM Press Ltd.

Trevitt, C. and MacKinlay, E. (2004) 'Just because I can't remember… Religiousness in older people with dementia.' In E. MacKinlay (ed.) *Spirituality in Later Life: On Humor and Despair*. New York: Haworth Pastoral Press.

Troll L.E. (2001) 'When the world narrows: Intimacy with the dead?' *Generations*, Summer, 55–58.

Vreugdenhil, E. (2004) 'Non-speech based pastoral care: A pastoral care program for aged care residents with little or no ability to speak.' In E. MacKinlay (ed.) *Spirituality of Later Life: On Humour and Despair*. New York: Haworth Pastoral Press.

Wahby, L., Born, W. and Montagnini, M. (2004) 'Physicians' attitudes and practices regarding spiritual assessment of palliative care patients.' *Journal of American Geriatric Society 52* (Supplement 1), S51.

Walsh, K., King, M., Jones, L., Tookman, A. and Blizard, R.(2002) 'Spiritual beliefs may affect outcome of bereavement: Prospective study.' *British Medical Journal (International edition) 324*, 7353, 1551–1554.

Weaver, A.J., Flannelly, L.T. and Flannelly, K.J. (2001) 'A review of research on religious and spiritual variables in two primary gerontological nursing journals: 1991–1997.' *Journal of Gerontological Nursing 27*, 9, 47–54.

Weaver, G. (2004) 'Embodied spirituality: Experiences of identity and spiritual suffering among persons with Alzheimer's dementia.' In M. Jeeves (ed.) *From Cells to Souls and Beyond*. Grand Rapids, Michigan: William B. Eerdmans Publishing Company.

Webster, J.D. and Haight, B.K. (eds) (2002) *Critical Advances in Reminiscence Work: From Theory to Application*. New York: Springer Publishing Company.

Wei, W., Sambamoorthi, U., Olfson, M., Walkup, J.T. and Crystal, S. (2005) 'Use of psychotherapy for depression in older adults.' *American Journal of Psychiatry 162*, 4, 711–718.

Williams, D.R. (1999) 'Commitment.' In Fetzer Institute (ed.) *Multidimensional Measurement of Religiousness/Spirituality for Use in Health Research*. Kalamazoo, MI: John E. Institute, 71–74.

Winslow, G.R. and Winslow, B.W. (2003) 'Examining the ethics of praying with patients.' *Holistic Nursing Practice 17*, 4, 170–177.

Worden, J.W. (1997) *Grief Counselling and Grief Therapy: A Handbook for the Mental Health Practitioner*. London: Routledge.

Wright, S. (2000) 'Spirited discussion.' *Nursing Standard 12*, 8, 24–26. Available at www.emedicine.com/NEURO/topic140.htm, accessed 18 April 2005.

Wright, S. (2004) 'A tool too far.' *Nursing Standard 18*, 26, 26–27.

Yesavage, J.A., Brink, T.L. and Rose, T.L. (1983) 'Development and validation of a geriatric depressions screening scale: A preliminary report.' *Journal of Psychiatric Research 17*, 37–49.

Zedek, M.R. (1998) 'Religion and mental health from the Jewish perspective.' In H.G. Koenig (ed.) (1998) *Handbook of Religion and Mental Health*. San Diego: Academic Press.

Subject Index

Author Index

CPSIA information can be obtained at www.ICGtesting.com
Printed in the USA
LVOW01s0005080715

445325LV00008B/24/P